GOD IS
FRIENDSHIP

GOD IS
FRIENDSHIP

A Theology of Spirituality, Community, and Society

BRIAN EDGAR

Printed in the United States of America

Paperback ISBN: 978-1-62824-034-4
Mobi ISBN: 978-1-62824-035-1
ePub ISBN: 978-1-62824-036-8
uPDF ISBN: 978-1-62824-037-5

Library of Congress Control Number: 2013938011

Cover design by Abe Goolsby—officinaabrahae.com
Page design by PerfecType, Nashville, TN

SEEDBED PUBLISHING
Sowing for a Great Awakening
204 N. Lexington Avenue, Wilmore, Kentucky 40390
www.seedbed.com

To Barbara, my best friend,
who has shown me more about
love and friendship than anyone.

CONTENTS

PREFACE

This book began when I started to take seriously the words the Lord Jesus spoke to his disciples, "I no longer call you servants but friends." The grace, the intimacy, and the freedom that emerged in understanding those words more fully was nothing other than profound. A relationship built upon friendship rather than servanthood can transform a life.

Friendship with God is a rewarding theme on which to write. It is so simple, so deep, and both enriching and challenging in terms of one's own friendship with God and with others. I hope this will also be the case for those who read these words. The fundamental message is that friendship can be a dynamic means of personal spiritual growth, a focus for a rich community life in the church and a vitally important public good.

I hope that others will see what is written here as I do: as a natural follow-up to my previous work on God as Trinity. The inner life of the Trinity may be expressed as one of deep and unique friendship and through the blessing of the Father, the ministry of the Son, and the inspiration of the Spirit believers are drawn into a life of friendship with God and others. The concepts of friendship and Trinity are inseparable.

The people and the congregations that responded so positively to those first preached messages about friendship with God are responsible for initially encouraging me to develop the theme, and numerous groups of students at Asbury Theological Seminary have provided helpful feedback and ideas along the way. Thanks especially to Paul Alvey for being able to use his story in chapter 4.

I am grateful to the president of Asbury Theological Seminary, Dr. Timothy Tennent, my colleagues on the faculty, and the members of the seminary Board for the semester sabbatical that enabled me to do much of the writing. It was a surprise to me that what began as one small part of the sabbatical gradually expanded to become a major project as the classical and biblical material that I was exploring grew and developed. I never did actually finish what I set out to do on that sabbatical, but this book, which came instead, is a far better result than what was planned!

It is a privilege to be able to publish through Asbury Theological Seminary and Seedbed. Particular thanks to J. D. Walt, the "chief sower" and the man with the vision for Seedbed who was encouraging and prepared to take on publishing this manuscript, Justin Barringer for his helpful comments, and Andrew B. Miller, the Director of Publishing, Holly Jones the Production Director, and all the rest of the team at Seedbed.

This only leaves me to thank my friends—every friend I have ever had, no less—for teaching me about friendship. Many friends, and frequently the best, are often more commonly known as "colleagues" or "family" but "friends" they are nonetheless. Special thanks to Barbara, my greatest friend.

The book is written with the prayer that the reader will be able to see that friendship with God in Jesus Christ is the most important friendship there can be.

PART I
Introduction to Friendship

Overture

The Changing Face of Friendship

1

> Here we are, you and I, and I hope a third,
> Christ, is in our midst.
>
> "SPIRITUAL FRIENDSHIP"—AELRED OF RIEVAULX

If a book were to symbolize the notion of friendship in modern culture, it would very likely be a small gift book filled with fine photographs of smiling faces and adorned with sayings such as, "A real friend is one who walks in when the rest of the world walks out," "A hug is worth a thousand words. A friend is worth more," and "Friends are the most important ingredient in this recipe of life." The book would probably have some pop cultural references from people like Lennon and McCartney ("I get by with a little help from my friends") or the television sitcom *Friends* ("I'll be there for you"). It is likely there would also be some room for rather more enigmatic quotes from philosophers such as Aristotle, "What is a friend? A single soul in two bodies."[1] And for the Christian market, it would include the wisdom of C. S. Lewis, "Friendship is unnecessary, like philosophy, like art . . . It has no survival value; rather it is one of those things which give value to survival."[2] There would be a biblical proverb or two, such as "The righteous gives good advice to friends, but the way of the wicked leads astray" and "One who dwells on disputes will alienate a friend" (Prov. 12:26; 17:9).

Presenting a gift book of quotations as a symbol of modern friendship is not intended to trivialize an important part of life, even though there is an element of underestimation of the concept when, for example, all contacts on Facebook are designated "friends." As one person said to another who was commenting about the number of friends that he had online, "How many of these 'friends' are willing to lend you a hundred dollars or help you move?" However, real friendships do exist widely, with real warmth, depth, and meaning. They are an important part of a very significant sphere of life for many people, but they are limited in scope. That is, friendship is generally not a public, political, theological, or philosophical issue. Friendship is seen primarily as a personal, even private, affective relationship, usually associated with high levels of intimacy and mutual sharing (especially for women) and recreational pursuits (especially for men). Friendship also involves expectations of care and concern and personal help in times of need. Friendship exists at all levels of intensity and extent, from the most casual to the most passionate, and from an exclusive friendship of two people through to the companionship of larger groups of mutual friends. Few would now agree with the idealism of Michel de Montaigne, who, in his essay on friendship, in a rather exaggerated fashion declared that a real soul-friendship occurred only once every three centuries![3] However, many would seek the kind of friendship sought by Anne of Green Gables:

> "Marilla," she demanded presently, "do you think that I shall ever have a bosom friend in Avonlea?"
>
> "A—a what kind of friend?"
>
> "A bosom friend—an intimate friend, you know—a really kindred spirit to whom I can confide my inmost soul. I've dreamed

of meeting her all my life. I never really supposed I would, but so many of my loveliest dreams have come true all at once that perhaps this one will, too. Do you think it's possible?"[4]

The intensely personal nature of modern friendship means that the observation that there are few contemporary references to the political, civic, international, philosophical, religious, or ethical dimensions of friendship would only occasion surprise that anyone would think there could or should be such dimensions to what is clearly a private, voluntary association! Friendship for politicians, amiability in public life, and thoughtfulness about all forms of interpersonal relationships are seen as right and proper, even helpful, but always essentially private. Moreover, in public life, the usual view is that one ought *not* be swayed by personal friendships or give preferential treatment to one's friends. That would be unjust and contrary to the egalitarian nature of public life, where all are treated fairly and equally. Indeed, there is a degree of disdain in Western culture for those societies where friendships do accord preferential treatment in public matters. In short, friendship has to remain a private rather than a public affair and is restricted to the personal rather than to the philosophical or ethical realms.

Nonetheless, our imaginary symbolic gift book on friendship hints at broader concerns through the inclusion of some quotes from Aristotle, C. S. Lewis, and the Bible. There are, indeed, some deeper, more thoughtful resources for those willing to explore the matter. There are some substantial essays, though, for example, by Ralph Waldo Emerson, Elizabeth Telfer, and C. S. Lewis.[5] However, not everything worth learning comes in the form of formal essays; actual accounts of friendships provide important insights that can extend one's understanding, encourage, and challenge. Sometimes these can come from the most unexpected sources, such as the apparently unlikely friendship between the playwright and giant of twentieth-century poetry T. S. Eliot, and comedian, film star, and quick-fire wit Groucho Marx. When they finally met, after some years of correspondence, Marx was fully ready to discuss *Murder in the Cathedral* or Eliot's study of modern despair, *The Waste Land,* but Eliot wanted to talk about Marx's comedies *Animal Crackers* and *A Night at the Opera.*[6] A healthy friendship will manage to incorporate discussions of both sets of interests. In a similar way, it is hoped that this exploration of friendship will draw together very different dimensions of friendship—connecting the philosophical and the practical, the theological and the popular.

It is my intention to consider the history, the philosophy, and, particularly, the theology of friendship, because it is not what it used to be, and it is not what it could be. I will be considering friendship as a *public,* civic relationship rather than simply as a private matter for one or two; as a serious topic of *philosophical* reflection as well as a personal preference; as a significant *ethical* virtue rather than only as a recreational activity; as a relationship which has *ontological* significance for our very nature as human beings rather than only an affective or emotional expression of character; as a relationship which is *contributory to the common good* and not merely a matter of personal disclosure and mutual sharing; and as a relationship which is *theologically grounded* and specifically Christian in form rather than simply a reflection of general secular principles. Friendship is biblically based and, in particular, has its shape and nature determined by friendship with God through Jesus Christ. It has implications for the form of the church and the nature of Christian relationships and the ministry and mission of the church.

The changing face of friendship

The nature of friendship and the way it is organized and expressed is significantly influenced by time and place. There are differences in the usual context for friendship (e.g., work or home) that vary according to socioeconomic class, and the form of friendship varies with age. Gender differences are also significant. Modern Western men are more emotionally reticent than women and more likely to find close friends at work. However, one has to be careful not to hold too tightly to these stereotypes. There have been significant changes in the understanding of friendship over long periods of time, with the ancients seeing male bonding through heroic, military activity as the highest form of friendship, and the ability of women to enter into real friendship has often been doubted: "the normal capacity of women is, in fact, unequal to the demands of that communion and intercourse on which the sacred bond (of friendship) is fit; their souls do not seem firm enough to bear the strain of so hard and lasting a tie."[7] Of course, the female reality may well always have been different to the male perception. However, even in more recent times there have been significant changes, for example, in the form of male friendship over the past century. A study of everyday photographs from the nineteenth century indicates a level of physical intimacy between men that would make most males uncomfortable today.[8] Obvious affection was expressed through holding hands, physical closeness, and intimacy. More intense and intimate relationships between males were perhaps to be expected in an era when men and women lived in very different ways. Until they got married, men and women basically lived in separate worlds.

What is very clear is that in modern Western cultures friendship, both for men and women, that functions according to traditional patterns is becoming more difficult and increasingly rare. However, the apparent decline of friendship may relate more to its changing forms rather than to a fundamental loss of intimacy. On the one hand, some sociological comparisons of "confidants with whom Americans discuss important matters" over the past twenty-five years indicate that these discussion networks are becoming smaller.[9] The number of people saying there is *no one* with whom they discuss important matters has nearly tripled. In 2004, the mean average number of confidants per individual was 2.08 compared to 2.94 in 1985. The significance of this decrease of almost a third, from virtually three to two confidants, is accentuated by the fact that the most common response is that the respondent has *no* confidants. The average of both kin-related and non-kin-related confidants has decreased, but the greater decrease of non-kin ties has produced a more pronounced reliance on spouses and parents, with fewer contacts through voluntary associations and neighborhoods. These shrinking networks reflect an important dimension of social change.

These changes in friendship patterns are connected with other changes in contemporary society including increased mobility; changing patterns of work; the deterioration of local, neighborhood community structures; increasing levels of depression; and a general sense of social alienation and fragmentation.[10] But one should not only consider the problem areas; any account of friendship must also deal with the positive dimensions of friendship today and the presence of many healthy, life-affirming personal relationships, as well as the positive aspects of many social trends. The constantly developing and extending information and communications technologies, for instance, can increase and enhance friendships in new and positive ways.

However, although there may be a discernible problem in friendship levels in certain forms of association, other studies indicate that significant levels of friendship are hidden from any research that does not take into account the changing patterns of relationship today. The work of Liz Spencer and Ray Pahl, for example, reported in *Rethinking Friendship: Hidden Solidarities Today*[11] provides a more optimistic assessment of the situation. Their research, which invited people to map their own friendship patterns, reveals the emergence of a new set of complex and multifaceted friendship repertoires with an enormous diversity of micro-social worlds.

However, although these trends are important and illustrative of the current situation, and even though I want this book to enhance the concept and practice of friendship, it is not my intention to address them directly, but rather indirectly. This is because I want to examine dimensions and possibilities of friendship that extend beyond a perception of friendship as a personal, affective relationship of mutual disclosure and activity. To operate on that basis would be too limiting and could not fundamentally alter the situation. It is not my intention to either critique or rehabilitate something that is purely perceived in such narrow terms. Rather, it is my intention to draw upon the rich history of friendship from biblical and classic traditions.

There is a rich history of friendship to draw on for this. The classic Greek philosopher, Plato of the fourth century BC, wrote a series of dialogues on important themes, and one of them, known as *Lysis,* between Socrates and several others, seeks to define friendship and clarify how one becomes a true friend. Friendship was the basis of society. Plato's student Aristotle, whose views are reckoned to be foundational for Western philosophy, logic, ethics, and politics, and whose influence extends from his time to the present, devoted two of the ten books of his seminal *Nicomachean Ethics* to the topic of friendship and its close relationship to virtue and the common good. This is one of the most important philosophical works we have, and friendship is described as central to ethics and to public life. Friendship that seeks the common good is the highest, the only true, friendship.

Cicero, the Roman philosopher, statesman, and lawyer of the first century BC wrote *De Amicitia* (On Friendship), a treatise in the form of a dialogue where friendship is grounded in virtuous love. The very existence of society, it is argued, depends upon the presence of friendship. This became perhaps the major source on friendship in the West—at least until there was a resurgence of interest in the *Nicomachean Ethics* in the thirteenth century.[12] Cicero's influence can be seen in the writing of the twelfth century's impressive advocate of friendship, Aelred of Rievaulx. His *De Spirituali Amicitia* (On Spiritual Friendship) is a classic description of friendship with God as the foundation for all friendship.[13] He spoke of friendship in the same way that John the gospel writer wrote of love in 1 John 4:16: that "God is friendship." His writing was influential on the spiritual life of monastic communities and, through that, on the whole church. The immensely influential

scholastic theologian Thomas Aquinas, the "angelic doctor" of the thirteenth century, revised Aristotle in a more theological context and he
made friendship with God the basis for his entire system of understanding the Christian love of God and neighbor. Friendship was
fundamental for social life, justice, and Christian community. "God is
our chief friend," he said.[14]

The decline of friendship

However, despite this honorable history, friendship has all but disappeared from sight in modern discourse. Theologians did not follow
Aquinas in making friendship a central theological concept, philosophers have not seen friendship as being essential to their concerns, and
friendship has not been a primary category for ethicists. Friendship is not
considered to have a public dimension, and there is no sustained treatment of friendship in political theory. Friendship in the public sphere is
not impossible, but it is by no means essential. The advertising tag for
the movie about the political implications of the relationship between
Bill Clinton and Tony Blair, *The Special Relationship*, makes a valid point
when it says, "Never underestimate the politics of friendship." Personal
friendships can have profound political ramifications, as they did in both
international and domestic politics, despite the presence of more formal
political and diplomatic processes. The proper role of friendship in politics will be discussed in the chapter "Public Friendship."

Friendship has all but disappeared from public life in the modern
era, and it is simply understood and practiced in terms of private, affectionate relationships. However, it has to be conceded that with this,
as in everything, there are exceptions. The topic does appear at times
in the most unexpected places, as in the thought of Nietzsche and
Kierkegaard. And in recent days there has been something of a resurgence in ethics as a result of the post–Alasdair MacIntyre shift toward
virtue ethics.[15] He called for a return to the virtue ethics exemplified
by Aristotle and Aquinas because of the failure of the Enlightenment

project to establish ethics on purely rational and objectively shared principles. This has necessitated some further reflection on friendship, but it has not yet had a significant impact. In fact, in terms of formal, academic study, friendship is generally restricted to psychology and sociology. It is definitely not a point of integration for social, cultural, religious, economic, philosophical, and political dimensions of life. So friendship remains theoretically undeveloped, and it exists as practiced in the everyday lives of ordinary people as a private, affective relationship generally divorced from public life.

There are three primary reasons for this. The first is that friendship, as an essentially communal concept, appears to conflict with the dominant starting point of post-Enlightenment rationalist thought, which is fundamentally grounded in a perception of the individual as a free, autonomous agent. For example, instead of starting with an Aristotelian conception of friendship, modern political theory is more likely to operate with assumptions about the essential independence or freedom of human nature. But of course, starting with such assumptions makes it virtually impossible to achieve real communion, and one has to be content instead with associations or pragmatic collaborations. If one begins with individualistic freedom, one may have a society but not a community. If one starts with the individual, then friendship can only come into the picture much later, as a private, voluntary relationship.

Secondly, the free exercise of the preferential dimension of friendship in public life appears to conflict with modern egalitarianism and its associated conception of justice. For example, while it is very appropriate for a public health official (perhaps a doctor in a hospital) to have a personal friendship that functions in the private realm, it is considered inappropriate and unjust if that friendship means that he gives his friend preferential medical treatment ahead of other patients. In other situations, a politician or public official who gave gifts to friends or did favors for them would be considered corrupt. Justice appears to demand a more impartial attitude than friendship provides.

Thirdly, theologically speaking, it appears that the personal, preferential love of friendship is in conflict with the Christian understanding of love as *agape* which is to be offered universally and indiscriminately (rather than to a select few people one knows very closely), and which is more volitional and active in practical care (rather than affective and predicated on mutual sharing) and ultimately epitomized by love of those who are *most distant* from oneself—love of one's enemies (rather than one's friends). In such a context, friendship-love appears too narrow and selective, perhaps even self-serving. This perception appears to be supported by a conspicuous absence of friendship-love in the New Testament. Kierkegaard claimed that friendship-love, like erotic-love, is essentially pagan and idolatrous. He also argued that it should not be seen as something to be taught in addition to agape love. He observed that if it was claimed that Christianity did affirm this form of friendship-love, it would have been considered remarkable "that in a whole [N]ew Testament there is not found a single word about friendship in the sense in which the poet sings of it and paganism cultivated it."[16]

Rediscovering friendship

The objective of this book is, as indicated earlier, to consider the history, the philosophy, and particularly the theology of friendship, and to view it as a public relationship, a serious topic of philosophical reflection, and as a significant ethical virtue, which contributes to the common good. It is a relationship that has implications for the life, ministry, and mission of the church. Consequently, my aim is, firstly, to explore further the history of friendship and show that is has existed as an important concept in premodern political thought, ancient ethics, and in biblical theology. It has had a public dimension that has been lost in recent times, and which needs to be restored in a manner suitable for today. However, although it is important to deal with the formal Western tradition of friendship from Plato, Aristotle, and Cicero through the other major writers, it is not my ultimate goal to write a history of friendship or establish in thorough detail precisely what the various theorists said. My analysis is a means toward the two ends that are expressed in the next two objectives.

My second and more significant goal is to establish a biblical-theological foundation for spiritual friendship. This means taking the biblical material about friendship with God as foundational and formative for an understanding of the nature and form of all friendship. Although insights from other sources may be illuminative, friendship with God as described in Scripture is determinative. This means moving from an examination of the biblical practice of friendship to an understanding of theory, rather than from a general theory of friendship to Scripture. As Ambrose of Milan pointed out, it is because God is true that friends can be true to each other.[17]

The third aim is to demonstrate the value of friendship—its value and extent for the life, ministry, and mission of the church, and for wider society as well. Christianity began with Jesus calling together a disparate group of people who became friends as well as disciples. Following Jesus' death, this group of friends became the foundation of the life and mission of the church. Friendship is not merely a cultural practice shared in common with all other people; it is a thoroughly Christian concept with its own distinct form, and it has profound spiritual, ecclesial, and missional consequences.

PART II
Friendship as Spiritual Formation

Beginning

No Longer Servants

2

"I no longer call you servants, ... [but] friends."

JOHN 15:15 NIV

S ervant imagery is such a vitally important and profoundly biblical part of Christian identity and such a dominant motif in Christian discipleship today that it is very difficult to write a chapter that criticizes it. This is an approach to the Christian life that has been stressed in preaching and discipleship, in theological education, and in thousands of books so that it is now practically impossible to conceive of being a follower of Jesus without employing this imagery. Every Christian is aware of Jesus' example of servanthood and his teaching that whoever wants to be great in the kingdom must be a servant of all (Mark 10:42–44). In worship we have all sung some form of the words of Francis of Assisi, such as "Brother, sister, let me serve you, let me be as Christ to you; pray that I may have the grace to let you be my servant too,"[1] or the hymn "From Heaven You Came," which praises Christ, who "came not to be served but to serve" and who calls us to follow him by making our lives a daily offering of service "to the Servant-King."[2]

17

The extent of the contemporary influence on servanthood and, it must be said, the strong foundation it has in biblical teaching makes it very difficult to critique the concept. Its position as the primary definition of Christian living makes it almost unassailable. It seems to run counter to the whole notion of the Christian life to suggest that servanthood may be misconstrued in the way in which it is presented, or that it can be unhelpful in the way it dominates discussions of discipleship, or that in contemporary teaching it is generally interpreted apart from its proper context. Nevertheless, these claims are not without foundation. If servanthood is to remain a vital part of the Christian life, it has to be properly understood. Specifically, it is very important that we do not ignore the teaching of Jesus concerning both servanthood and friendship, nor reverse his understanding of their relationship. Simply put, it is necessary to take seriously the words of Jesus to the disciples, "I no longer call you servants, . . . [but] friends" (John 15:15 NIV) and locate servanthood within the context of divine friendship.

Unfortunately, the general tendency is to do precisely the opposite and place servanthood above friendship. One may be forgiven for assuming that in most churches friendship with Jesus is seen as a childlike, rather than an adult, way of expressing one's relationship to the Savior. It is an image that functions at a level suitable for children; Jesus is, after all, "Jesus, friend of little children."[3] And while it is an important stage in one's spiritual journey, friendship is seen as only one step along the way to adopting a more dutiful and responsible form of relationship, such as that of servanthood. Taking on the role of a servant is perceived as something much more serious. It marks a genuine commitment and involves the adult dimensions of duty and responsibility. Mature faith, it seems, must leave behind the childish approach. It is just as though Jesus had called the disciples to a new level of relationship by saying, "I no longer call you friends, but servants." However, to think in this way is to reverse the actual trend of Jesus' thought and to guarantee the development of a works-related and duty-orientated view of discipleship, rather than one permeated by the grace and love of friendship.

This contrast—between the Christian life interpreted primarily in terms of friendship compared with servanthood—should not be taken as implying a disregard for the concept of servanthood. Properly understood, the two concepts are not in conflict, yet neither are they the same. The relationship between them needs to be clarified for the sake of the life and ministry of the church. How different might the church be today if, over the past twenty or more years, there had been a focus on exploring the implications of friendship with God to the same intensity with which we have explored servanthood? Comparatively speaking, there has been little development of the concept of friendship, yet it has great potential for enhancing Christian life and ministry in every respect. It is central to each person's relationship with God in Christ; it is a vital part of the community relationship of the body of Christ; and it has great value as a mode of relationship with the wider community. All three of these areas need to be explored.

From lordship to servanthood

The critical passage of Jesus' teaching that relates friendship and servanthood is recorded in John 15:10–15 (emphasis added):

> "If you keep my commandments, you will abide in my love, just as I have kept my Father's commandments and abide in his love. I have said these things to you so that my joy may be in you, and that your joy may be complete. This is my commandment, that you love one another as I have loved you. No one has greater love than this, to lay down one's life for one's friends. *You are my friends* if you do what I command you. *I do not call you servants any longer*, because the servant does not know what the master is doing; *but I have called you friends*, because I have made known to you everything that I have heard from my Father."

It is well understood that in the teaching of Jesus there is a great revolution in social relationships. Attempts to communicate the radical nature of the message of Jesus, which so often contradicts ordinary, human ways of thinking, appropriately include references to "the great reversal," "the upside-down kingdom," "the church inside out," and "the Jesus revolution." These all refer to the way in which Jesus reinterprets "greatness" in terms of "servanthood." However, understanding this means recognizing only half of what is actually a double revolution that not only involves reinterpreting *greatness in terms of servanthood* but also reinterpreting *servanthood in terms of friendship*. This latter revolution is as remarkable and transforming as the former, though less well comprehended. The kind of transformation Jesus proposes can be compared with the most sweeping political revolutions that do not occur simply when one president or king is replaced by another. They occur when there is a double change—not only of person but of the system as a whole—as when, for example, a tyrant leading a dictatorship is replaced by a new leader, elected by the people. When Jesus challenges human perceptions of power, authority, and lordship, there is a double revolution of both status and system.

The first part of the revolution involves substituting servanthood for lordship as the goal of the Christian life. The disciples James and John showed they did not initially understand this when they asked Jesus, "Grant us to sit, one at your right hand and one at your left, in your glory" (Mark 10:37). They assumed that they were to have the best seats in the house and were perhaps surprised by Jesus' response to this:

> So Jesus called them and said to them, "You know that among the Gentiles those whom they recognize as their rulers lord it over them, and their great ones are tyrants over them. But it is not so among you; but whoever wishes to become great among you must be your servant, and whoever wishes to be first among you must be slave of all. For the Son of Man came not to be served but to serve, and to give his life a ransom for many." (Mark 10:42–45)

This is a revolutionary step that subverts existing notions of power and lordship. However, radical as these words are, they do not constitute the whole of Christ's revolution. There is, indeed, a reversal of position and status in what Jesus says—when the lord becomes the servant and greatness is measured by humility—but what if the whole structure of lordship and servanthood was overthrown? Would that not be even more radical? The interpretation of lordship in terms of servanthood is only the first part of a revolution that reorientates the believer's relationship with God onto a different, nonhierarchical foundation of friendship, with an extensive change of personal identity and social perspective. When friendship becomes a dominant image of the form of divine-human relationship, then it is as though the old structures have been done away with, and everything shifts into a new way of being.

From servanthood to friendship

The disciples began by assuming that they would share in lordship and power, and found they had to learn to be *servants*, but beyond that they had another lesson to learn, one that was potentially more disconcerting—that they were to become *friends*: "I do not call you servants any longer, because the servant does not know what the master is doing; but I have called you friends, because I have made known to you everything that I have heard from my Father" (John 15:15).

In this double revolution, not only is lordship or "greatness" to be interpreted in the light of servanthood,[4] but servanthood is to be interpreted within the context of friendship. It is important to note the line of development in Jesus' own thought, which moved *from servanthood* as an early stage of ministry *to friendship* as the more mature form of relationship. Unfortunately, all too often this development has been reversed. And perhaps this is not too surprising as it is very easy to unconsciously resist the simplicity of grace. It is as though the idea of friendship is nothing other than childish imagery (Matt. 18:3) and preliminary to the more serious, mature notions of service and leadership that are more appropriate for those further advanced in Christian life and ministry. So often the focus in Christian teaching falls upon reminding believers of the need to be a servant, as though everyone knows what it means to be a friend of Jesus and that what everyone really needs is to be taught what it means to be a servant. But this is a complete reversal of the biblical imagery. It is true that friendship is a good and easy concept with which to help a child begin a relationship with Jesus, but it is wrong to think that it is a concept that belongs primarily to children; and it is a serious mistake to reverse the direction of Jesus' own thought and imply, in any way, that friendship is superseded by servanthood as a more appropriate and mature form of relationship for teenagers or adults. Indeed, Jesus' line of thought works in precisely the opposite direction. Friendship with Jesus is a more mature relationship than servanthood.

Of course, someone may point out that Jesus' declaration of friendship begins with the words, "You are my friends if you do what I command you" and protest that this still sounds like a form of servitude and not like the concept of friendship that most people have. But given the context, this statement of Jesus' is best understood as consequential rather than conditional. I say to my students that a conditional statement is like this: "You are an Asbury seminary student if you have paid your tuition fees," but a consequential statement is like this: "You are an Asbury seminary student if you love the Lord and work hard at your studies." The Asbury seminary student shows his or her commitment to being a real Asbury student by behaving in particular ways that are much more important than simply fulfilling the formal requirements of enrolling and paying fees. Similarly, the disciples are real friends if they live in Jesus' way.

The problem that some people have is that friendship with God can appear to be a view of discipleship that is too lightweight (when compared with the glorious sacrifices of servanthood); too ordinary a relationship to have with God in Christ (as it is the kind of relationship we have with many other people); and perhaps too arrogant a relationship to elevate over servanthood (given that the greatest thing that can be said about God is that he is the Lord of the universe). But as I have suggested, the greatest difficulty in accepting friendship as the basic form of relationship with God can be precisely *the difficulty of accepting grace*. To think of it as too simple or lightweight is to fall into a legalism, which suggests that we are saved by the radical sacrifices of our discipleship. To think of friendship as too ordinary or unworthy for the unique relationship we ought to have with God is a failure to understand the depth of God's grace, as though the incarnation brought God near but not too close. To think of friendship with God as too great a relationship for mere human beings is to underestimate the extent of God's grace shown to us. One of our primary tasks in the Christian life is to overcome the temptation to revert to a works-based form of relationship with God and, instead, to seek to restore the concept of friendship to its rightful place as a primary definition of Christian life and ministry.

The implications for the mode of Christian life are significant. As well as being able to say, "Jesus is *my* friend," it can also be said that he is "*our* friend" as well as "*the world's* friend" and even "friend *of sinners.*" The concept of friendship has implications for the way believers relate to others as well as to God. It is a very close, intimate egalitarian relationship. The image of God as friend is one that is fully Christian and also eminently suitable for our postmodern times, where intimate experiences are sought and valued. The notion of God as friend offers an intimacy that is not based on the expectations inherent in family relationships, but is grounded in the free act of one who chooses to embark on a journey of personal exploration. Friendship is an inclusive relationship that can be adult in form, reflecting a partnership rather than childish reliance. It is gender-neutral and completely unrelated to any office or position. It is an expression of faithfulness and even of the kind of sacrifice where the greatest love is to die for one's friends. In addition to all this, friendship can provide a theoretical and practical foundation for ecclesiology and mission; it is relevant to the life of the church in wider society, and it can become a vision of God's future for the world. No model can express everything, and a friendship model may not be able to represent the more transcendent notions of awe, holiness, majesty, or the fear of the Lord, but it should take its place as a significant model for Christian life, ministry, and mission.

Friendship also has many other advantages as a relational model. It is a concept that crosses cultures easily; it is simple enough to be understood by everyone, and yet it is also profound, with such depth of meaning that the implications deserve to be explored in detail. It is a universal image of the Christian life that can be applied to every Christian—not all are pastors or apostles, not everyone is a deacon, a bishop or an evangelist, but everyone can be a friend of God. Unlike many of the other images that describe the relationship of the believer to God (master-disciple, father-son/daughter, Lord-servant), it is symmetrical in its reciprocity (friend-friend), something that introduces a new dimension to the whole relationship of believers with God. It is also a personal relationship, much more personal than the servant-master relationship. This image is of particular importance because Jesus himself gave it a priority, and thus it is applicable to all. It also has particular value for certain groups of people. For some people, hierarchical relationships are difficult to identify with because they represent previously held abusive relationships. The friendship image may also be more easily adopted by those who have difficulties with father-son/daughter imagery because of experience with dysfunctional or abusive parental relationships.

As we shall see in the following chapters, friendship with Jesus is a robust concept that has public, civic, political, ethical, and missiological dimensions. Gregory of Nyssa said plainly, "Christ is our true friend" and through friendship with him one becomes friends with God. Ambrose of Milan identified friendship with God with the "perfection" of voluntary poverty and celibacy—that is, those acts of discipleship which extend beyond the ordinary obligations of Christian friendship to love one's enemies. Friendship with God is thus an intimate relationship; it is no cozy, lightweight affair. Friendship is a model of relationship with God that deserves the same degree of attention that servant-leadership has received over the past fifteen or more years, for it can speak powerfully about the way evangelism, pastoral care, community life, education, administration, leadership, and every other area of the Christian life should function. Christian community will be enhanced if there is an in-depth and wide-ranging exploration of the implications of the concept of life and ministry as "friendship with God." This friendship is a direct implication of the grace and the love of God that influences every aspect of our relationship with others. As the apostle John said, "Dear friends, since God so loved us, we also ought to love one another" (1 John 4:11 NIV).

The messianic significance of friendship

It is appropriate to stress the role of friendship in the Christian life because Jesus' declaration of friendship with the disciples was no incidental or ordinary action. Friendship with Jesus had eschatological significance as part of Jesus' messianic ministry. Up to the point in the narrative of his gospel where Jesus had declared the disciples to be his friends, John has recounted how Jesus and the disciples had shared in a wedding together, eaten together, lived together, and had argued and been through storms and rough weather (both literally and metaphorically). They had stayed together and demonstrated many of the characteristics of friends, and so, after spending considerable time together in this way, there should have been no surprise, at a human level, that he declares that they are his loving friends. But the disciples' new friendship with Jesus does not have its origin in times of mutual sharing, conversation, and experience, but more specifically in the decision and call of Jesus and generally as a sign of Jesus' understanding of his role as the messianic suffering servant.

The number of parallels between John 15:15–17 and Isaiah 41:8–10 make it clear that Jesus' words concerning friendship and servanthood are to be interpreted with Isaiah in mind. One of the most enduring aspects of the Christian tradition's understanding of Jesus is the way it has consistently interpreted his person and work in the light of the Servant material in Isaiah 40–55, and despite contemporary debates about the extent to which this material influenced the Christology of the early church, the prevailing consensus sees the influence of Isaiah everywhere in the New Testament. Isaiah, and especially Isaiah 53 and the redemptive-healing work of the Servant, are important influences on the interpretation of the significance of Jesus.[5] In John 15:15–17 he says to the disciples:

> "I do not call you servants any longer, because the servant does not know what the master is doing; but I have called you friends, because I have made known to you everything that I have heard from my Father. You did not choose me but I chose you. And I appointed you to go and bear fruit, fruit that will last, so that the Father will give you whatever you ask him in my name. I am giving you these commands so that you may love one another."

The themes of *choosing, servanthood,* and *friendship* are linked together in this passage in such a way that it is strongly reminiscent of these words in Isaiah 41:8–10 (NIV):

> "But you, O Israel, my servant, Jacob, whom I have chosen, you descendants of Abraham my friend, I took you from the ends of the earth, from its farthest corners I called you. I said, 'You are my servant'; I have chosen you and have not rejected you. So do not fear, for I am with you; do not be dismayed, for I am your God. I will strengthen you and help you; I will uphold you with my righteous right hand."

First, the passages in John and Isaiah both function within a general context of imminent suffering. The relevant passage in Isaiah is God's assurance of the election of Israel in the context of the Suffering Servant (Isa. 41:8a, 9b), while Jesus' words are an assurance of the election of the disciples in the context of his imminent suffering on the cross. Second, for both Israel and the disciples, their assurance is based on the fact of their being chosen. In Isaiah the Lord God reminds Israel "I have chosen you," while Jesus' words to the disciples are "You did not choose me but I chose you." Third, the presupposition about their relationship is that both Israel and the disciples are servants. (Yahweh refers to "Israel, my servant," while Jesus reminds the disciples, "You are my servants.") Fourth, there are explicit promises of ongoing help in both passages. (The Lord God says to the Israelites in Isaiah 41:10, "I will strengthen you, I will help you" while Jesus says in John 15:16, "The Father will give you whatever you ask him in my name.") Finally and most importantly, both passages speak of the establishment of a new relationship based on friendship. The people of Israel are reminded they are "offspring of Abraham, my friend" (Isa. 41:8), with the implication that they will, at least, be treated well on the basis of Abraham's friendship. Jesus' words to the disciples are more direct; they can have confidence because, he says, "You are my friends." In short, the material from Isaiah concerning Israel as God's Servant provides the primary background for the interpretation of Jesus' declaration of friendship ministry in the passage in John.

Even though it may seem relatively normal for someone who has traveled with a group of people for several years to declare his friendship with them, this friendship cannot be seen simply as the inevitable result of spending time together. Friendship with the messianic servant of God cannot be automatically assumed; the equality that is essential to friendship cannot be earned or created by the disciples. This friendship has an eschatological character and significance beyond that of other typically close relationships, and it had to be established by an act of grace. Those who become friends of Jesus are nothing other than friends of the Messiah, and they have been chosen or elected to participate in those momentous events that mark the beginning of the end of all things. The disciples are representatives of those who will come, as foretold in Isaiah, "from the ends of the earth, . . . from its farthest corners" and who are not friends primarily as a result of their own abilities, characters, or their own choice (although that is also necessary), but because of God: "You did not choose me but I chose you" (Isa. 41:9; John 15:16).

Moreover, Jesus' words constitute a promise that can be claimed by all those who are disciples of Jesus: they will be his friends. It is a profound, unexpected, gracious, and powerful promise, for a master does not have to treat his slave or servant as a friend. In his *Nicomachean Ethics,* Aristotle discussed the possibility of friendship between a citizen and a slave. Friendship comes in different forms but is always predicated on a form of equality between persons; therefore, it is not possible for there to be a genuine friendship between a citizen and a slave. But, he eventually conceded, while a citizen could not have a friendship *with a slave,* there could be friendship with the slave *as a man,* "for there seems to be some justice between any man and any other who can share in a system of law or be a party to an agreement; therefore there can also be friendship with him in so far as he is a man."[6] Their shared humanity opened up the possibility of a friendship, but only of sorts, and it does not come close to the New Testament notion of the radical transformation of the status of a slave described here, and which is also reflected in practice in Paul's request to Philemon to treat the slave Onesimus "no longer as a slave, but better than a slave, as a dear brother" (Philem. 16 NIV; see Gal. 3:28).

Servanthood and friendship compared

This then is the second of the two revolutions of thought. The first meant leaving lordship behind and embracing servanthood; the second means leaving servanthood behind and embracing friendship. The first revolutionary call to reverse the positions of authority and to give up power and control in favor of humility and service is certainly dramatic. It is a complete reversal of human tendencies. But it is, according to Christ, an insufficiently radical step. The more challenging approach is not merely to reverse, but to do away with all forms of hierarchical relationship and all concepts of *greater* and *lesser*. Friendship with God is a truly awesome, almost scandalous concept, one the church often resists. Of course, Jesus always remains as our "Lord" and "King" and "Master," but this only serves to stress the magnitude of the grace offered—that every believer can be treated as a *friend* of the King!

The essential themes and principles bound up in servanthood are not, however, to be rejected, and the idea of "friendship with God" embraces many of them, although the motivation for action is different. Consider the similarities and the contrasts in the following table.

Servant-master relationship	Friend-friend relationship
Does what the master wants	Does what the friend wants
Acts out of duty	Acts out of friendship
Obedience is the central virtue	Friendship and love are central virtues
Does not really know the master	Knows the friend intimately
A relationship defined by doing	A relationship defined by being
Servanthood is a requirement	Friendship is a gift of grace
Work orientated	Relationship orientated
Hierarchical in form	Egalitarian in form

The servant model has the very real danger of developing an unhealthy sense of unworthiness on the part of the servant, compared to the sense of privilege and the simple joy that are part and parcel of being called a friend. As the table indicates, the servant model is work orientated and less intimate. The friendship model does not imply that the friend does not do what the other wants; indeed, the sacrifices offered by a friend are likely to be even greater than those offered to a master. Consequently, the friendship model should not be seen as an easy way of opting out of the serious demands of discipleship or the hard work of service. What it does do is change the attitude and the motivation involved. No longer is obligation at the heart of the relationship; instead, the free act of love that comes from a close friendship is the key. Unlike servants, friends are not justified by their work; they are appreciated for their friendship.

Lordship and leadership

This discussion of the double revolution from lordship to servanthood and then from servanthood to friendship can be related to the present situation with regard to leadership. The general parallels between biblical "lordship" and contemporary "leadership" are obvious. In the New Testament, "lord" was a broad term that could mean owner, employer, or superior. It could be used of husbands in relation to their wives, masters in relation to slaves, angels in relation to those they address, and God in relation to people. Its range extended from simple politeness in everyday affairs to a designation appropriate for an emperor, but it consistently denotes superiority and has implicitly within it the right of the lord to direct, control, and lead in a manner appropriate to the particular relationship (Matt. 10:24; Mark 12:9; Luke 16:3; 1 Peter 3:6). Leadership in the modern era is a different, though overlapping and equally multifaceted term potentially referring to a wide variety of military, political, community, business, and voluntary associations. The mode of functioning for lords and leaders varies considerably within the usage range of both terms, and yet there is a correlation that makes the comparison appropriate.

"Leadership" has only recently become a significant ministry concept within the life of the modern church. Over the past two thousand years of Christian history, the church has worked with a number of different models of Christian ministry—always linking together biblical images with local cultural convictions. For example, soon after the period of the New Testament, the dominant model of ministry was that of the *bishop* or "overseer," who was God's representative to the people. It was a role with biblical justification (1 and 2 Tim.) but was also significantly influenced in its form by the existing, hierarchical model of government of the Roman Empire. Similarly, in the medieval era, the dominant model of ministry was that of the *priest*, who administered the sacraments, while at the time of the Reformation the dominant ministry model shifted to become that of the *teaching pastor* (the shepherd who feeds the sheep). The suitability of the teaching-pastor model was undoubtedly related to the overall development of humanism and the importance attributed to the general spread of education at that time. The point is that the selection and use of biblical imagery concerning the Christian life and ministry is always correlated with current needs and cultural understandings. Therefore, it is no surprise that in the contemporary era, the dominant model of ministry has become that of the *leader;* and while this has a biblical justification, it is also a concept heavily influenced by cultural principles, which shape it in, for example, an individualistic and success-orientated manner. Certainly, leadership as it is understood and practiced today is something that would, I suggest, have appeared as very strange to those of other times and places, including the fathers of the early church, such as Athanasius and Augustine, the reformer Martin Luther, and the puritan Richard Baxter.

The dominance of this model of ministry is seen in the way "leaders" has become the preferred generic term for those previously identified as "pastors," "preachers," "priests," "ministers," and "full-time Christian workers." The older, "clergy-laity" distinction (which certainly created some problems) gave way to a "leader-follower" way of talking. Similarly, within individual local congregations "leadership team" has become for many the preferred way of grouping together those otherwise referred to as "elders," "deacons," or "pastors." "Leader" is also used for those involved in Christian education and worship. It has become an all-purpose word, and so it is not surprising that training in leadership proliferated in all types of resources (books, magazines, journals, tapes, seminars, courses, and other materials) in such a way that the implication is that leadership *is* ministry, or that ministry without leadership is inadequate. So, for a long time now, seminaries and Bible and theological colleges have stressed the development of leadership skills in formal ministry training. Good leadership has not only become an essential part or prerequisite for competent and successful ministry; ministry is, in fact, primarily to be defined in terms of effective leadership. Therefore, the essence of Christian leadership tends to become a clear, measurable success in achieving objectives that have been laid out beforehand, albeit done with a servant attitude. If one is to be a good leader, one also has to be a good manager, for good leadership requires good management. Leadership not only involves the ability to envision the future and to motivate and lead people; it requires the necessary ability to organize and to make this come about. A vision has to become a plan, and a plan has to be implemented.

Of course, if ministry is defined primarily in terms of leadership, then there are two alternatives for those who are *not* leaders. The first is that they are logically seen primarily in terms of being *followers*. This has the effect of perpetuating the problem concerning the ambiguity of the term "the ministry of the church," which has been used to refer to both the ministry of "the people of God as a whole" and, more narrowly, to the ministry of "the minister" (the ordained minister, the pastor, the preacher, or the clergy, depending on the particular tradition). This ambiguity has been confusing and disenfranchising for many people because the terminology suggests that the *real* ministry is what the pastor, minister, or priest does. Biblically speaking, however, every baptized person is a minister of Christ. If "the ministry" is replaced by "the leadership" it does little to enhance the ministry role of the laity.

The alternative to this leader-follower distinction has been to develop the idea of ministry as leadership as a model for *all* ministry, and to seek to train *everyone* to become a leader in their own sphere of life and ministry. It can be argued though, that while universal leadership training enhances many people's confidence and awareness of their abilities, it also has the potential to reduce an emphasis on the diversity of forms of ministry and the gifts of the Spirit by turning everyone toward leadership. Nonetheless, the concept of ministry as leadership is one that has been well accepted culturally and it has now been exercising considerable influence for many years. It has been able to do this because some of the obvious problems associated with certain forms of leadership, especially domineering attitudes and behaviors, have been mitigated by attempts to Christianize leadership through the adoption of servant attitudes utilizing the teaching of Jesus.

This means taking seriously Jesus' injunction that "whoever wants to be first must be slave of all" (Mark 10:44 NIV). The leader, therefore, has to be a servant rather than a lord. Gradually, in the modern manifestation of the Christian life, servanthood and contemporary conceptions of leadership have become fused. Together they have influenced the perception of Christians with regard to the way God and Christian self-identity, as well as the way Christian community and mission are to be understood. The connection of leadership with servanthood has produced "servant-leadership," a term that is familiar throughout the church. This owes much to Robert Greenleaf's influential *Servant Leadership: A Journey into the Nature of Legitimate Power and Greatness*,[7] and "servant-leadership" has become, arguably, the most dominant model of ministry in recent years. One of the great advantages of this correlation of terms is that it has ensured that purely secular approaches to leadership have not provided the only content for Christian leadership. Nonetheless, the movement as a whole has had the effect of reinforcing the notion that ministers and full-time Christian workers are essentially to be *leaders*. The basic concept is leadership, with *servant* being a qualifying term. That is, the reference is always to "servant-leaders" rather than to "leading-servants." The implication is that Christians need to be leaders in order to be good ministers of Christ.

Servant-leadership

The emergence of servant-leadership as a leading understanding of ministry is not really surprising, as strong, decisive leadership is a well-regarded and much sought-after factor in contemporary culture, as it promises security in the midst of uncertainty. This is what many seek, within the church as well as society. It reflects the situation of the children of Israel, who asked for a king to be appointed so they could feel safe and be "like other nations" (1 Sam. 8:5–8). The same desire exists today. Almost every organization wants dynamic, charismatic, visionary leaders, and there is a whole industry that revolves around writing about, searching for, and training leaders. This generates higher and higher expectations and increasing levels of responsibility for leaders—and the Christian community is not exempt from this. Pastors are expected to demonstrate high levels of leadership. The call to high-quality, dynamic, charismatic leadership is such that many do not feel up to this task and so, inevitably, even more is expected of fewer people. This, in turn, leads to the problems of stress and burnout among church leaders. As Craig Blomberg comments,

> Ours is an age that delights to exalt Christian celebrities, to demand that our pastors entertain, have charismatic personalities, and display more spiritual gifts than any one Bible character ever had! Little wonder that burn-out from full-time ministry seems to be at an all time high and that moral failure often results from stress.[8]

As long as ministry is defined in terms of leadership, there will be a constant tendency to define *successful* leadership as the mark of authentic ministry because a need to succeed is built into the very concept of leadership. The extent of the identification of leadership skills with Christian ministry is seen in the way management skills become determinative in the appointment of pastors to larger and, thus, more complex congregations. The top-management skills required for leading a congregation of five thousand are very different from those needed in a congregation of fifty where a competency equivalent to that of a general supervisor is required. Such assessments are necessary as long as the understanding is that the fundamental role of the pastor is to "manage" or "run" or "lead" the congregation in a manner comparable to that of the managing director of a business. The inevitable consequence is that the minister becomes less and less of a pastor and more and more of an executive, with the exercise of spiritual gifts being supplanted by the need to demonstrate leadership and management skills. The secular principle of "management by objective" is spiritualized and becomes the measure of ministry.

In a secular context, the exercise of modern, charismatic, effective, visionary leadership is difficult. And within the church, which is primarily a voluntary association, it takes on additional challenges relating to motivation and inspiration in order to achieve measurable success. And in addition to that, the expectation that leaders be *servant-leaders* creates a new and particular difficulty for ministers. There is not only the stress of seeking to be an empowered, visionary, and successful leader, but there is also the difficulty of being a willing and eternally gracious servant at the same time. The expectations associated with this form of ministry undoubtedly add a high level of personal obligation on the leader in terms of character to the already extensive, often almost unlimited range of responsibilities that they are expected to engage in or oversee. The success of leadership has to be accompanied by a similar "success" in personal life and manner.

The inherent difficulties in servant-leadership are compounded by some culturally influenced interpretations of biblical narratives concerning biblical characters such as Moses, Joshua, Nehemiah, David, and Paul. The problem emerges when the fundamental intent of the narrative as a whole is ignored and it is interpreted in terms of lessons in leadership. This can overshadow the covenantal, messianic, soteriological, and eschatological intentions to be found in the biblical narrative. No book is included in the canon of Scripture primarily because it is a good handbook on spiritual leadership. The fundamental interpretation of the written material should always be related to God's salvific intentions. It is inadequately treated if taken as nothing other than a case study in leadership. A second problem occurs when significant contextual differences between biblical and contemporary times are ignored. Lessons are drawn about Nehemiah's leadership which pay little attention to the significant differences between the essential nature of leadership by a military commander in ancient times defending a beleaguered city-state and the needs and situations faced by church leaders with people genuinely seeking to be responsible citizens of the kingdom of God in a postmodern context. Parallels are possible, but great care must be taken.

Altogether, servant-leadership is an exceedingly difficult concept to practice. Lean too far to the leadership side (with all the attendant notions of what it means to be a leader as defined in a secular context), and the leader becomes (albeit unintentionally) dominant and controlling. Lean too far to the servant side, and you become an over-worked, stressed-out doormat whose life is controlled by everyone else. These two concepts of leadership and servanthood have been put together precisely because they are seen to represent opposite aspects of ministry—one is needed to counter the worst tendencies of the other. However, this can produce a personal tension that is unbearable for the one who tries to live it out. It is possible to feel inadequate both as a leader and as a servant—and to be criticized for it as well.

Is this stating the matter too harshly? Not for many ministers and full-time Christian workers, and especially not for the large proportion that have dropped out of ministry. The issue is particularly sharp for evangelicals, younger people, and those involved in church growth strategies. It is they who have been particularly enthusiastic about adopting these servant-leadership expectations. Much of the literature related to the idea of servant-leadership addresses these difficulties, and it is true that many useful, appropriate, and helpful biblical principles can be applied to minimize the problems. However, it is possible to ask the potentially subversive and dangerous question as to whether the basic servant-leadership model of ministry actually creates these problems and whether it deserves the extensive attention it has received in recent years. From both biblical and practical points of view, both the leader and the servant dimensions of servant-leadership need to be rethought, though not rejected. The practical implications of this principle for every minister, even (perhaps especially) those called and set apart by the church as ordained or full-time workers, are very clear. The task of the minister-servant will always include the most humble service and may include unclogging the church toilets as much as preaching fine sermons. Those who profess to follow one who washed dirty feet must be prepared to do likewise. However, although the importance of this servanthood cannot be overestimated, it is vitally important that it be placed within the context in which Jesus placed it—as functioning within the orbit of a divine-human relationship that is described in terms of friend-friend rather than master-servant, because Jesus said, "I no longer call you servants, . . . [but] friends" (John 15:15 NIV). However, this is not always the actual situation, and the difficulty of accepting the friendship model of relationship rather than the servant-leader model is nothing other than the difficulty of accepting grace.

The grace of friendship

God's offer of friendship is sheer grace. Indeed, nothing could be more gracious. This friendship is an expression of the evangelical doctrine of justification by grace through faith. It is the recognition that no human activity of work or worship can earn salvation, which is a sheer gift of grace. However, there are many people, including pastors and other Christian leaders, who, although they well understand that one cannot work one's way into God's kingdom, find it hard to apply this doctrine to their own lives. It is not that they have refused to accept the grace of God for their own salvation, but they then find it hard to live that grace out in the way they minister for Christ. It is something they teach to new Christians, but it is a lesson they find difficult to accept for themselves; they minister as though it all depended upon them. This, of course, is often perceived as a fine Christian life, which can accentuate the problem. The ones who find it hardest to accept the grace of friendship rather than servanthood are precisely those who see themselves as strong and talented, those with strong egos, intellectuals and high achievers who believe they can think or work their way through, and those who are ordained. They find it most difficult to surrender and experience God in a new and different way.

This point is well made in Janet Hagberg and Robert Guelich's description of the life of faith in *The Critical Journey*. In their terms, people with the most success have the greatest difficulty when they "hit the wall."[9] This happens in what they refer to as the third stage of faith—the productive phase—a time primarily involving ministry and leadership. This is the stage of faith beyond the first stage (one of discovery, where people enter into a relationship with God) and the second stage (a time of discipleship). In the productive phase of faith involving leadership, productivity, and success in achieving goals, many people eventually "hit the wall" in the same way that marathon runners do when, deep into the race, they have to confront the feeling that they are worn-out and that it is impossible to continue. And unless the runner can find the right mental attitude, he or she will not be able to finish. Hitting the wall for the Christian means confronting a developing sense that all of their personal successes really do not count for much as they previously thought. It is a difficult time because it means letting go of the need for success and accomplishment, and instead of having an identity bound up almost entirely with being a hardworking servant for God, it means knowing God and talking face-to-face with God "as one speaks to a friend" (as it is said of Moses and God in Exodus 33:11).

Productivity, activity, servanthood, and leadership do not cease, but the notion that our relationship with God is predicated on achievement and success has to be released. It means shifting from a self-perception based primarily on servanthood to one predicated on friendship with Christ. The movement that is essential at this point is an inward journey that can be seen as the process of accepting the friendship of Jesus in a new and mature fashion. This developing friendship with Jesus does not disconnect one from the world—a friendship with Jesus means developing friendships with his friends—but the focus is certainly changed to have a looser grip on self and a greater confidence in God. The primary motivation is to love and to live according to God's purposes. It includes a greater acceptance of self and a strong sense of God's unconditional love. Treating success in ministry as of lesser importance is, for some people, very hard. It runs counter to the whole ethos of the productive life. It is one thing to learn that failure is not final and that God loves and uses us anyway; it is quite another to learn that success is not everything either. Maturity comes, as Rudyard Kipling suggested in his poem "If," when triumph and disaster (or, we might say, success and failure) can *both* be treated as imposters. Success and achievement count for little more than failure in comparison with the depth of one's relationship with God.

Conclusion

The result of this situation is that the church today needs to take seriously the words of Jesus, "I no longer call you servants, . . . [but] friends" (John 15:15 NIV). This means accepting the grace of God and shifting one's primary focus from working *for* Christ to being *with* Christ. Achieving this form of deep, personal, spiritual friendship with Christ is essential. It is grounded firmly in the words of Jesus, has profound implications for Christian life and ministry, and it is a foretaste of the final communion that is eternal life in God. One example of an approach to the Christian life that embraces friendship is found in the writings of the twelfth-century Cistercian monk Aelred of Rievaulx, who produced the classic Christian treatise *Spiritual Friendship*. He sought to guide his readers toward what monasticism then referred to as a "perfect" relationship with God,[10] and he argued that "among the stages leading to perfection friendship is the highest."[11] It is "a stage bordering upon that perfection which consists in the love and knowledge of God, so that men from being a friend of his fellow man becomes the friend of God."[12]

Through friendship one learns of the love of Christ, and then through Christ one's love of others is perfected.

The remaining chapters examine both the way that this friendship with God, of which Aelred spoke so powerfully, can be achieved and the implications it has for one's personal relationship *with God*, relationships with others within the life of *the church*, and for the good of *the wider community* as well.

Growing

Friends of the King

3

> God is our chief Friend.
>
> THOMAS AQUINAS

When Barack Obama's longtime friend Reggie Love went full-time as his assistant, responsible for anticipating his personal needs, acting as a confidant, playing basketball with him, organizing his music, and guaranteeing at least some time for relaxation, he may not have known it, but he was fulfilling a very traditional role that has existed in many ages and cultures. In ancient Israel he would have been known as "the king's friend."

It was quite common, in the ancient Near East, for kings to have a variety of officials to help in the task of governance: commanders for the army, governors for regions, priests for the cult, administrators for government, and most important, friends for advice and relaxation. For example, in the listing of Solomon's senior officials, there are the high priest, the secretaries, the recorder, the commander of the army, the priests, and the head of the officials, and right in the midst of them is Zabud the son of Nathan, whose role is described as "priest and king's

41

friend." In a similar listing of the officials of King David there is, among the various counselors, scribes, attendants, and the king's counselor, a reference to Hushai the Archite, who is the king's friend. Moreover, it was not only Hebrew kings who had special friends. In Genesis, King Abimelech of Philistia had Ahuzzath acting in an official capacity as "a friend of the king" along with other commanders and advisers.[1]

The friends of the king

The role of "friend of the king" merged personal and official dimensions of the king's life, and it had a status that varied over time. In earlier days, the official dimension was grounded in a preexisting personal relationship the king had with his friend, but in later times the position became much more formalized and was grounded in the system of favors and paybacks one finds in most political systems. By Maccabean times, the idea of "friends of the king" had become a system involving an especially privileged class of people who were "Members of the Order of the King's Friends." The first two chapters of Maccabees records how, under Antiochus Epiphanes, the Jews were directed to engage in prohibited Gentile customs and were forbidden to circumcise their sons or to offer burnt offerings and sacrifices. They were to build altars and shrines for idols and were commanded to sacrifice swine and other unclean animals. In short, they were to forget the law and make themselves unclean according to traditional practices. Inspectors were appointed to see that this happened. Many people forsook the law and did evil; but others, like Mattathias and his sons, resisted. The king's officers who were enforcing this apostasy came to the town of Modein to force the people to offer unclean sacrifices. When they saw that Mattathias and his sons had influence over the others, they tried to bribe them into apostasy, saying,

> You are a respected leader, a great man in this town; you have
> sons and brothers to support you. Be the first to step forward and

conform to the king's decree, as all the nations have done, and the leaders of Judah and the survivors in Jerusalem; *you and your sons shall be reckoned among the Friends of the King,* you and your sons shall be honored with gold and silver and many presents. (1 Macc. 2:17–18, Jerusalem Bible; emphasis added)

The very practical and largely informal role of being a friend to the king had become a formalized position of honor that could be bestowed upon people for political benefit. As it was enlarged in number and raised in status, it was simultaneously reduced in terms of real significance and purpose. The Privy Council in the British system of government is an example of the transformation of a position such as this. It began in the Norman period as a council of trusted people close to the king who assisted in the running of the affairs of state. It grew in significance to become the executive arm of government and then was gradually replaced by the cabinet system that reduced its power. Membership of the council became a reward for service rendered, and it grew steadily to around four hundred, all the while becoming more a position of honor than real service, with most of its functions being symbolic. In the case of the Order of King's Friends, it grew in number and developed various grades of honor. For example, Jonathan, the brother of Judas Maccabeus, was honored by being enrolled in the "first class of the order of King's Friends" (1 Macc. 3:38; 6:10; 10:65; 14:18).

This was a position that declined in real significance as it grew in number and honor, but if one considers it in its undistorted form, the logic behind it is obvious and it is relevant to every high-ranking and stressful leadership position; every king or president needs a best friend or two, someone with whom he can relax and get some perspective on life. The "first friends" of the US president operate in this way. They are the link to normal life, and usually they are long-standing friends, like Bush's Texan buddies and Clinton's friends from Arkansas, who therefore tend to have the president's best interests at heart. They have a level of access denied even to senior officials. These friends are people to relax or go on vacation with. Above all, they have to be people with discretion, who will talk to the president about whatever is needed, but who will not talk to others about it. Recently, writers researching the history of such friends found it frustrating precisely because it was so hard to get anyone to say anything at all.[2] A highly valued characteristic of first friends is that they are honest and frank in their speech, providing a contrast to the flattery, adulation, formal respect, bureaucratic language, ambiguous statements, and veiled threats that a leader is likely to meet with on a regular basis. These responsibilities are nothing other than the normal responsibilities of friends; however, with a leader, they need to be exercised much more intensively than in normal situations, and the responsibilities that the king has means it becomes an extraordinarily important and influential relationship.

Abraham and Moses as friends of the king

If being "the friend of the king" is a special relationship, then being a friend of Yahweh, the King of kings is even more remarkable. There were two people, and two only, who are explicitly described as having this particular role: Abraham and Moses. The tradition of Abraham being recognized as a special friend of God is noted in the New Testament letter of James. The point is made that Abraham's faith in God, in being willing to sacrifice Isaac, was not only rewarded with the life of his son but also with the declaration that his actions were "reckoned to him as righteousness,' *and he was called the friend of God.*"[3] *Moses* was also specifically described as a friend of God as the children of Israel journeyed to the Promised Land. Moses would pitch the tent of meeting outside the camp, and those who sought the Lord would go there, a pillar of cloud would descend, and "the Lord used to speak to Moses face to face, as *one speaks to a friend*" (Ex. 33:7–11; emphasis added). As special confidants of the Lord God, Abraham and Moses were in a privileged position. They were no longer servants, but friends. A servant does not tell the master what to do, nor does a subject instruct the king, and so bargaining with God and reminding the Lord of what should be done is scandalous, but this is the right, even the duty, of the friends of the king (Gen. 18:16–33; Ex. 3:11; 4:1, 10, 13). Throughout his life, Moses was able to speak to God without reserve. It was a robust relationship in which he was continually taken into the confidence of God and was of such a nature that when the nation was facing divine judgment because they worshiped the golden calf, he was bold enough to remind God of his promises. Moses' reminder had such an effect that "the LORD changed his mind about the disaster that he planned to bring on his people" (Ex. 32:14).

The close and intimate relationship that Abraham and Moses had with God was not the typical form of relationship that the people of Israel had with God. The robustly intimate prayer in which Abraham and Moses engaged, which is also appropriate for those called to be friends of King Jesus, stands in sharp contrast to all personal prayer that treats God as remote or uninvolved, or that exhibits little expectation of any direct response from God. While there is certainly a spiritual danger in overly insistent and enthusiastic prayers that imply that one has a direct line to God, it is a form of spiritual malaise when there is a lack of certainty that God will say or do anything. Between the two lies the confidence of a friend that God has heard and will respond.

The shock of intimacy

It should be noted that the remarkable intimacy of the face-to-face relationship between Moses and God described in Exodus 33 appears to be almost immediately repudiated by contrary statements. Even though Moses has just been specifically described as relating to God *face-to-face*, when he then asks (as part of his intercession for the people) to see God's glory, he is told that while God would reveal his goodness, his name, his grace, and his mercy, he would *not* reveal his face, "for no one may see me and live" (v. 20 NIV). Verse 20 seems to take away what was given in verse 11. The danger involved in a face-to-face meeting with God is also expressed in the account of Jacob's special night of wrestling, after which he called the place Peniel (meaning "face of God") "because I saw God face to face, and yet my life was spared" (Gen. 32:30 NIV). And when Gideon realized who the mysterious stranger under the oak at Ophrah was, he exclaimed, "Help me, Lord GOD! For I have seen the angel of the LORD face to face," and he was glad to be reassured when the Lord said to him, "Peace be to you; do not fear, you shall not die" (Judg. 6:22–23).

These all speak of the danger of intimacy with God and stress divine transcendence, and so it is no surprise that it is the friendship dimension of the relationship that is usually most difficult for people to comprehend. It is very easy for the message about divine transcendence to overwhelm the message about immanence and intimacy, not least because of the very common and innate difficulty in believing that the almighty God would want to come close to sinful humanity. Paul, a former student of mine, described his own reaction to this when, in preparing together for some studies, his pastor read the verse about the Lord speaking to Moses face-to-face, as one speaks to a friend. Paul said, "I couldn't believe what I heard my pastor utter. I was more than astonished. Had he written blasphemy? What was going on? My mind was spinning!" Paul insisted on checking different translations, but that did not change the situation. "I thought my world had just crashed. I believed that no one could look upon the face of God and live. I recounted the story of God placing Moses in the cleft of the rock, and if this passage were true, then it would fundamentally change some of my core beliefs. My mind was trying to make sense out of what I had just heard and read. I was thinking to myself, 'I know I must look ridiculous and this response must seem childish, but I must somehow figure out how to make meaning out of this apparent contradiction. Is it just a play on words?'"

It is possible for people to live in faith for many years without understanding or experiencing the closeness of a friendship relationship with God. The shock of true intimacy with the almighty God is, rightly understood, almost too much to bear. Paul's reaction may seem strange to those who have adjusted to this truth, but his response is, in one sense, very appropriate. Those who fail to be astounded by the idea of friendship with the Almighty do not perceive the real significance of it. Even for those who have become familiar with this, it can remain virtually incomprehensible. There is a human tendency to stay with the image of God as Lord and self as servant because it seems to be easier to comprehend and a more appropriate form of relationship. Friendship like this runs counter to culturally formed perceptions of the appropriate structure of power relationships between persons of very different status. And it also seems to run counter to biblical teaching about the majesty of God and the lordship of Jesus Christ.

What this resistance to intimacy does is demonstrate the inherent human difficulty in accepting grace for what it really is. In fact, a correlation of transcendence and intimacy is absolutely essential for the proper understanding of both. Transcendence without intimacy and personal friendship is simply naked and dangerous power, and friendship without transcendence and a sense of awe becomes trivial and sentimental. Transcendence and immanence, majesty and friendship are not opposites but correlates that are essential to their mutual definition. It is a correlation that is biblically grounded and a part of the reflection of almost all the great spiritual writers, whatever tradition they come from. It is vital for a biblical understanding of friendship, for without it one is left with friendship as a pleasant but relatively minor relationship.

The almighty, transcendent God, the one hidden by the cloud of unknowing may be said to dwell in darkness, or in silence (1 Kings 8:12; Ps. 18:11; 1 Kings 19:12), or, as in the words of the hymn, "in light inaccessible"—all images seeking to express the utter difference of God.

Walter C. Smith's hymn is perhaps the best-known expression of this hidden character of God:

> Immortal, invisible, God only wise,
> In light inaccessible, hid from our eyes,
> Most blessed, most glorious, the Ancient of Days,
> Almighty, victorious. Thy great Name we praise.

But it is precisely this majestic God who is closer to us than anyone else and who, through Christ, may be described as a friend who fulfills the sentiment of the proverb, "Some friends play at friendship but a true friend sticks closer than one's nearest kin" (Prov. 18:24). The otherness of transcendence has as its corollary the grace of friendship, and the designation of God as Friend is as much needed as the more formal titles of transcendence, dignity, and office, such as Yahweh, the Most High God (*El-Elyon*), King, and Lord. The point of this friendship is that it is friendship with the Almighty. Truth often involves the recognition of opposites, and sometimes the best approach is moderation and balance. However, at other times, as when relating divine transcendence and immanence, the greatest truth is not obtained by finding a middle position but by stressing both extremes: in this case, that it is possible to have friendship with the Creator of the universe!

Graeco-Roman friends of the King

This history of special friends of the king lies behind Jesus' declaration that his disciples were now to be known as his friends. They were "friends of the King of kings" and had all the rights, privileges, and responsibilities that go with that position. It is this background that explains the formal declaration of the friendship ("I have called you friends"), the way it is rather one-sided ("you did not choose me but I chose you"), and the fact that this friendship, rather unusually, involves obedience ("you are my friends if you do what I command you"). All of this seems out of place according to modern notions of friendship, but it makes good sense when seen against not only the Hebrew background of a royal relationship but also the contemporary Graeco-Roman understanding of friendship.

There were, for instance, "friendships" that were essentially political alliances but which entailed personal obligations. Herod the Great had been a friend and supporter of Mark Antony, which created problems for him when Augustus gained control of the empire. Nevertheless, Herod dealt with the issue head-on, arguing to Augustus that he had tried, unsuccessfully, to persuade Antony to be reconciled with Augustus (while conveniently ignoring the real reason for this, which was that he was concerned about his own head). And he claimed that just as he had been loyal to Antony, he would be loyal to Augustus. Fortunately for Herod, Augustus took the view that he could be a useful ally, and he declared that Herod was, indeed, his "friend," and thus that Herod would rule as king of Judea.[4] Being declared "a friend of Caesar" (whether or not one was personally intimate with him) was a way to guarantee success. On the other hand, not being a friend of the emperor was a guarantee of having a problem. After the trial of Jesus, John 19:12 recounts the threat made to Pilate when he found no fault in Jesus and proposed releasing him: the Jews cried out, "If you release this man, you are no friend of the emperor. Everyone who claims to be a king sets himself against the emperor." Not to be a friend of Caesar meant being his enemy, and that spelled political doom.

Even though royal friendships could become self-centered means of obtaining political power and status and could be formed and broken depending upon who could offer the most advantages, these formal forms of friendship still play an important part in understanding the friendship Jesus had with his disciples. The possibility of the manipulation of friendship with the king ought not detract from the significance it could have when properly exercised. The concept of the "friends of the king" helps us understand what Jesus was doing when, after having been received into Jerusalem in triumph as "the King of Israel," he declares that the disciples are now his friends. They are now the special friends of King Jesus; and even though there is a sense in which this friendship always remains as a relationship between persons of very different status, its institution as a friend-friend relationship means that it is clearly and deliberately differentiated from king-subject or master-servant relationships. A relationship of equality has been created between them.

The conviction that servants or slaves could be treated as equals and given this knowledge is not entirely unknown, for it is found in the early second-century-BC Jewish writing Ecclesiasticus, the Wisdom of Ben Sira, which said, "If you have but one slave, treat him like yourself, because you have bought him with blood. If you have but one slave, treat him like a brother" (33:30–31). However, this was not the norm; it was quite radical, and what Jesus has done extends it further—the King of kings is treating his servants as friends. The disciples are treated as most trustworthy friends, who can have important and normally hidden knowledge revealed to them. In any friendship one may expect some personally sensitive information to be disclosed, but here we have the friends of Jesus being introduced to the mysteries of God!

Friendship and metaphoric theology

This, then, is the biblical background to Jesus' declaration of friendship. However, while it is one thing to examine the biblical background of this concept, it is quite another to consider the implications of it for the relationship that a present-day believer has with Jesus. It leads into a relationship with God that is primarily defined in terms of friend-friend, and this is to engage in an exercise in metaphoric theology. In general terms, this is the analysis of the various images and metaphors used for God and the way they function as attempts to name God and to describe the relationship of God with humanity.[5] The images and the way they are used not only have implications for the character of God but also the nature of salvation, the self-identity of the believer, and the form of Christian life and ministry. Friend-friend imagery is, of course, only one of a number of sets of images that are used to express the nature of a relationship with God, including father-son or daughter; lord-servant; lover-beloved; husband-wife; master-slave; shepherd-sheep; head-body; judge-sinner; king-subject; mother-child; and creator-creature. None of them are literal descriptions of a relationship that is, by definition, beyond human understanding. As Sallie McFague says, "No words or phrases refer directly to God, for God-language can refer only through the detour of a description that properly belongs elsewhere."[6]

Some are perceived as expressing more authoritarian aspects of God's holy, transcendent nature (Lord, Master, Creator, King), while others are seen as representing the more personal dimensions of God's immanent and intimate character (father, mother, lover, friend). Each of them expresses a specific cluster of attributes of God: the image of God as shepherd speaks of care, compassion, guidance, and protection, while the idea of God as king speaks of divine authority, rule, and leadership.

It is helpful to note that different images tend to come to the fore at different times, and both cultural and theological factors influence the ones that become dominant. Preachers and teachers have a significant level of responsibility in regard to the selection, interpretation, and use of the various metaphors that Scripture makes available. The way Jesus is perceived is central to any understanding of God, and so the critical question is: What does it mean to say that Jesus is my friend? And tied up with that is the mode in which the question is asked, whether it is "What does it mean for me to call Jesus my friend?" or "What are the implications for the life of the church if Jesus is our friend?" or even "What does Jesus' friendship mean for society as a whole?" Personal, ecclesial, and social dimensions flow from this central perception. The argument being made here is that it would undoubtedly be helpful to the life of the church if, over the next twenty years, the implications of being a friend of Jesus were to be explored with at least the same kind of enthusiasm and commitment as the idea of servanthood has been explored over the past twenty.

Some objections considered

The latter part of this chapter and the rest of the book will explore the benefits of doing this, but before proceeding with that, it is necessary to consider some objections to any use of this imagery at all.

Friendship with God as too spiritual?

It has been argued that the imagery of friendship with God is a theologically inappropriate model of relationship with God and that it is not biblically substantiated. C. S. Lewis noted the general infrequency of references to divine-human friendship within the New Testament as a whole, observing that "friendship is very rarely the image under which Scripture represents the love between God and Man,"[7] but his main problem was that friendship is "too spiritual" to be a helpful model of relationship. He regarded friendship as a valuable form of human relationship that raises humanity above the animal. It is a means of developing virtue, though it can also be "a school of vice" and in that sense is ambivalent: "it makes good men better and better men worse."[8] Yet despite this problem, and the fact that there can be undue pride in friendship, he argued that it is one of those important dimensions of living which gives value to life. So why is it not used of the divine-human relationship? It is, in fact, "too spiritual to be a good symbol of Spiritual things." That is,

> God can safely represent Himself to us as Father and Husband because only a lunatic would think that He is physically our sire or that His marriage with the Church is other than mystical. But if Friendship were used for this purpose we might mistake the symbol for the things symbolized.[9]

Lewis's argument is based on the metaphorical nature of our language about God and shows a concern that there is to be no confusion about this. The danger of friendship language is that it does not appear to be as metaphorical as, say, Father or Husband; it may be assumed, therefore, that people can really have this sort of friendship.

The issue revolves around the extent to which friendship is a metaphor, and there is a sense in which all language, let alone all theological language, is metaphorical. When Lewis observed that "friendship with God" is not suitable because we might think we can actually have that sort of relationship, he was right if it is assumed that friendship with Christ means we can have the same kind of friendship we have with other friends, where we go for a walk, talk over coffee, or play pool. Clearly it is not that kind of friendship that is envisaged. Nevertheless, the whole point of friendship is that it is flexible in form. Every friendship is unique, and no friendship is excluded from being a friendship because the friends do not, say, have coffee together or play golf or pray together. Some metaphors have more fixed parameters (kings rule, for example, and fathers have children), but friendship is a flexible relationship with a reciprocity that allows both parties to be involved in creating its form. The whole point of Jesus' remarkable teaching about friendship is that he wants to enter into such a relationship that is formed by both parties together.

Friendship with God is not reciprocal?

Questioning the biblical validity of using the imagery of friendship may seem a little strange given the explicit declaration of friendship in John's gospel that has been at the center throughout the whole of the present discussion. However, D. A. Carson has noted that although John's gospel describes various people (including Lazarus and the disciples; John 11:11; 15:15) as *friends of Jesus,* the reverse—that *Jesus is friends with some person* or persons—is not found: "Neither God nor Jesus is ever referred to in Scripture as the 'friend' of anyone."[10]

The intention is not to minimize either the value of friendship or the "friendliness" of God; the point is simply that Carson is not convinced that it represents the appropriate form of relationship with God or Jesus. Carson says the distinction between various people being friends of Jesus and the absence of references to Jesus being friend of anyone is intended to mark an important difference in terms of friendship with God. It does not mean that God is unfriendly or unloving in any way; "if one measures friendship strictly on the basis of who loves most, guilty sinners can find no better and truer friend than in the God and Father of our Lord Jesus Christ, and in the Son whom he has sent."

Nonetheless, according to Carson, the absence of any reference to the friendship of God or Christ is an important indication that this is not "mutual, reciprocal friendship of the modern variety" because this "cannot be without demeaning God."[11]

If the distinction that is being made here—between Jesus *having* friends and *being* a friend—is valid, then it is significant and calls into question the use of friendship as a primary description of the divine-human relationship. It would be necessary to reject it in favor of other metaphors, such as Father, Lord, and Creator. However, the validity of the distinction between Jesus being described as having particular friends, compared with people being friends with Jesus, has to be questioned. While some relationships are based on the status of one of the parties and exists irrespective of the knowledge or attitude of the other (a king is the king even when a particular subject is not aware of it or even resists it), this is not possible with a reciprocal relationship like friendship. It is of the essence of friendship that it is freely chosen by both parties. It is doubtful that John can be a friend of Jesus if Jesus is not a friend of John. Moreover, it really cannot be argued that it is any more inappropriate or unbecoming as a description of the divine-human relationship than the use of other intimate and reciprocal terms, such as the relationship between bridegroom and bride (John 3:27–30).

It is possible that the distinction that Carson observes reflects the initiative involved in the relationship that can only occur with the calling of Christ. This friendship is genuinely reciprocal, but it has an asymmetry that lies in the fact that these disciples are not friends by right but *by grace*. The problem of the inequality between people of unequal status, such as between the disciples and Christ or between believers and God, is one that had been explored previously. Aristotle, for one, argued that friendship requires some form of equality. It need not be absolute, and there can be considerable variation between the parties with friendship remaining; but, he argued, when one party is removed to a great distance, as God is, then the possibility of friendship ceases.[12] However, here the problem is overcome by grace. Such a relationship certainly could not be assumed without the prior calling of Christ. Even then, one has to bear in mind that there remains a difference of kind between humanity and God, but one ought not deny the capacity of God to be gracious in such a way that friendship is a divinely given possibility. People are not friends of Jesus because they are pleasant or competent people but because they are *called* to be friends. This is only possible within the context of the New Covenant, and so it is only in the epistle of James—rather than in the Old Testament— that the broader implications of the tradition of Abraham's friendship with God are observed. James does this when he notes two implications of Abraham's faith, which were "active along with his works" when he offered Isaac on the altar (James 2:22).

The first, concerning his status, is that his faith was "reckoned to him as righteousness" and, secondly, concerning their relationship, that he was "called the friend of God" (James 2:23). James extrapolated the first of these—that he was righteous through faith—to become a general principle for *all* believers that both faith and works are involved in one's salvation (James 2:24), and this is widely recognized and discussed. Unfortunately, many discussions of what James said stop right there and ignore the second part of what he said concerning the implications of the ongoing relationship that Abraham had with God: that because of his faith he was "called the friend of God." Consequently, although it is common to hear that the idea of righteousness through faith can be extrapolated beyond Abraham to all believers, it is far less common to hear a similar account of friendship with God. Many believers today still think that the kind of relationship Abraham had with God is special and unattainable for the ordinary Christian. However, this is not so. This special friendship with God is now, as a result of the new covenant established by Christ, open to all believers. Friendship with God is the fulfillment of the promise that was given through Jeremiah that there would be a new and distinctive form of relationship with God when the people would know God and the law directly, rather than through another: "I will put my law within them, and I will write it on their hearts. . . . for they shall all know me, from the least of them to the greatest" (Jer. 31:33–34). This comes to fruition in friendship with God through the ministry of Jesus and his declaration of friendship with the disciples.

Friendship with groups but not individuals?

One final point in regard to this is that some argue against the use of a friendship metaphor on the basis that the Gospels do not describe Jesus as having particular friends—in distinction from others being described as friends of Jesus. But this is only partially true. There is some reserve in describing individuals—even people like John and Lazarus—as Jesus' friend (although Jesus does speak to the disciples about "*our* friend Lazarus" in John 11:11; emphasis added), but several categories of people are clearly described as being Jesus' friend (and not only friends of Jesus).

Ironically, in the two situations where Jesus does specifically refer to individuals as friends, one of them is definitely a traitor to him, and the other is dead. One of them occurs in Matthew's account of the arrest of Jesus when he says to Judas, who has come from the chief priests and elders with armed men, "Friend, do what you are here to do," which was, of course, to betray him with a kiss (Matt. 26:50). Given the situation, it would seem more logical for Jesus to have said, "Traitor, do what you are here to do," but at the very point where one who had been so close to Jesus is about to betray him, Jesus chooses to call him "friend." This emphatically makes the point that Jesus' offer of friendship has been extended to Judas and that this act of betrayal is a definite and calculated rejection of it. The motive, according to Matthew, was thirty pieces of silver. Judas is the prime example of the effect of rejecting the friendship of Jesus—it keeps one, unnecessarily, outside the realm of eternal life and love that is friendship with Jesus and peace with God. But it is very clear that this is not what Jesus wants. He offers friendship to Judas to the very end. His friendship is offered to all, but it can be rejected. By its very nature friendship is not compulsory.

The other occasion takes place when Jesus announces to the disciples that they will go to Bethany because "our friend Lazarus" has died (John 11:11). The significance of the use of the term "friend" in this situation cannot be separated from the fact that Lazarus is dead. It is, in fact, a demonstration of the way that even death cannot break a bond of friendship with Jesus and unwillingly separate one who loves Jesus. The subsequent raising of Lazarus is a symbol of "the resurrection and the life" that is for all who are friends of Jesus (John 11:25). Nothing, not even death, can take a person away from Jesus if he or she wishes to remain with him. It is extremely important to note that this is not because of the individual's own strength, but because of the power over life and death that Jesus holds in his hands. There are many who love Jesus but who fear that under spiritual stress and temptation they may not be able to hold on to faith. However, such a one should be reassured that it does not finally depend on his own strength: God is faithful and will hold fast to all who love him. No one who wants to remain with Jesus can be taken away from him.

Overall, the reserve about focusing upon individuals like John and Lazarus as Jesus' friends probably relates to the desire to go beyond the older pattern of royal friendship that was limited to just a few, like Abraham and Moses, and to emphasize the fact that every person among the groups of people described specifically as Jesus' friends was actually a friend. This was said, firstly, of the disciples, of whom Jesus said, "I call you friends." Reciprocal friendship with Jesus is an integral part of being a disciple. Disciples are no longer treated as servants but as friends who know everything that the Father has revealed to Jesus. Secondly, Jesus is most clearly described as the friend of tax collectors and sinners (Luke 7:34; Matt. 11:19). He is the one who said to the paralyzed man, "Friend, your sins are forgiven you" (Luke 5:20). Perhaps most surprisingly of all, he is the one who named Judas as "friend"—significantly the only individual in the Gospels described this way—just when he was about to betray him with a kiss: "Friend, do what you are here to do" (Matt. 26:50). This is probably intended to accentuate the nature of his actions as nothing other than the worst form of betrayal, but it nonetheless reflects the truth that Jesus is a friend of sinners.

After considering these various objections, the conclusion is that there are no insuperable problems with the imagery of "friendship with Jesus" or "friendship with God." The distinction between Jesus "having friends" and "being a friend" is not convincing, and friendship is, by grace, an eminently appropriate description of the mutual and reciprocal relationship of love that believers can have with God through Christ. The objections to the use of friendship imagery arise from a very proper regard for the difference in status between the friends; but the very point of the divine friendship is that it overcomes the barriers and establishes a relationship that is accessible to all.

With the biblical foundation for friendship imagery thus established and some of the theological and formational implications addressed in the discussion of the significance of friendships with God (such as those of Abraham and Moses), it is now possible to turn to four other main characteristics of friendship with Christ that emerge from the narrative associated with Jesus' declaration of friendship with the disciples. The narrative connects "friendship with Jesus" with *calling, obedience, love,* and *death.* These, it will be shown, are themes that speak to us today about the nature of the messianic friendship we have with God and with others.

Election in the light of friendship

In John's gospel, Jesus' friendship with the disciples has to be understood in the light of the depiction of Jesus as the promised King (John 1:49; 3:3; 12:13; 18:36; 19:21). For those who have the eyes to see and the ears to hear, Jesus is revealed as a royal figure. This begins with Nathaniel's declaration at the very beginning of Jesus' ministry, "You are the king of Israel!" It continues through to his royal entry into Jerusalem, and includes his claim to kingship of a kingdom that is "not of this world" (NIV). John specifically notes that he was crucified under a sign referring to him as "Jesus of Nazareth, the King of the Jews" (John 19:19). Consequently, he is able to elevate his disciples (who by rights are his subjects; see John 13:1–20) into "the Order of King's Friends" as those with a special status and awareness of the king's plans: "I have called you friends, because I have made known to you everything that I have heard from my Father" (John 15:15).

Jesus' call to the disciples to become friends is nothing less than a profound image of the gift of salvation. By becoming friends, the disciples have been transported to the very heart of the kingdom of God. The work of salvation is presented in Scripture almost entirely through the use of images and metaphors, each of which contributes to the overall message of the atonement. There is the language of redemption (derived from the imagery of the release of slaves and prisoners of war), reconciliation (derived from the imagery of personal relationships), justification (derived from the courtroom), sacrifice (derived from the imagery of priesthood and religious practice), and victory (derived from the imagery of war). Now there is the language of friendship with the king. Each of these images presents the truth of salvation from a different perspective, stressing different dimensions of God's activity, human response, the effect of sin, and the transformation brought by salvation. In the call to friendship, there are dimensions of the atonement that are not so prominent in the other images: the *intimacy* of the personal relationship with God that is involved; the utter *graciousness* of God; and the way that the friend *shares in divine mysteries.*

Salvation is a *victory won* (over sin and death), a *status achieved* (from guilty to innocent), a *freedom granted* (a release from sin), and also, without doubt, a *friendship entered into.* The imagery of becoming friends with Jesus needs to stand alongside these other, more commonly utilized images of salvation. Jesus' election of the disciples as his friends is the most loving and generous call of God that seeks a response, an answer that says, "Yes, I will be your friend!"

This means that calling will be seen in a very different light. Understanding election as one friend calling to another is very different from understanding election as a *King* calling his subjects or a Lord calling his servants. The connotations involved with the call in each situation are very different. If God is perceived as King, then it is inevitable that election will be identified with "the sovereign will of God," and thus as a royal decree that is issued unconditionally so that it is effective irrespective of the situation of those subject to the decree. After all, subjects and servants have no choice in royal decrees. However, when the relationship that God has with his people is expressed in terms of the imagery of friendship, then the divine choosing becomes a call to friendship that begins with the free choice of God, but which does not dominate in the manner of an unconditional decree. It can only be properly realized as a friendship through the free and loving response it seeks in return. Friendship imagery teaches us that if God's gracious choosing overwhelms us, it is with love and not with power or compulsion. Friendship calls for a willing response; it cannot be compelled. Election understood in the form of friendship is a fundamentally gracious relationship. The attitude is that which is expressed in this prayer, which appears in various forms in a number of liturgies:

> Come, not because you are strong, but because you are weak.
> Come, not because of any goodness of your own but because you need mercy and help.
> Come, because you love the Lord a little and would like to love him more.
> Come, because he loves you and gave himself for you.

Friendship and the knowledge of divine purpose

The next distinctive characteristic of divine friendship is that Jesus' friends know what Jesus has been told by the Father: "I have made known to you everything that I have heard from my Father" (John 15:15). Friends of Jesus are no longer servants, and they now share in a deeper understanding of divine purposes. This is the kind of knowledge of important affairs that a friend of the king in the ancient Near East would have. When Jesus calls the disciples to be his friends, they, too, share in knowledge of the affairs of state of King Jesus.

The connection between friendship and the revelation of inner secrets was expressed in the Wisdom of Ben Sira (written c. 195–175 BC), which has extensive material dealing with friendship.[13] It extols the virtue of good friends, saying, for example, "Faithful friends are a sturdy shelter: whoever finds one has found a treasure." It warns against faithless ones, "For there are friends who are such when it suits them, but they will not stand by you in time of trouble." Shared knowledge is important for friends, and the maintenance of trust is critical: "Whoever betrays secrets destroys confidence, and will never find a congenial friend. Love your friend and keep faith with him; but if you betray his secrets, do not follow after him" (see Sir. 6:14; 6:8; 27:16–17).

Jesus' friendship introduces the disciples to extensive knowledge that involves "everything that I have heard from my Father" (John 15:15). This sharing includes a revelation of the ultimate plan, the wisdom of God (1 Cor. 2:7; Col. 2:3). Early in John's gospel, unbelievers are presented as rejecting him because they "did not know him" and then, throughout the gospel others come to "know" him as the Savior, the Holy One of God, the Messiah, the good shepherd, and the one from (or "in") the Father (John 1:10; 4:42; 6:69; 7:26, 28–29; 10:14; 14:20). This knowledge that Jesus shares with his friends is not trivial; it concerns God's character and God's purposes. It is not knowledge or information about some specific, local circumstances or about some other person; it is a more fundamental understanding of God's desires and plans for the world. This knowledge enables a deeper understanding of the situation and the events of the world.

Those who know Jesus can "read" the world according to the standards and principles of Jesus. This means being able to recognize good and evil for what they are. Many people, unfortunately, get confused by evil and do not understand good. Having an insight into the purposes of God does not mean having something like an astrological chart or the prophecies of Nostradamus; it is practical wisdom that makes it possible to discern faith and feel compassion for a world that is filled with turmoil. It enables us to value things, people, and relationships appropriately. In short, becoming a friend of the King of kings relocates one to the point where one shares, as a friend, in the life, the privileges, the secrets, the power, and the authority of the King. In friendship, God comes to meet his people in the most accessible and the most gracious of all relationships. It is unique and precious friendship and, as Gregory of Nyssa said, "we regard falling from God's friendship is the only thing dreadful and we consider becoming God's friend the only thing worth of honor and desire."[14]

Obedience as the mark of friendship

The next characteristic of friendship with Christ is that it is connected with obedience. Once again, understanding obedience in the context of friendship, rather than servanthood, gives us a different insight into the nature of our relationship with God.

Jesus says to the disciples that they are his friends, "*if you do what I command*" (John 15:14). This creates something of a tension, as it seems to imply a conditional, rather than a gracious friendship. Friends do not normally say, "I will be your friend if you do whatever I want."

It is possible, on the one hand, to simply see this as appropriate for a relationship that is not only friend-friend but also king-subject, but it is also possible to interpret the phrase "if you do what I command" more as a sign, a *result,* of friendship rather than as a cause or prerequisite of friendship. It is conditional in the sense that if they do what he wants, then they show themselves to be his friends. This is perhaps seen more clearly in the related comments by Jesus that "they who have my commands and keep them are those who love me" and, conversely, "whoever does not love me does not keep my words" (John 14:21, 24).

The point is that friends will naturally discern the good in the life of their friends and will not need to be overtly instructed on the implications. Out of love and appreciation they will be influenced toward the good. For example, Jim Stynes came to Australia as a tall, athletic, Irish youth who, despite never having played this particular form of football before, had been recruited to become a professional player at the highest level of Australian rules football. The scout's judgment proved to be astute, for Stynes became part of football folklore as one of the finest exponents of the game, holding (among other achievements) a record for playing 244 consecutive senior league games. However, he was not only highly regarded for his playing ability but also for his way of life and the responsibility, respect, tolerance, and genuine care for others that he showed. A teammate turned football commentator wrote in a tribute to Stynes, who was at that time battling a serious cancer, "the best way I can describe it now is that in so many ways Jim led his life in such a way that it challenged the way I live mine."[15] Hopefully this challenge led to changes in the way Jim's teammate actually lived. If it did, then it would show that he was a real friend. So, too, changing our way of life because of the example of Jesus indicates that we are his friends.

Dietrich Bonhoeffer made a similar point in his book *The Cost of Discipleship* when he wrote against "cheap grace."[16] He stressed not only the obvious principle—*that only the one who believes will obey*—but also the more challenging corollary—*that only the one who obeys really believes.* His concern was to overcome the notion that there could be belief without obedience. Those who thought they could receive the grace and forgiveness that came from belief in Christ without actually being obedient to his commands were mistaken. Their inaction showed their lack of belief. The same can be said of friendship and following Jesus' way of life. Only friends of Jesus will want to follow his way of life, but equally, *only those who follow his way of life are actually his friends.* The challenge of friendship is to allow our Friend to change us. The grace of God means this is possible.

The cross as the foundation of friendship

The final characteristic of divine friendship is revealed when Christ dies for his friends: "No one has greater love than this, to lay down one's life for one's friends" (John 15:13). There is a soteriological foundation for Christian friendship. Without the cross of Christ, there can be no friendship. He laid down his life for his friends.

Of course, the death of Christ is always central to soteriology, but the way the death is understood depends upon the imagery that is invoked. If Christ is King, then atonement is seen in terms of a victory in battle or the redemption of a prisoner, and if Christ is High Priest, then the atonement is understood in terms of priestly sacrifice.

The death of Christ has thus been variously interpreted as a sacrificial offering, a demand of justice, the payment of a ransom, and the requirement of reconciliation. However, when related to the imagery of Christ as our Friend, it is seen purely and simply as an act of love. It is love that leads one to lay down one's life for one's friend. This makes the point very strongly that the central dynamic for the cross is love. It is not an act compelled by the requirements of law or justice; it is not undertaken unwillingly or begrudgingly; it is done freely and lovingly.

This imagery can stand on its own as a complement to the other images of atonement, and it can influence the way atonement is understood when other images are utilized. The general tendency has been for the atonement to be interpreted in terms related to those images that stress status, authority, and hierarchy, as in John Calvin's influential description of the saving activity of Christ that is expressed in terms of the threefold messianic office of prophet, king, and priest. Prophets were to declare the word of the Lord and teach his ways; kings were to govern as God's representatives, exercising justice and providing protection to the people; and priests were to be mediators between the people and God, dealing with sin and seeking divine favor. These three offices come together in the title "Christ" (taken literally as "anointed") because all three were anointed to their ministry. The Lord Jesus is the prophet of God who proclaims a message of healing and liberation; the heavenly king who enriches his people and protects the church; and the sinless high priest whose sacrifice and eternal intercession reconcile us to God.[17] However, these offices can be understood in terms of friendship as well as in terms of the lordship of Christ because he not only fulfilled these ancient offices, but he also transformed them in terms of the way they were exercised.[18]

First, as the prophet of the kingdom of God, Jesus challenged those who neglected their responsibilities or oppressed the poor. However, he also went well beyond the role of the prophet by becoming a friend of the poor.

Second, as the spiritual King of Israel, Jesus came to govern justly, to liberate people from slavery to sin, and to protect his subjects from the Evil One. However, he also transformed the relationship between the people and their king by inviting them to become "friends" of the King and making known to them "everything that I have heard from my Father" (John 15:15).

Finally, as the High Priest, he not only came to offer a sacrifice, but in particular, he offered the sacrifice of his own life as an expiation for sin for the salvation of the world. This sacrifice is described as the greatest love that one can have, and it is precisely the love involved when a person lays down his life for his friends.

In each of these ways, an impersonal office is turned into a personal relationship. The important roles of Prophet, Priest, and King, when seen in the light of divine friendship, instead of only in terms of divine lordship, take on a different light. The atonement is not like a commercial transaction, a political victory, or a cultic experience; it is part of a personal relationship without which there is no real humanity. Christ's death is the revelation of the nature and character of God as Friend. God is revealed in Christ, who shows the greatest love that there can be by giving up his life for his friends. Above all else, Christ is the Friend of sinners, and the most distinctive sign of friendship is Jesus' willingness to die for his friends: "greater love has no one than this, that he lay down his life for his friends" (John 15:13 NIV). The cross is the foundation of friendship.

The full significance of Christ's death as a friend can only be appreciated by taking into account the different biblical perceptions of the way Jesus' friendship operates. In John, as we have seen, the greatest love is "to lay down one's life for one's friends" and Jesus is the one who lays down his life willingly for his "own" (John 10:7–18; 15:13); but whereas in John, Christ's death is for his *friends,* in Paul, Christ's death is for his *enemies,* and it is offered as a sacrifice in order *to make them his friends.* In Paul, the great love of God is shown in the way Christ died for those who were actually opposed to God. This is the shock of the gospel: "Rarely will anyone die for a righteous person—though perhaps for a good person someone might actually dare to die. But God proves his love for us in that while we still were sinners Christ died for us" (Rom. 5:7–8).

According to the classic view, the ultimate test of friendship lies in being willing to die for one's friends. As Aristotle said, "It is true of the good man too that he does many acts for the sake of his friends and his country, and if necessary dies for them."[19] This is a noble death that brings honor to the one making the sacrifice. Paul, however, describes Jesus as going beyond what are usually considered to be the limits of friendship. His is a friendship that overcomes the inequality of status and radically extends the love that joins the friends together and which actually creates friendship through sacrifice.

Only through understanding both John and Paul is it possible to see the full implications of messianic friendship, and only through the effect of Christ's friendship-making death does the possibility arise of loving those who hate us. Humanly speaking, this is impossible; but God's befriending love makes it possible. Christians should aspire to love as God has loved us. This is at the core of the Christian life.

Conclusion

We have seen how the ancient Near Eastern concept of "friends of the king" relates to the special friendships that Abraham and Moses had with Yahweh and how this lies behind Jesus' offer of friendship to his disciples. No longer is close friendship with God in Christ limited to some; it is, in fact, the defining mark of belonging to Jesus. Friends of Jesus are called by him to an intimate relationship in which they can know the deep things of God. This friendship changes the lives of his friends and the way they live and relate to others. Jesus is the best Friend anyone can have, for in his death he has shown the greatest love of friendship. With the cross it becomes clearer that not only are disciples friends of God in Christ, but also that God in Christ is Friend to us. This is a deeply profound and transforming revelation of God in Christ. The shift of emphasis from God as Lord to God as Friend transforms our perception of God, our personal relationship with God, our perception of our own identity, and the form of our ministry. Everything is changed. If, as Paul affirms in Acts 17:28, it is in relation with God that we exist as persons ("In him we live and move and have our being"), then it is now clear that the form of our existence is to be understood in terms of friendship and its inner life of love and communion.

Learning

God Is Friendship

4

> God is friendship.
>
> Aelred of Rievaulx

B elievers in some of the earliest Christian communities were known simply as "the friends." At the end of the short letter known as 3 John, the writer says to Gaius,

> I hope to see you soon, and we will talk together face to face. Peace to you. *The friends* send you their greetings. Greet *the friends there*, each by name. (vv. 14–15; emphasis added)

He does not say, "*Your* friends send you their greetings" or "Greet *our* friends there," which would have been more natural if all that was meant was a reference to a few people who happened to be known to both parties. However, the references to "*the* friends" who send greetings and "the friends" who receive them suggest that he is referring to *the community* of believers. "The friends" had become a shorthand way of referring to all those who were part of the church of Jesus Christ, and was a term that could be used instead of "disciples" or "the believers."

This is a point that was taken up by the Society of Friends (more informally known as the Quakers), who are following a rich tradition in which friendship is understood as a key description of relationship with God through Christ and with the other members of the body of Christ.

This chapter will describe the main elements of the development of the theology of friendship. From the time of the apologist and evangelist Justin Martyr (c. 100–165) spiritual friendship grew in significance. The developing tradition drew on Jewish wisdom literature, the Graeco-Roman philosophical tradition, popular stories of friendships, accounts of friendships in business and politics as well as, of course, the gospel material about Jesus, his teaching, and his friendships. The tradition of Christian spiritual friendship particularly developed from the fourth century with Ambrose of Milan and John Cassian, who both wrote short pieces on friendship, through to the twelfth-century work of Aelred of Rieuvaulx. Not many wrote specific treatises on the topic, but the overall tradition includes Paulinus of Nola, Augustine of Hippo, Basil of Caesarea, Benedict of Nursia, Gregory the Great, Anselm of Canterbury, Bernard of Clairveaux, William of St. Thierry, and Thomas Aquinas. There is a relative constancy of approach within this medieval monastic tradition but never a dominant influence, and historically, it came to an end around the thirteenth century, after Aelred's influence declined.

The primary aim is neither a complete historical reconstruction nor an analysis of the individual sources, their methodology, or the relative degree of influence of particular figures involved. The aim is to draw out aspects of the early history of Christian friendship for contemporary Christians who wish to explore the notion of spiritual friendship for today. This is a journey undertaken in seven steps.

The first step involves noting the way in which friendship was seen, in both biblical tradition and contemporary culture, as an important dimension of a holy life. The second step goes further and interprets friendship both as a virtue in its own right and as an important means for developing other virtues. Friendship is thus a major component of a holy life. It is important for every individual. The third step involves recognizing the role friendship plays in ecclesiology. This requires a more developed theology of friendship, and it becomes a concept located at the heart of the idea of Christian community. The fourth step continues to move friendship to the center of theology as a whole, so that it has a preeminent position, not only at the core of the church but at the heart of our understanding of God. The nature of God, the nature of friendship, and the nature of love are interwoven, and Aelred declares, "God is friendship." This is the high point of the discussion, and the remaining steps consider various implications of this. The fifth step discusses the centrality of spiritual friendship and certain objections to it. The sixth step considers the implications of friendship in terms of eternity, while the final step is to return to a consideration of the role friendship now plays in spiritual formation.

Step one: spiritual friendship at the center of a holy life

The use of the terms "friends," "friends of Christ," and "friends of God" continued within the life of the church in the post-apostolic era. Justin Martyr testified that he was, at least in part, led to faith by the example of "the friends of Christ."

> A flame was kindled in my soul; and a love of the prophets, and of those men who are friends of Christ, possessed me . . . I found this philosophy alone to be safe and profitable.[1]

He pointed out that anyone, whether Scythian or Persian, who gained a knowledge of God in Christ and who sought to follow him would become "a friend of God," and God would rejoice in this.[2] Clement of Alexandria (c. 150–215) encouraged believers to have spiritual confidence because "through the mediation of the Word" they have been "made the friend of God." Thus they are able to share in everything that belongs to God, because, as everyone understands, friends have all things in common.[3] And although he did not use the phrase, Origen (c. 185–254) was familiar with the Pythagorean writing known as the Sentences of Sextus, which was popular among Christians, and he would have known of Sextus's declaration that "the goal of godly living is friendship with God."[4]

It is not surprising that Ambrose of Milan (c. 337–397) could write thoughtfully about friendship. He was so popular and highly regarded for his personal qualities among the people of Milan that he was spontaneously elected archbishop despite being a layman. After some hesitation, he accepted the position and threw himself into the study of theology. He proved to be a good choice—pastoral in approach, eloquent in preaching, courageous in dealing with emperors, orthodox, and theologically astute. He became one of the four traditional doctors of the Latin Church. He was, among other things, an influence on his friend, the notable Augustine of Hippo (354–430). Along with another friend, Paulinus of Nola (c. 353–431) who, with his wife, gave up great wealth to become a monk, and others, such as John Cassian (c. 360–435), he promoted the concept of spiritual friendship. Paulinus was the first to use the specific term *spiritalis amicitia*,[5] but it was Ambrose who was the greater influence, albeit in close connection with the general movement of the day.

Ambrose brought with him to his role as a leader of the church a classical education, and so he was familiar with the work of Marcus Tullius Cicero (106–43 BC), the Roman philosopher and statesman whose treatise *On Friendship (de Amicitia)* had already been influential for centuries. It was presented as a dramatic dialogue on many themes found in Plato and Aristotle, although Cicero had a broader interest in friendship than Aristotle and he went even further in bringing it to the forefront of social interaction, attributing to it a central place in society.

Cicero located friendship right at the center of a well-lived life, arguing that with the exception of wisdom, nothing is better than friendship: not riches, sensual pleasure, good health, power, or office (all of which are frail and uncertain and dependent on the caprice of fortune), and not even virtue. Aristotle had placed intellectual virtue (including wisdom, science, and understanding) and ethical virtue (justice, courage, temperament, and so forth) at the center. But Cicero argued that while it is more noble to find the "chief good" in virtue than in many other possibilities, even this is misconstrued; for virtue is that which leads to the final goal of friendship: "the very virtue they talk of is the parent and preserver of friendship, and without it friendship cannot possibly exist." Therefore, he said, "All I can do is to urge on you to regard friendship as the greatest thing in the world; for there is nothing which so fits in with our nature, or is so exactly what we want in prosperity or adversity."[6]

Life is not worth living without "the mutual good" of friends. Nothing is more pleasurable than friendship—prosperity is pointless unless shared, and friendship halves the burden of misfortune.[7] Ambrose took this understanding of friendship and merged it with biblical notions of love and friendship both in his own dealings with the clergy and in his writing in *On the Duties of the Clergy,* which he based on Cicero's *On Duties (de Officiis,* c. 44 BC) which dealt with the ideal public life, including discussions of the four major virtues: prudence, justice, courage (or fortitude), and moderation (or temperance).[8] He felt justified in integrating the ideas of the ancient Greeks and Cicero's basic structure with Christian principles because, after all, "whence have they got such ideas but out of the holy Scriptures?" That is, it seemed obvious to Ambrose that Cicero had learned about virtue and friendship from Moses and David and the other writers of the Old Testament.[9]

Step two: spiritual friendship as a virtue and the way to develop virtue

Ambrose developed Cicero's work by saying that friendship itself was a virtue. This was something new; no previous writer had unequivocally called friendship, or love in any form, "a virtue."[10] Friendship was a virtue because it was the expression of kindness and goodwill to God and others. Indeed, it was the guardian of virtues, and thus an important part of "the duties of the clergy" (and other Christians). He also connected virtue, and therefore friendship (*amicitia*), to the love (*caritas*) that is at the heart of the Christian life so that, for example, justice, which prefers the well-being of the other to the promotion of the self, is an expression of the true love of God.[11] Therefore, both love and friendship are important for the virtuous life.

His discussion of friendship in *On the Duties of the Clergy* begins with an illustration of friendship from the book of Esther. The Persian king Ahasuerus hanged Haman his "chief friend" for betraying his position of authority, and Ambrose uses this to make the point that friendship is not an excuse for abusing privilege or gaining honor or power. In a passage that shows his integration of Cicero and Scripture, Ambrose agrees that it is actually necessary to rebuke a friend who suggests otherwise,

> For rebukes are good, (*as Cicero had declared in his "On Duties"*) and often better than a silent friendship. Even if a friend thinks himself hurt, still rebuke him; and if the bitterness of the correction wounds his mind, still rebuke him and fear not. "The wounds of a friend are better than the kisses of flatterers." (*as according to Proverbs 27:6*). Rebuke, then, thy erring friend; forsake not an innocent one. For friendship ought to be steadfast. (*Cicero again, from "On Friendship"*) "[12]

However, the context of the rebuke is that of friendship, and therefore it is done with love, avoiding harshness and bitterness as much as flattery and arrogance. "Let the other warn and reprove like a friend, not from a desire to show off, but with a deep feeling of love."[13]

Negatively speaking, friendship is to help avoid sin, and positively, the point of friendship is to develop virtue. It is not primarily about personal pleasure, amusement, conversation, or shared activities; it is not even really about education, empathy, or encouragement—though these are not bad aspects of a friendship. Much more than this, friendship is about the development of personal, and even communal, character. It is to be concerned with virtue and goodness and the spiritual life, and a friendship that does not address these matters is no real friendship. Altogether, in Ambrose's terms, friendship should exhibit the classic virtues which are interpreted in the light of the Christian "fruit of the Spirit"—love, joy, peace, patience, kindness, goodness, faithfulness, gentleness, and self-control (Gal. 5:22 NIV). The lesson in this for every age, but perhaps particularly the present, is that the importance of friendship lies in the way it can mediate virtue, rather than in the way it can amuse or entertain us. The fruit of the Spirit simply cannot be learned in isolation; they are essentially relational, and growth in the Christian life depends on having close companions who can help develop them.

Most people find it hard to be too different from those around them; there is a tendency for attitudes and behaviors to be held in common and to become a community standard. Just as the tallest trees are those found in a forest, so, too, in order to grow spiritually taller, we need tall people around us who will encourage growth. This encouragement is vital for the moral development of the person. Ambrose understood this and stressed its importance when he said not only that "friendship is the support of life," but also that "a faithful friend is the medicine of life and the grace of immortality." The road to holiness is not taken alone.

Social transformation through friendship

There are, thankfully, some people who are able to do what is right when they perceive that a society is engaged in some injustice. These are people who stand up for the oppressed in the face of opposition. They are the people who are able to be different from those around them who tend to go with the prevailing standards. Edmund Burke's aphorism, "all that is required for evil to triumph is for good people to do nothing," is relevant here. A certain strength of character is required in order to be radically different from others, and few people achieve it. Not everyone can be a Wilberforce, a Mother Teresa, or a Martin Luther King, but the leadership of such people is important and can lead to significant transformation. Others can follow where they have led, and so through this ministry it is possible to turn a community into a just society. This is *social* transformation through what we might call *prophetic* leadership.

There *is* a need for prophetic figures who are able to stand out as being radically different and who oppose the worst forms of evil, but there is perhaps an even greater need for friends who are prepared to make friendship a spiritual relationship that challenges people to overcome their satisfaction with a mediocre Christian life. This form of personal transformation through friendship contrasts with, but complements, prophetic leadership.

Friendship is a simpler form of transformation than the prophetic, but it is one that is accessible to everyone, and there is no shortage of need for spiritual friendships that builds up the friends of God. There are, unfortunately, many who are satisfied with what is merely good (rather than the best), often mediocre, and sometimes morally dubious. The difficulty the prophet faces with outright injustice is not in recognizing it, but in being prepared to be the first to do something about it, and this can require people of remarkable courage. The difficulty with mediocrity lies in recognizing it for what it is and being willing to show and encourage oneself and one's friends to a better way of living. One may be tempted to think that such people are as rare as those individuals who stand out within a society as a whole.

When an individual (or the community as a whole) is unaware of the possibility of a greater good, or is self-satisfied with a life that is not as enriching or as joyful or as faithful as it might otherwise be, then one needs a friend who can remind one, in the words of another aphorism, that "the good is the enemy of the best." The whole point of friendship in the monastic tradition is that it is not satisfied with the average; it seeks nothing but the best in the other, and that means the greatest possible faith and love. Spiritual friendship that seeks the best in the other is the primary means of overcoming the natural tendency to be satisfied with that which is relatively easy to achieve.

Step three: spiritual friendship as the heart of Christian community

Ambrose's description of friendship as both a virtue and as a means to virtue is important not only because of the conclusions it comes to about individual friendship, but also because it establishes a pattern of theological reflection on friendship. In this tradition, friendship is now located toward the center of the Christian spiritual life, and the notions of friendship with God and of being a community of friends are not merely superficial terms but part of a developed theology of friendship. However, despite the teaching of Ambrose and Cassian, it was not until the time of Anselm of Canterbury in the eleventh century that the concept of spiritual friendship developed any further. Monastic friendships certainly existed, but there was great reservation, even suspicion, about them because of the possibility of abuses. So friendship did not, generally at least, go beyond formal and polite expressions of friendship consistent with the conventions of the day. But with Anselm, comments Douglass Roby, "We suddenly see the rhetoric of epistolary friendship fuse with the inarticulate friendship of monks to become genuine spiritual friendship."[14]

Anselm is famous for his writing on God and the atonement. He was responsible for changing the way the work of Christ was understood, which, until his *Cur Deus Homo* (*Why God Became Man*), was largely focused on the ransom theory (Christ's death was a ransom paid to release us from the power of the devil). However, he related the atonement to medieval concepts of honor and satisfaction, and friendship played an important role in this.

The feudal concept of status involved paying appropriate honor to people according to their rank. Satisfaction (an apology, a payment, or punishment) was required whenever a superior's honor was slighted. God, naturally, was considered to have the greatest honor, and all human disobedience and sin could be seen as an infringement of it. It was, therefore, necessary that satisfaction should be made to God. Anselm's conclusion was that because this payment *ought* to be made by man (who is the cause of the dishonor), but *can only* be made by God (the only one who can make such a great reparation), it necessarily has to be made by the God-man, Jesus Christ.[15] As the one man who does not have to make any satisfaction, Jesus becomes a substitute for the whole of humanity. This substitution is only possible because of the spiritual union with Christ that occurs through friendship. Christ, as our friend, is at one with us. It is important to note that for Anselm the idea of friendship with Christ was not merely an image or a metaphor but a spiritual reality. The biblical concept of union with Christ is interpreted in the light of the ancient Greek tradition of friendship as a linking of souls in complete harmony. Aristotle spoke of the friend as "another self"; indeed, a man "is related to his friend as to himself (for his friend is another self)."[16] At least from the time of Aristotle it was proverbial that "a friend is one soul in two bodies." This was important for Anselm because it made possible the substitution of one person for another, and this was central to his theology of atonement.

A remarkable illustration of the degree to which this fusion of souls was adopted by Anselm is found in a letter he wrote to Henry, the prior at the Monastery of Canterbury. It concerned a youthful monk called Moses who, Anselm believed, had been deceived into taking money belonging to someone else, which he then spent. He had deserted the monastery but now wished to return, and Anselm wrote on his behalf, taking advantage of the parable of the prodigal son to encourage Henry to be like the loving father. But in addition to this, Anselm wrote that

> Master Moses, from the sole of his foot to the crown of his head, is covered entirely with the skin of your servant brother Anselm . . . if therefore, there should be anyone among you whom I have ever willfully offended, let him first scourge my skin in Moses for that aforesaid fault . . . But after that I commend my skin to brother Moses to guard as he loves his own; and to you that you not merely spare it. For if for his fault my skin be struck or severely injured, of him will I require it; but if any should spare him, I will be grateful to him . . . know that I have no other skin, since his safety is mine: his soul is my soul.[17]

The idea of substitution is clearly seen here. It is as though two souls share the one body (or at least the same skin), for Moses is now a friend of Anselm. It is possible for one friend to stand in for another. This way of speaking may seem unusual to those of us today who operate from within a very different context and who do not share the same cultural or philosophical background, and yet it is possible to see the spiritual zeal involved in being willing to stand with a friend. It gives depth to the notion of friendship with Christ that cannot be seen as mere imagery or metaphor but rather as a real spiritual relationship. In regard to our own relationship with Christ, we do not have to speak the way Anselm spoke about Moses in order to be reminded of the spiritual connection that there is between Christ and his friends. The cross is indeed the basis of salvation, and its benefits are available because of friendship with Jesus. He laid down his life for his friends to bring salvation to them, and the friends of Jesus are to imitate this level of love in their own relationships.

Step four: God is friendship

At this point, the friendship tradition came to its climax in the claim that "God is friendship" in Aelred of Rievaulx (1110–1167). Aelred was one of a trio of friends whose work, when combined, brought together contemplation, love, grace, the Trinity, and friendship. Bernard of Clairveaux (1090–1153) was an influential Cistercian teacher and spiritual leader of the age. He was a theological mystic with a deep understanding of love and grace who stressed the fact that God should be loved simply because God is God. William of St. Thierry (near Reims; 1085–1148) was a Benedictine monk who later joined a Cistercian monastery, and he reflected on the spiritual implications of the nature of the Trinity and redemption. Aelred was born in Hexham, Northumbria, into a well-educated and religious family. As part of the common practice of the time, as a youth he was sent away from home to live and learn with another family. He went to the court of King David I of Scotland to be a companion to one of his sons. Part of his education involved familiarity with Cicero's *On Friendship*. During a mission to York on behalf of the king in 1132, Aelred visited a new Cistercian monastery at Rievaulx. After considering the matter overnight, he returned the next day and joined the community. He subsequently became abbot and was known for his appreciation of monastic friendships, and he wrote *Spiritual Friendship* (*de Spiritali Amicitia*).

Spiritual Friendship is one of the great works of medieval spirituality, and yet its influence has been limited to a remarkable degree. Until relatively recent times, it has largely been unknown. Aelred was well known among monastic communities during his lifetime, although his books and his teaching were basically limited to England and the Low Countries. Even Bernard at Clairveaux only had an abbreviated compendium of Aelred's work. He was known for a century or so after his death, but thereafter his teaching was generally lost even to those in the monastic tradition. When he was quoted, it was often without attribution or incorrectly attributed to Bernard or another writer. No other monastic writers followed his lead and wrote on spiritual friendship. His writings were first published in 1616, but interest only began when he was included in the *Lives of the English Saints* in 1845,[18] and he has only been widely known since the middle of the twentieth century.

Why was there such an apparent lack of interest in what has been such a highly regarded piece of spiritual writing? It is because close friendship—even as a part of spiritual formation—was no longer seen as a part of monastic life. The tradition of spiritual friendship from Ambrose, Cassian, and Basil of Caesarea to Aelred has always been the perspective of a minority. By and large, intimate friendships were not expected, generally not discussed, and were frequently distrusted as opening doors to cliques that damaged the community as a whole, and to specific relationships that were open to abuse. The fear of spiritually damaging relationships meant that the many, significant spiritual advantages described by Aelred were usually not realized within the life of the community. This is a loss that cannot be measured.

Aelred's high view of friendship began explicitly with Cicero's *On Friendship*, with up to a third of his work based on what was widely considered a classic expression of social relations. Consequently, his work gained a degree of authority from this association, but he was no slave to Cicero, and he readily adapted and extended Cicero's view in his own way. And he specifically related his teaching to Scripture where, although there is no formal discussion of friendship, there is wisdom about being a friend and there are illustrations and practical examples of friendship as well as the teaching of Jesus.

Aelred began by accepting Cicero's basic definition that "friendship is mutual harmony in affairs human and divine coupled with benevolence and charity (*caritas*)"[19] which may be interpreted as saying that friends (a) share a common view about life, (b) share in affection or love, and (c) seek the good (for the friend, for themselves, and for the wider community). However, Aelred thought of friendship entirely from a theological point of view and so he pointed out, at the very start, that true friendship of this kind only exists in Christ. His point was illustrated even before he expounded it by way of the famous first words of his treatise, when he said to his friend Ivo, "Here we are, you and I, and I hope a third, Christ, is in our midst."[20]

In this opening sentence he summarized the essence of friendship: being together in Christ. If the inclusion of Christ as the most important element of friendship is the most fundamental step, then the subsequent connection of love and friendship is not much less significant. It is only by being in Christ that friendship has the love that is the dynamic for benevolent behavior. As the very words point out, said Aelred, friendship (*amicitia*) is grounded in love (*amor*). And so, by definition, all friendships involve this affection, and this in turn derives from friendship (*amicitia*) with God. This connection of *amicitia* with God has two implications of great significance for Aelred's distinctive view.

Passion in the love of God

The first is that in relating *amicitia* to our relationship with God, he was describing a relationship of great intimacy and affection. He held to a view of the divine-human relationship that is predicated on a remarkable closeness. This love between God and his friends is passionate, warm, affectionate, and intimate. Sometimes, in other traditions, God's love is interpreted more intellectually than passionately, more volitionally than emotionally, more action oriented than affectively, and more sacrificially and tragically than in the almost romantic manner in which Aelred portrayed it. However, there was no such reserve in Aelred, who said,

> Friendship, therefore, is that virtue by which spirits are bound by ties of love and sweetness, and that of many are made one[21] [and] . . . in friendship are joined honor and charm, truth and joy, sweetness and goodwill, affection and action *(and, of course)* all these take their beginning from Christ, advance through Christ, and are perfected in Christ.[22]

Here is a description of relationship with God that is full of passion, love, and delight. This relationship is not primarily based on obedience and service (although these are by no means excluded), but on fervent feelings, extreme ardor, unbridled enthusiasm, extreme zeal, and great delight. The affections described are those usually applied only to those few whom one loves most deeply, but in Aelred they are applied to God and understood to be reciprocated, for God is the one who loves with the greatest passion. It represents the intensity of the love expressed in the Song of Solomon,

> Let him kiss me with the kisses of his mouth! For your love is better than wine . . . Your name is perfume poured out; therefore the maidens love you . . . We will exult and rejoice in you; we will extol your love more than wine; rightly do they love you. (1:2–4)

Throughout this "Song of Songs" or "Greatest Song," the lover praises the beloved ("you whom my soul loves . . . you are beautiful"; 1:7, 15) in such earthy, romantic, passionate, human language that many have had difficulty understanding how it can be applied to a relationship with the almighty God. In much the same way, some have questioned the romanticism of Aelred and, in like manner, those expressions of love and passion that emerge in some forms of corporate prayer and worship.

There are at least three factors involved in the reservations and criticisms concerning this sort of emotional expression. The first is *cultural*, and it is obvious that emotion and passion are demonstrated according to conventions that vary between cultures and even within cultures, depending on social grouping and context. Therefore, for some the expression of passion of the kind attributed to Aelred and the Song of Solomon is problematic because of the reserve of their culture or their class or individual personality. The issue here does not lie in the passion itself, but in the nature of public expression. In some situations, it is appropriate for the praise of God to be loud, enthusiastic, and bold, while for others this is something best expressed in private or in the measured, corporate reading of a psalm of praise. While respect for cultural norms is appropriate, Aelred is reminding us of the importance of not denying the depth of one's relationship with God and of the importance of expressing it fully in worship.

Others have deeper questions, not so much with the appropriate cultural expression of emotion as with the spiritual appropriateness of intimate relationship of which Aelred spoke. As we have seen, for a long time there was in the monastic tradition significant reserve about the notion of spiritual friendship, and there are always those who prefer a more transcendent understanding of the divine nature and forms of divine-human relationship that are more oriented toward "discipleship" or "service" and worship that stresses difference, majesty, and divine authority. Although the different approaches are not fundamentally opposed, it can be difficult to coordinate them, and there are those who, for example, speak scathingly of "Jesus is my boyfriend" approaches to worship, which stress emotion and deep passion. It is true that the words that Aelred used to express his deep passion can be used in other romantic and even sentimental associations. A statement such as "I love you" can be maudlin, sentimental, trivial, or even code for lust. These possibilities make it difficult for some to apply the same words to a relationship with God. But the words "I love you" can also be used within a deep, loving relationship of husband and wife of many years and may be a summation of a life of shared experiences of faithfulness, sacrifice, sadness, and joy, and an expression of a genuinely deep feeling. Or, it can be an equally deep expression of a real friendship. One cannot necessarily tell their significance from the words alone, and there simply are no other words available that have the potential to be as profound or as deep as these. Nothing else can speak of a relationship with God that is as deep and as rich as this, or even deeper and richer. Aelred was right to encourage believers to explore the depth of their relationship with God in Christ in this way.

A third reservation about the form of spiritual friendship of which Aelred spoke is theological and is a repercussion of the classic theological tradition of the impassibility of God. This is the doctrine that

God is not affected emotionally by anything and is impassible or apathetic. The rationale behind this is that a being subject to passions of any kind is one who can be affected or changed by someone else whose behavior makes him sad or happy or angry, and this challenges the ultimate power of God. Historically, this doctrine is one that was imported from Greek philosophy, and it has created internal theological conflicts because it does not (unless one assumes all such biblical statements about God showing passion are anthropomorphisms) fit with the biblical tradition of God who loves, becomes incarnate, and dies for the world. The alleged philosophical problems associated with such a God have to give way to the incarnate, loving, passionate God. And yet the effects of the impassibility doctrine have lingered on in various contexts, though not in Aelred, for whom intimate relationship with Jesus Christ was at the heart of everything. It is not merely passion that is central but precisely a passion for Christ. This should not be misunderstood, for it is not a passion of the kind that may be commonly found and which may be oriented toward the trivial as much as toward that which is magnificent. This is a passion for the transcendent, almighty God, and what makes it so passionate is that this awesome God is the very one who has come close to us. This is the astonishing truth of the gospel of Jesus Christ. This passion is not just about personal feeling or private emotion; it is love of the one who is great and good, loving and gracious. One can get emotional intensity, and one can appear to get intimacy, in many other ways, but it is only through a relationship with God that real intimacy and real passion emerge. This is the message of Aelred. As the American theologian of revival, Jonathan Edwards, said, "If persons have the true light of heaven let into their souls, it is not a light without heat."[23]

Friendship as the highest love

The second implication of Aelred's connection of friendship-love (*amicitia*) with God is that he drew a distinction between two related senses of love. In addition to the intense, personal, affective *amicitia,* there is *caritas,* which is that sacrificial love to be shown in care and service to all. It represents the Greek New Testament notion of love as *agape.* At this point he was dealing with the difference between a general love (*caritas*) of neighbor and specific friendships (*amicitia*), and he observed that "in the perfection of charity we love very many who . . . we do not admit to the intimacy of our friendship."[24] There is a distinction between charity-love and friendship-love,

> For divine authority approves that more are to be received into the bosom of charity than into the embrace of friendship. For we are compelled by the law of charity to receive in the embrace of love not only our friends but also our enemies. But only those do we call friends to whom we can fearlessly entrust our heart and all its secrets; those, too, who, in turn, are bound to us by the same law of faith and security.[25]

But one should not draw this distinction too sharply as though these two loves are not connected, nor should one assume that friendship is, therefore, a lower grade of love compared with the sacrificial love of caritas. It is not at all like that. The fact that we are only able to love some within the bonds of friendship is a limitation that is a result of the Fall, a derogation from the original and perfect state of the world.[26] Friendship, therefore, is actually the truest remnant of a genuinely full and universally mutual love. Thus, friendship is a superior expression of love, a representation of that perfection which God intended at the beginning, which will one day be restored to all in eternity, and which, in the meantime, is the calling and the privilege for all those who follow Christ. The connection between that universal love of all and friendship is observed when he says, "The fountain and source of friendship is love. There can be love without friendship, but friendship without love is impossible."[27]

Friendship is the epitome of love. The implication of this is that while believers have a responsibility to love all, especially neighbors, no one can love everyone fully or comprehensively, but everyone can love some people in that way. The love of friends, therefore, is an important part and expression of our love for God. It was most certainly *not* the case for Aelred that one loves God primarily and others secondarily. For through friendship-love, one is expressing the highest love. And all such love is founded upon and points toward the love of God. There is, therefore, no conflict between the love of God and the love of friends because all love, including its highest form of friendship-love, has its origin in God.

So it was that Aelred came to his famous definition, that "God is friendship." Aelred was able to lift friendship to a higher level than it held for Ambrose in much the same way that Cicero was able to promote friendship above the position it held for the ancient Greeks. For the ancient Greeks, friendship was a means toward virtue, and both friendship and virtue contributed—together with pleasure, honor, wealth, and wisdom—to a good life. However, in Cicero, friendship was promoted to being the goal or chief end of a well-lived life. Subsequently, Ambrose interpreted the all-important virtue in terms of the fruit of the Spirit and, especially, love (*caritas*) which, in turn, produced friendship (*amicitia*). He was thus able to see friendship itself as one of the virtues. However, within this monastic spiritual tradition of friendship, Aelred followed Cicero's example and advanced friendship so that it became the highest expression of love. In this way he appreciated the work of Cicero on friendship, but as he said, Cicero

> was unacquainted with the virtue of true friendship, since he was completely unaware of its beginning and end, Christ . . . for what more sublime can be said of friendship, what more true, what more profitable, than that it ought to, and is proved to, begin in Christ, continue in Christ, and be perfected in Christ?[28]

It is a very significant point that in Aelred the form of love that lies at the heart of the divine-human relationship is friendship-love—an intimate, affective love that transcends, without denying, the more active love of care, justice, and charity which is due to all. And in this intimacy, a real friendship is found only with Christ involved, "you and I, and I hope a third, Christ, in our midst." For Aelred, the biblical evidence for this lay in the eternal nature of friendship as described in Proverbs 17:17, which says, "He that is a friend loveth at all times" (DRB), and by Jerome, who said, "Friendship which can end was never true friendship."[29] Because the only eternal one is God, the only conclusion is to say of friendship what John, the friend of Jesus, said of love—"God is friendship." Aelred admitted to reservations about this conclusion:

> That would be unusual, to be sure, nor does it have the sanction of the Scriptures. But still what is true of charity, I surely do not hesitate to grant to friendship, since "he that abides in friendship, abides in God, and God in him."[30]

The focus of the spiritual life is none other than Jesus Christ. He is the focus of Christian formation, and knowing Christ and growing in love is the whole point. This friendship with Christ connects all his friends together as one community of friendship—the church. Mutual friendship is the primary means for understanding relationships within the church, and it is within the church that one establishes those friendships that lead to Christian formation. Friendship with all who are within the community does not mean that one will be close or most intimate with everyone, but it is within this context that one finds the friends that will be of greatest assistance. It is of incalculable value to have a friend who shares life with us and who thinks in terms of spiritual growth.

Step five: friendship and love

The claim that friendship is the primary expression of love with God and others is not beyond challenge. For some, Christian love clearly has to be something more than friendship. The British writer, critic, and devout Anglican Samuel Johnson (1709–1784), argued that friendship and Christian love were mutually exclusive:

All friendship is preferring the interest of a friend, to the neglect, or, perhaps, against the interest of others; so that as an old Greek said, "He that has friends has no friend." Now Christianity recommends universal benevolence, to consider all men as our brethren, which is contrary to the virtue of friendship, as described by the ancient philosophers.[31]

This was an argument also utilized by both Kant (for whom the particularity of friendship was in conflict with the categorical imperative) and Kierkegaard, for whom friendship became idolatrous as it deepened. For Kierkegaard, friendship is not intrinsically bad; it is a human necessity, but not a specifically Christian virtue. Friendship (*philia*) and Christian love (*agape*) take the person in different directions. Friendship is preferential and based on human attraction, agape is self-sacrificing and based on God's command to love the one who is different or in need. This differentiation was also the essence of Anders Nygren's distinction between *agape* and *eros* with *philia* as a subset of *eros*.[32] They represent contradictory worldviews, with *agape* being theocentric and *eros* being egocentric. While these various arguments have been influential, they have also been recognized as unnecessarily divisive. They also fail to fully comprehend the nature of Christian friendship.

First, there is no need for a sharp distinction that separates love and friendship. While C. S. Lewis's discussion of "the Four Loves" (unconditional love, affection, friendship, and erotic love) is not so highly polarized, it nonetheless demonstrates the problems inherent in any attempt to categorize the complexities of both human nature and language. He helpfully delineates the varied nature of love and shows the importance of the various terms, but love and friendship (as well as other personal affections and impulses) are perhaps more complex than suggested by a fourfold categorization. The distinctions made, for instance, between unconditional love (agape) and friendship mean that he has little place for friendship as a spiritual relationship. Friendship is a valuable, even central human relationship[33] but is clearly distinguished, by linguistic means, from unconditional, Christian love.

Despite the differences in their range of meaning, neither contemporary Greek literature nor the New Testament maintains a sharp
distinction between agape/love and friendship/philia, and friendship
is frequently used as an entirely appropriate theological word to use of
the form of both God's relationship with people and the relationship of
believers. The flexibility between the various forms of *agape* and *philia* is
seen in the way both can be used in the nontheological sense of those
who "love" the seats of honor at a banquet (as in Matt. 23:6, which uses
the cognate of *philia*), or in the synagogue (as in Luke 11:43, which uses
the cognate of *agape*), and in Jesus' use of both, apparently interchange-
ably, in his dialogue with Peter about tending his sheep, in John 21:15–19.
And the theological use of *philia* is seen in references to the Father's love
for the Son, the Father's love for disciples, and the disciples, love for "the
Lord" (John 5:20; 16:27; Matt. 10:37; 1 Cor. 16:22). It is also seen in
the various friendships: Jesus is friend of both sinners and the disciples, Theophilus is a friend of God, and God is the friend of all people
(Matt. 11:19; Luke 7:34; Luke 1:3; Acts 1:1; John 15:14; Titus 3:4).

Secondly, a theological or spiritual dimension to friendship is only
problematic when friendship is defined too narrowly and not from the
perspective of faith, that is, when friendship is understood without
reference to its fulfillment in love for God. When love for God is introduced into friendship, then there is no conflict between friendship
and universal or unconditional love; rather, friendship is the means for
developing this love, and universal, unconditional love is friendship's
ultimate goal. The claim that preferential love is necessarily exclusive
and unjust does not stand when the love that is experienced in a friendship is one that takes the person beyond self-centered concerns. There
is a certain appropriateness in giving to a close friend (as to a husband,
wife, or colleague) the love, care, or time that is due to that friend by
virtue of his or her position. But such a preference need not be exclusive, any more than the "exclusiveness" that is intrinsic to the finitude of
life as a whole, because of which it is simply impossible to relate fully to

every single person. It is certainly true that some friendships are exclusive, narrow, and unhelpful, but this need not be seen as the normal definition of friendship. Good friendships enable and encourage the befriending of others and develop love and compassion. Friendship that is filled with grace is a training school for divine friendship. It is neither fulfilled in itself without the transformation of grace (contrary to the self-love and self-sufficiency of friendship in Aristotle and the Greek fathers), nor is it to be dismissed as un-transformable. In friendship, Christians can develop a habit of love that eventually becomes a principle of life.

This issue was addressed in the sermon "Love of Relations and Friends" by John Henry Newman (1801–1890). According to Newman, the idea that Christian love is contrary to the preferential love of a few in friendship is not only mistaken but precisely the reverse of the truth. The best—indeed, the only—way to go about loving the world at large is to develop friendships with those near to us and, through them, to learn to love. "The love of our private friends is the *only* preparatory exercise for the love of all men."[34] The principle that "whoever is faithful in a very little is faithful also in much" (Luke 16:10) applies, and what is learned early in faith will be developed later. It is a matter of learning habits for a lifetime, habits that can only be learned in the context of personal relationships. The call to love the world—to love enemies as well as neighbors, the poor as well as family, the weak and the alienated—can be intimidating, but in friendship God has provided a means of help by reducing the initial scope of the call. As Newman says, in friendship "he has given us a clue"; we are to begin with loving the friends around us, and then we will be enabled to enlarge the circle of love and compassion until it reaches all people.

The love of friends—if it is authentically Christian love—will create an attitude, a life-orientation, or a disposition toward others that will enable us to be ready to help whenever and wherever we can. Friendship nurtures the love that can change the world; it is the means to learning compassion, care, patience, kindness, gentleness, and all the virtues. Friendship is not merely advantageous in this way; it is essential; it is *the* way to learn. Those who have not learned about loving others at close quarters will take no interest in helping or caring for people for their own sake. "Private virtue," Newman suggests, "is the only sure foundation of public virtue."[35]

This avoids any trivialization of friendship. When God and Christ are introduced into friendship, it cannot be a self-centered or cozy relationship. There can be no reduction of friendship to human standards, but rather a reevaluation of friendship according to the friendship of Jesus Christ. In friendship, Christians can develop a habit of love that eventually becomes a principle of life.

Step six: friendship, eternity, and the communion of saints

Although Ambrose did not, as Aelred did later, come to the conclusion that "God is friendship," he nonetheless had a high view of friendship as a blessing that develops one's moral life, helps lead to life with God, and is itself a relationship grounded in God. The connection, in both writers, of friendship with Christ took friendship into the realm of the eternal. Their understanding of human friendship lived in Christ was that it was a present experience of an eternal union. The experience of friendship is the means by which it is possible to anticipate future glory here and now. All dimensions of life will be transformed through the resurrection and will be found in eternity in a renewed fashion. Yet, if there is one aspect of our present lives of love in Christ that will be seen most directly in this future life, it is friendship. Other relationships, such as marriage, may change,[36] but friendship will certainly continue and will be changed only in that the present limitation of friendship to a few will be removed and friendship will become the universal form of relationship: "With salvation secured, we shall rejoice in the eternal possession of Supreme Goodness; and this friendship, to which here we admit but few, will be outpoured upon all and by all outpoured upon God, and God shall be all in all."[37]

Friendship, then, is the heavenly form of love and a relationship experienced in eternity that can also be experienced now. Because friendship was seen as a present anticipation of eternity, it created a strong sense of the immediacy of heaven and of the communion of saints. One illustration of this, concerning the use of wealth, shows not only how the believer is to relate to others as friends, but also how *friendship connects us to eternity*. Ambrose's discussion of wealth again begins with, but soon supersedes Cicero's understanding of the need to share earthly possessions. While Cicero utilizes the proverb "friends have everything in common"[38] to make his point, Ambrose prefers to make use of Jesus' instruction at the end of the parable of the dishonest manager that the disciples should "make friends" for themselves by their use of wealth (Luke 16:9). But for Ambrose, the friends that are made through the use of money are *not only* the earthly recipients of the suggested generosity, but *the saints who are in heaven* who observe these acts of generosity: "If you bring the stranger under your roof, if you support the needy, he procures for you the friendship of the saints and eternal habitations. That is no small recompense. You sow earthly things and receive heavenly."[39]

Friendship is thus grounded in Christ, expressed in relationship to others and experienced in relation to all the saints in heaven. Friendship is not just an earthly relationship, but something which emerges from a spiritual relationship with God in Christ and, as a spiritual relationship, it is the form of connection of "the communion of saints."

This eschatological dimension of friendship as the eternal form of community is, today, frequently neglected, although it is important for our understanding of the life and mission of the church. This is seen, I would suggest, in the rather limited popular perception of the church that is commonly seen as "the community of believers" or "a gathering of the people of God" or "a congregation of saints." The biblical images associated with a definition such as "the people of God," or "the body of Christ" do, in biblical usage, have an eschatological dimension, but this is often neglected in practice, in favor of an understanding of the church as the present gathering of believers. The problem is accentuated by the common tendency for Christians to think about the church sociologically rather than theologically. In *sociological* terms the world or *the culture* is the broader concept, and the church, one voluntary association among many, is one component of it. That is, the focus falls upon the gathered people of God. In itself, that is good and correct, but without an obvious reference to the broader Christian hope, it becomes too present-oriented, lacking a genuinely eschatological dimension. Nevertheless, theologically, the church as the body of Christ is the greater, broader concept; it is nothing less than the future and the destiny of all things! The world was created so that there might be a church, a community worshiping God, a body of Christ. The church, as the body of Christ, is the primary category, and it is nothing less than the future of the world. A sociological mind-set that views the church as a part of the culture diminishes what ought to be a more substantial theological perception of the grandeur and the ultimate destiny of the body of Christ. The church needs to see itself as the present, proleptic anticipation of what God is going to do for the whole of creation, which is nothing less than the incorporation of all things in the Trinitarian life of God with all the saints, something that is expressed in terms of friendship.

Step seven: holy friendship as spiritual formation

Naturally, the writers on friendship, from Ambrose to Aelred, located friendship within the discipleship structure of their time. This means it was understood within the broad framework of the ascetic, medieval monastic tradition. This led to the introduction, as we have already seen, of a number of dimensions to the relationship that *enhanced* the role of friendship as a spiritual relationship both with God and other people. At the same time, it initiated a process that was partially responsible for *limiting* its role to those seeking the perfection they saw as the preserve of those set apart within the religious disciplines. This was the result of there being various levels of the Christian life. It was understood that there were *commandments* that were the responsibility of all believers and *counsels of perfection* that were expected only of some. The Ten Commandments, for example, were for all followers of Christ, while Jesus' counsel to the rich young ruler to embrace voluntary poverty was only for some. Specifically, it was for those who wished to achieve the "perfection" ("If you wish to be perfect, go, sell your possessions, and give the money to the poor, and you will have treasure in heaven; then come, follow me"; Matt. 19:21) at which the monastic life was aimed. Similarly, Paul's words about virginity are taken as specific counsel rather than general command ("Now concerning virgins, I have no command of the Lord, but I give my opinion . . . that, in view of the impending crisis, it is well for you to remain as you are"; 1 Cor. 7:25–26).

Given this dualistic ethic, the modern reader may well expect Ambrose and Cassian, for example, to treat friendship as one of the general expectations of all believers while treating the more onerous expectations of poverty, chastity, and obedience as the obligations of those few who seek to live according to the principles of the higher, monastic stage of the Christian life. This would fit with many popular perceptions of monasticism as being primarily characterized by self-discipline, asceticism, and sacrifice. However, the actual situation is the reverse of this because the instructions that the monastics understood Jesus to be giving to *all* believers are described as "commandments," and they reasoned that commandments are given to servants rather than to friends. Friends, on the other hand, are given counsel, but, Ambrose and Cassian argued, this counsel (concerning poverty, chastity, and obedience) that Jesus gave to some of his followers was *more* challenging than the commandments given to all. This could only be so because they operated within the context of friendship—a relationship of love, openness, and encouragement that enabled one to achieve the highest reaches of the spiritual life—rather than merely servanthood.

The role of discipline and sacrifice in their monasticism should not be misunderstood, for there was, in fact, a deep understanding of friendship and intimacy with God, which lies beyond the mere performance of ascetic disciplines. This is also seen in the writing of John Cassian (c. 360–435), who learned about the monastic life in communities near Bethlehem and in Egypt before founding two monasteries near Marseilles. It was there that he produced his *Conferences*, which are written as a series of dialogues on various topics with a number of Eastern fathers and became influential in Western monasticism. According to Cassian, it is the first stage of relationship with God, which is that of a servant to a master ("that first stage of fear which we rightly term servile, of which it is said: 'When you have done all things say: we are unprofitable servants'"), and those seeking perfection should advance higher and go beyond this.[40]

Cassian distinguished the final goal of the monastic life as attaining the kingdom of God from "the immediate aim or goal" which is the "purity of heart, without which no one can gain that end"[41] and from the means of achieving this purity of heart (which include self-denial and charity). The final goal, which is that "the soul may ever cleave to God and to heavenly things,"[42] is not achieved when the believer perceives his or her relationship in terms of servanthood. Indeed, the responsibilities of a servant (such as fasting, vigils, withdrawal from the world, and meditation on Scripture) are all "of secondary importance" and meant to be practiced only with a view to developing "purity of heart, which is love." The disciple, according to Cassian, will not be hurt if any of the things that are of secondary importance have to be omitted since it will not be of the slightest use to have done everything if the main goal is left undone ("He then will practice these exercises to no purpose, who is contented with these as if they were the highest good").[43] The ultimate goal of "cleaving to God and heavenly things" is achieved by those who learn they are friends of Christ.

Cassian initially described the movement of the believer from that of a servant to that of an employee (hireling), and then to the intimacy and privilege of being a *son*; but elsewhere, he spoke of the highest relationship with God in terms of friendship.[44] He preferred to use the Latin *caritas* for the Greek *agape* that is love for all, and *diathesis* for this more specific love of a few, such as family and friends. This specific form of love does not indicate any lack of love for others, but it does indicate "a fuller and more abundant love" for some. This love hates no one, "yet loves some still more" whom love embraces with a special affection.[45] It is important to note that a special friendship with one or a few need not operate to the detriment of anyone else. Friendship is not a zero-sum game in which the gain of one is matched by a loss to another. Indeed, the creation of one friendship is likely to lead to yet another and another, and ultimately, to a benefit for many.

The challenge for contemporary friendship is not to simply adopt this form of monastic thought about discipleship and friendship, yet there are profound lessons to be learned and applied. The monastic view of the Christian life valued friendship deeply and saw it as an essential part of the development of that purity of heart that is love and intimacy with God. They gave friendship a strong theological foundation by grounding it in friendship with Christ, and this had the double effect of connecting the believer to God in a particular way and of providing a model for relationships with others. They rightly saw friendship as a higher level of relationship than either servanthood or asceticism, and therefore located it within the higher counsels of Christ as the primary means for achieving the perfection of love and intimacy with God. It is possible that Christian, spiritual friendship today could be as enriching and edifying as this.

The dangers of friendship

At the same time that friendship was elevated to a spiritual practice within the monastic tradition, it also suffered a serious setback. The notion that this step into friendship with God is actually part and parcel of the journey for *every* believer was negated by the way it was seen as part of the specific counsel of God and, therefore, a religious rather than a universal calling. Perhaps inevitably, the notion of friendship as spiritual formation was limited to the specifically religious person— alongside voluntary poverty, chastity, and obedience. What could have been universalized was limited.

Of course, this was not the view of the monastics themselves. From their perspective, although not all were able to take up a religious life, the monastic life was really the model and guide for all life. Their life was not a separation from real life—it *was* real life. Nonetheless, the overall effect in regard to friendship was to place limitations on the exercise of spiritual friendship.

The general situation today is the opposite of this. That is, friend- ship is *universalized* as a broad, all-encompassing, casual relationship, ranging from fairly trivial associations through to more substan- tial and personally enriching relationships, but *not* seen so much as an ecclesial reality and the context for spiritual growth. Some of the significant dimensions of the monastic form of friendship can, however, be discerned in other relationships, such as mentor, counselor, spiritual director, advisor, and teacher. But these are often professionalized, and none of them quite replaces the spiritual ministry of friendship and its distinctive combination of elements: it is a freely chosen and mutual association (not based on kinship or obligation) of love and friend- ship, which is grounded specifically in friendship with God in Christ, and which seeks for both oneself and the other a deeper intimacy with Christ and love for God, and a continuing development of virtue and personal character, all achieved in such a way that it is of benefit to the community as a whole. This is a form of friendship that would enrich the life of the church and the world today.

In addition to the limitation of friendship to the monastic community, there was also a degree of ambivalence about the value of friendship within the community. Friendship was valued, but it also presented particular challenges. There was the danger of a distortion of the community if particular friendships isolated some people and fragmented the community and, without due care, there was also the danger of a distraction from spiritual matters if specific friendships became focused on anything other than purely spiritual matters. This made the active promotion of friendships rather rare.

Two important influences on monastic spirituality in this regard were Basil of Caesarea (c. 330–379), one of the renowned Cappadocean Fathers, who was a primary influence on Eastern monasticism, and Benedict of Nursia (c. 480–540), a towering figure in the West. Benedict's Rule drew on Cassian, among others, and he also commended the reading of Basil's *Rule* (or *Asketikon* which, although providing guidance for the spiritual life, is not really a "rule" in the same sense as Benedict's). The potential for a distortion of community life existed whenever friends separated themselves from the rest of the community. It was possible for friendship to become a rival to the community though the formation of cliques and the generation of jealousies and suspicions about the conversation and behavior of friends. Consequently, Basil's vision of the community being united by love and friendship placed limitations on specific friendships—all members of the community must be treated equally and without any particular appreciation or dislike.

He also addressed the problem of distraction from spiritual matters that could come about through physical attraction under the guise of spiritual love or simply from conversation for pleasure, which should be avoided. No conversation, "with either friend or stranger" should be permitted "unless we are persuaded that in their conversation they

mean to pursue what builds up souls and will help them to make progress."[46] Benedict allowed that special friendships could exist, but at the
same time he advised people to read Basil carefully. Moreover, Cassian,
who stressed the notion that friendships had to be oriented toward
spiritual and moral growth, remained an important influence.

The first two of Cassian's six rules for friendships[47] placed the friend
ahead of possessions and the self. The first rule involved contempt for
worldly possessions. It was, he argued, utterly wrong for those who had
renounced the world in order to embark on a monastic life to regard
whatever they had left more than the love of a friend. The second
required humility, to avoid imagining oneself to be a wise or experienced person with better opinions than one's friend.

The next four rules were aimed at maintaining the relationship in
a state of love and peace. The third rule called for a recognition that
everything, even the useful and necessary, must come after the blessing
of love and.peace. The fourth called for the realization that one should
never be angry with one's friend for any reason, good or bad; and the
fifth involved a desire to deal with any anger a friend may have, however
unreasonable. For Cassian, it made no difference who had the anger,
it would damage the relationship. The final rule, which is "undoubtedly generally decisive" in regard to all problems, is for each one to
"remember that he is to pass away from this world; as the realization
of this not only permits no vexation to linger in the heart, but also
represses all the motions of lusts and sins of all kinds."[48]

There is a lot for us today to learn from monastic friendship,
including this teaching about its dangers and problems, even though
the present context is very different. The first point is that if friendship is
defined in terms of its distinctly *spiritual* nature, then potential or actual
friendships cannot be prevented or damaged by anything other than
unspirituality. Although friendships often come about as the result of
shared interests, any differences between friends concerning their interests, or differences in politics, age, gender, or social background should

not interfere with the spiritual possibilities inherent in a close relationship. Unspiritual attitudes, however, are potentially fatal. Cassian saw anger as one of the great barriers to friendship, and it is certainly true than many spiritual disorders (one could list any of the "works of the flesh" of Galatians 5:19–21) emerge in a relationship in the form of anger. Hence, his concern was to overcome it, which necessarily meant getting to the root cause. His desire for this to be dealt with, irrespective of where the problem lies, is a reflection of the friendship that Christ has shown to his friends. It is not Christ's fault that a barrier has been created, but he is the one who has worked—and paid the cost—to remove it. Human friendship should reflect the friendship of Christ in all circumstances.

The monastic fathers remind us of the unpleasant truth that there are many Christians who are divided by great anger and jealousy, but the reality is that there are many more who are divided by far more trivial dissensions, resentments and long-held disappointment. There are many people waiting for some other person to take the initiative in restoring a relationship. Cassian's approach is to remind people to take "the long view," that is, that everyone is ultimately to pass away from this world, and recognizing this ought to allow "no vexation to linger in the heart." The difficulty has been expressed in the ditty

> To dwell above with saints we love,
> That will be grace and glory.
> To live below with saints we know;
> Now, that's another story!

Both Cassian and the writer of this quatrain remind us that living here and now is closely connected with living in the future. Friendship can also be a danger to the community if it involves the formation of cliques or exclusive groups. While friendships necessarily involve particular people, a Christian view of them incorporates a broader dimension that means that they are to work for the good of the community as a whole. If they detract from community life in any way, then they are not functioning as Christian spiritual friendship should.

Monastic friendship will, necessarily, be different from friendship expressed in modern Western church culture. The monastic community operated in such a way that formal rules and principles were set down to be studied and practiced. While this is unlikely today, there still should be some recognition of the problems, as well as the benefits, of spiritual friendship. And it is unlikely that many people will adopt the notion that the *only* point of friendship is spiritual growth and that friendships for other pleasures are to be avoided. The idea of friendship for pleasure is well established and unlikely to change; nor is that necessary since it was a specific attribute of monastic discipline. However, the writing of the Fathers ought to challenge notions of friendship as *nothing other* than pleasure or entertainment or common activity for personal amusement. Engagement in friendship for fun is by no means inappropriate, but if that is the only form of friendship, then one is impoverished.

Three forms of friendship

The final observations in this discussion of holy friendship belong to Aelred, who was less pessimistic about the dangers of friendship and consequently did not major upon them. In Cassian, the focus was upon avoiding sin and anger in close relationships rather than on their spiritual advantages, and the monastic tradition as a whole was ambivalent about friendship, out of fear of factions and sexual and other temptation. However, Aelred preferred to stress the blessings; he spoke more of "the excellence of friendship" and the ways it could remain unbroken. Nonetheless, he did describe different levels of friendship, with the lower levels either to be avoided or to be perfected. In Aelred there are three forms of friendship, the lowest being the *carnal*, which "springs from mutual harmony in vice,"[49] the *worldly*, which may or may not be helpful, and the *spiritual*, which is perfection.

Carnal friendship

Of the various forms of friendship, perhaps the least needs to be said about the carnal, for it is nothing other than association for sinful purposes. Such relationships are to be avoided or ended, for no good can come of them. Yet it is helpful to comment on this in relation to the fact that Jesus was known as a "friend of . . . sinners" (Matt. 11:19). He did not shrink away from associating with all manner of people, including—perhaps especially—those perceived to be the most unacceptable members of society.

Of course, the pharisaic complaint that Jesus was a friend of sinners has to be interpreted in the light of their perception of who it was that comprised the group known as "sinners." In Jesus' eyes it would seem that the Pharisees were more culpable. However, this sort of association and friendship is not "carnal" in Aelred's terms. It is not an association for the purposes of sinful behavior, and Christians have a responsibility to engage with the world in order to share the good news of Jesus in every way possible. But neither are these "spiritual friendships" in Aelred's terms, for they are not mutual relationships grounded in Christ (though they may be entered into *for* Christ), with both seeking the development of love and virtue. These are friendships that are still in need of union in and through Christ, to be entered into in faith and hope, that through them the Spirit of God will make new friends of God. Such friendships will, inevitably at times, create problems that arise from the presence of different foundations and varying expectations. There was a pastor/evangelist who was well known and widely respected for his ministry with those people whom society has rejected or deemed to be less worthy, including bikers and addicts, and as part of his ministry, he developed an ongoing association with a stripper who was interested in talking about life and faith. After some time of this, she suggested he come to her workplace to see her strip. From her point of view, this was simply her normal work, and the invitation was issued in an open, honest way with a degree of pride in expecting to demonstrate, much as many others would, a job well done. Negotiating one's way through tricky situations like that can take time, but even though there are situations and associations that are difficult, it is still important not to use a very appropriate aversion to carnal relationships to avoid engaging with the world.

Worldly friendship

Aelred's advice is focused on avoiding those relationships that are inherently oriented toward sin. These are relationships that begin with an appeal to the senses: there is something ostensibly pleasurable to be achieved, but they are predicated on sinful attitudes or actions. They are to be rejected, and the only advantage is that they are more recognizable for what they are than the second kind of friendship that Aelred designated as "worldly." These are friendships that are "born of a desire for temporal advantage or possessions," and they are also to be rejected. The difference with the carnal is that the end that is sought, which may be status, wealth, possessions or any form of advantage, is not intrinsically sinful. That is, it is not always wrong to seek to be well educated, to be promoted in employment, to gain an advantage in business, to play on a good sports team, or to associate with people to whom you are attracted. However, worldly friendships are those where these are the aim and goal in themselves; they are done purely to benefit one's own pleasure, without thought to God's will, the benefit of the other, the alternative use of time and effort, or the effect on one's spiritual life. It is very possible to seek something good for the wrong reason and more difficult to identify this as such than it is to identify a carnal relationship.

Aelred may have thought of spiritual friendship in contrast with the worldly friendships that existed within the court in Scotland, where he spent many years. There is no doubt such friendships always exist in political circles, but equally, they can be found within churches, the workplace, and business and community groups. The problem is the subtlety of it all. Why, for example, does one want to develop or avoid certain relationships within the church community? It is necessary to consider the desires of the heart, and a good spiritual friendship can help clarify this by example as well as by conversation. A worldly friendship, in Aelred's thinking, is either to be rejected or developed, for although it is problematic, "yet this friendship can lead to a certain degree of true friendship."[50] It can become the basis for a more spiritual friendship.

Spiritual friendship

Spiritual friendship is, of course, the perfect friendship. Negatively, it does not seek any worldly advantage, and positively, like wisdom or any virtue, such as goodness, love, or patience, it is to be sought simply for its own sake.[51] The advantage of friendship is friendship. It is its own reward. It is an intrinsic good in itself. It is possible to take what Aelred said about spiritual friendship and structure a brief summary of its main elements in this way:

(a) *Concerning pleasure:* Spiritual friendship may well begin with the usual activities of friends, including enjoyable conversation and various shared activities, all undertaken with goodwill and humor. It will also, no doubt, result in the benefits of being able to heighten joys and halve griefs through sharing.[52]

(b) *Concerning empathy and care:* But to be a spiritual friendship, it must move on to greater heights and involve being solicitous for one another, praying for them, and seeing their failings and progressions in life as one's own.[53] Aelred nominated four qualities that will assist in this: loyalty, good intention, discretion, and patience.

(c) *Concerning sharing and spiritual formation:* Beyond the qualities of loyalty and patience, spiritual friendship needs to enhance the spiritual life of the friend through actions that may be challenging to both. This can include, for example, radical sharing. Aelred followed existing

tradition, saying, "Men would lead a very happy life, says the Wise
Man, if these two words were taken from their midst: namely, 'mine'
and 'yours.'" A friend also ought to not hide from sharing his or her
insights ("let friend counsel friend as to what is right, securely, openly,
and freely") even when that is difficult and may hurt one's friend: "for
the wounds inflicted by a friend are more tolerable than the kisses of
flatterers. Therefore, correct the erring friend." This is because friendship does not excuse a failure of virtue, for it is friendship that is the
primary means of developing virtue. It is not uncommon to find people
thinking that friendship is an excuse for doing something that is wrong
("they'll do it for *me*"), but spiritual friendship is oriented in precisely
the opposite direction, toward the moral good of all.[54]

(d) *Concerning Christ:* Finally, and most importantly, there needs to
be a clear understanding of what is truly central to spiritual friendship.
The various "advantages" enumerated in the three previous sections of
this summary must be seen primarily as the *effect* of friendship rather
than as the *essence* of it ("they ought to follow friendship, not precede
it").[55] They are all part and parcel of "spiritual friendship," but they flow
out of that which is perfect and which is at its heart.

> Friendship is a stage bordering upon that perfection which consists
> in the love and knowledge of God, so that man from being a friend
> of his fellow man becomes the friend of God, according to the
> words of the Savior in the Gospel: "I will now not call you servants,
> but my friends."[56]

In short, friendship leads to the love and knowledge of God through
Christ, and the fundamental question which emerges from this review
of monastic spiritual friendship is whether it is possible today to recover
this central focus and enhance our love of God and neighbor by intentionally developing friendships that take us to a new and more mature
level of relationship with God and our friends.

PART III
Friendship as the Life of the Church

History

The Privatization of Friendship

5

> Friendship is the most perfect among all things
> pertaining to love.
>
> Thomas Aquinas

Despite the formation of a tradition of Christian spiritual friendship, it has always been surprisingly difficult to persuade the church as a whole of the value of seeing friendship as more than an essentially private and personally beneficial relationship. It seems, for example, that at the turn of the thirteenth century, the distance across Europe, from Rievaulx to Rome, was too great for Aelred's teaching on spiritual friendship to travel, so when Thomas Aquinas (1225–1274) was preparing to write about the goal of human life in terms of friendship with God, he appears to have been completely unaware of Aelred's previous work and influence.[1] The fact that he did not know of what would have been a useful resource is an indication of the difficulty that the concept of friendship had in holding its place in spiritual theology.

An even more notable illustration of the capacity of the church to lose track of the role friendship can play is seen in the way that even after Aquinas—independently of Aelred—very deliberately placed friendship in a theologically central position in his theological scheme, it appears to have had almost no effect on those who followed or on the subsequent teaching of the church. This is particularly remarkable given the otherwise profound impact Aquinas has had on both Catholic theology in particular and Western philosophy and culture in general. Thomas had adopted friendship as the primary form of spiritual relationship and declared, "God is our chief friend."[2] For Aquinas, friendship was the best way to describe what our life with God should be like, not only now but also eternally. Moreover, he was willing to make friendship the center of the ethical life (for friendship is love and the means to the development of all virtue) and critical to an understanding of the human person (because relationships, especially friendship, are in a real sense, constitutive of the person). Aquinas's scholastic use of friendship as part of his theological system—with its primarily intellectual, logical, and philosophical approach to God—contrasted with, and yet also complemented, Aelred's monastic and more contemplative approach to spiritual friendship, which stressed desire and personal experience. Despite their differences, their writings overlapped considerably as they sought, in their own way, to lead people to the ultimate goal of union with God. However, the reality is that even the combined efforts of Aelred and Aquinas, in monastic and scholastic contexts respectively, were not enough to generate ongoing spiritual and theological interest in friendship.

Consequently, Western concepts of friendship had to develop in the absence of any active Christian tradition, and so, from the fourteenth century on, with the specifically *Christian* tradition lacking in influence, the *classical* or Graeco-Roman tradition continued to provide a more influential background to the development of the modern or contemporary perception of friendship. The interaction between classical influences and contemporary trends can best be understood in terms of the correlation between self-discovery and self-disclosure. They are correlated because both aim to uncover what it means to be a person-in-relationship, but they differ on how this takes place. The classic, Graeco-Roman approach may be designated as a *Discovery* mode of understanding and the modern or contemporary view as a *Disclosure* mode of understanding. The models agree on many aspects of friendship (including the role of mutual attraction, shared trust, affection, benevolence, and reciprocity), but stress these elements differently.

The classical approach: friendship as the discovery of the self

One version of the Discovery model of friendship is found in Aristotle's classic assessment of friendship in books 8 and 9 of his *Nicomachean Ethics*. The books were originally separate and are based on lectures dedicated to his son, Nicomachus. The question throughout them all concerns how one should live. Aristotle's thoughts on this matter became foundational for medieval philosophy, and his ongoing significance, in the opinion of contemporary Western philosophers, has hardly waned. Friendship is described as central to ethics and to public life. Friendship that seeks the common good is the highest, the best form of friendship.[3]

Aristotle defines friendship as a virtuous relationship that is based on mutuality and reciprocity. There are three types of friendship, representing different levels of virtue and mutuality. The first type of friendship involves those who are friends for some utilitarian purpose. That is, they are friends insofar as they gain some good for themselves. They are not manipulative, but simply mutually beneficial in that they involve some activity or occupation in which both wish to engage. The second form of friendship involves those who are friends because of what is good or pleasant for themselves. This may be a friendship based, for example, on the pleasure of a relationship where the presence of the other person is appreciated for their sense of humor or knowledge or their sexual prowess.

The third, and really the only genuine form of friendship, is a friendship of virtue. "Complete friendship is the friendship of good people similar in virtue."[4] This is the most reciprocal friendship of all because in a complete friendship *everything* is held in common. Aristotle sees this as the fulfillment of the proverb "what friends have is common." In such a friendship, the friends both wish the best for the other. This form of friendship is complete and enduring, though likely to be rare. It is the friendship of good people.

Aristotle connects this form of complete friendship, which seeks the good of the other, with the concept of the common good of a society and with the very public practice of politics. In the absence of political parties to organize those relationships and alliances that can provide good government, personal, virtuous friendships that seek the common good are a necessity. Most importantly, this form of friendship also involves the discovery of one's own nature and character. There are three lessons to be learned here. The first concerns the need for friendship in order for the individual to be able to achieve self-understanding. In a complete friendship, according to Aristotle, the good that one wishes for a friend is also desired for oneself.

> Each of these features is found in the decent person's relation to himself . . . the excellent person is of one mind with himself, and desires the same things in his whole soul . . . hence the good person must be a self-lover, since he will both help himself and benefit others by doing fine actions.[5]

The commonality of virtue and the reciprocity of desire and intention means it is possible to learn about oneself by looking at, and considering, this "other self" who is so similar in character. "We are able to observe our neighbors more than ourselves, and to observe their actions more than our own."[6] In short, without friendship one cannot achieve the self-knowledge that is essential for happiness and a good life. We cannot fully know ourselves without our friends. A person can come to know his own character only by studying that of his friends. A friend is "another self" who can be examined with a degree of objectivity. Yet intuition tells us that we are fundamentally the same. A person is able to see his own character reflected, as in a mirror, in his friends.

This process of self-discovery is then enhanced by the way that friendship can be a means for building up the moral character of the person in a way that is not possible for the individual alone. In the Discovery model, complete friendships are predicated on a similarity of virtue, and they look for benefit to the common good through the development of virtue. Friends can model positive and virtuous aspects of life, and this can encourage friends to imitate these attitudes and behaviors. Friends can also, implicitly or explicitly, rebuke and challenge inappropriate conduct. Virtue cannot be achieved in solitude. Friendship, specifically virtuous friendship, is at the heart of Christian community. One needs friends in order to be holy.

If the first theological insight of the Discovery model of friendship is growth in self-knowledge and the second is moral transformation, then the third involves a change of nature that comes about when friendship with God is under consideration. Aristotle had doubts that friendship could take place between those who are not similar or equal. This includes relationships between parents and children, older and younger, and those who are separated by a wide gap in virtue, vice, or wealth. This problem "is most evident with gods, since they have the greatest superiority in all goods."[7] Yet "there is no exact definition in this," and parents do indeed love their children and can be friends with them, and there can be friendships of people of different ages. These sorts of friendships can involve the pleasure and utility of the first two types of friendship, and though they cannot be complete friendships, a form of equality can be achieved if the loving is proportional to the difference in status between the two. That is,

> the better person, and of the more beneficial, and each of the others likewise, must be loved more than he loves; for when the loving reflects the comparative worth of the friends, equality is achieved in a way, and this seems to be proper to friendship.[8]

Therefore, "it is perhaps enough, as it is with the gods and with one's parents, to give them what one can."[9] That is, a form of friendship can exist despite inequality, although he remained ambivalent about this, and it does, indeed, point to a problem: how can friendship *with God* be a possibility? Theologically, for the Christian the answer lies in grace alone, expressed in creation, incarnation, and redemption.

Something of the significance of friendship with God is illustrated in the relationship between the unconventional speech therapist Lionel Logue and King George VI that is recounted in the book *The King's Speech: How One Man Saved the British Monarchy* and the subsequent film. The problem the king faced was serious because, as he put it, "The nation believes when I speak, I speak for them. Well, I can't speak!" Logue was successful in helping the king, and the slow, measured pace he developed made his wartime speeches particularly affecting. In the process, they became close friends. However, Logue, at least at the beginning of the relationship, had very little status. He was simply the son of a brewery accountant, a former actor, and a self-taught teacher of elocution. Consequently, there was "a certain amount of antipathy from the royal family," especially the Queen Mother, at the way George and Lionel maintained a close friendship, rather than simply a professional relationship, right through until the king's death. It seemed to some to be an inappropriate friendship given the disparity of status, but at least in this case, this does not seem to have been an issue for a gracious king, and it produced a friendship that was the greatest pleasure of Logue's life. Friendships such as this, that cross all status boundaries, are always possible with the King of kings. The biblical concept of the *imago dei* relates the nature of humanity very directly to God: "so God created humankind in his image, in the image of God he created them" (Gen. 1:27). Therefore, despite the fundamental difference between human and divine, there is a point of connection; it is this connection that underlies the possibility of God's friendship with Abraham and Moses.

In the incarnation, and through the believer's friendship with Christ, God in Christ can be seen as "another self," one who relates to believers as a friend. And in terms of redemption, the epistle to the Colossians says, "you have taken off your old self with its practices and have put on the new self, which is being renewed in knowledge in the image of its Creator" (3:9–10 NIV). By grace, the friend of Christ is being formed into the image of Christ, a fully redeemed person, which means becoming one's true self.

The contemporary approach: friendship as the disclosure of the self

In classic thinking, the Discovery model of friendship focuses upon self-knowledge, virtue, and moral transformation, but with the shift to a Disclosure model of friendship in the modern era, friendship has become a more private, affective relationship based upon mutual sharing.

This is true, as a general statement, notwithstanding the presence of two influences that run counter to this. The first is that in ethical debate there has been a resurgence of the virtue ethic exemplified by Aristotle and Aquinas, which tends to allow for a reconsideration of the possibility of virtuous friendship.[10] The second is that in the political realm some attention has been paid to the public dimension of the concept by writers such as Jacques Derrida. However, despite these, the overall assessment is that in the modern era, friendship is not a key public or philosophical concept. As an essentially communal concept, it conflicts with the dominant starting point of post-Enlightenment rationalist thought, which is fundamentally grounded in a perception of the individual as a free, autonomous agent. Friendship, therefore, is perceived as a private, affective connection lacking the status of an essentially virtuous relationship seeking the common good. Whether actual friendships have changed or not, the perception has.

Those familiar with the view of friendship as a virtue tend to see the more popular contemporary interpretation as involving a deterioration (a fall from grace) from the lofty standards of the ancients. However, others are willing to see a more positive aspect to it. The Aristotelian view of friendship, which only exists where there is unity, virtue, and a concern for the common good, can be seen as making it the preserve of the "the implausibly pure in heart" rather than a real-life relationship.

> Friendship is interesting when it has to handle mixed motives, psychological conflicts, terrible character flaws, inconsistencies, inexplicable changes of direction, moral lapses, and the rest. We don't always approve of our friends.[11]

Popularly speaking, friendships today are not primarily seen in terms of the development of virtue but in intimate sharing, characterized by the vulnerability that comes from privileged sharing and support through life's experiences and difficulties. Friendship involves significant, high-level personal disclosure.

The change is connected with the fundamental shift toward a more interior view of the self who functions as an autonomous individual. This is usually associated with René Descartes (1596–1650), often referred to as the "Father of Modern Philosophy," who believed that the truth of the self, like the truths of mathematics, is best established and defined by a pure, rational process of thinking, rather than by reference to either the traditions of old or the more contemporary scientific method of empirical observation. Certainty was established through a process of doubt that eliminated all foundations except the undeniable certainty: the interior awareness of the thinking (i.e., doubting) self.

Romantic and amoral friendship

However, it is possible to see the turning point, specifically in terms of friendship, occurring prior to Descartes: in the essays of French Renaissance writer Michel de Montaigne (1533–1592) and English philosopher Francis Bacon (1561–1626), who, although still connected to the older view, nonetheless wrote of friendship in a way that modern people find much more recognizable. The increasingly individual, private, and emotional view of friendship came to the fore.

In Montaigne, friendship is "being truly perfect . . . the complete fusion of wills" with "everything actually being in common between them—wills, thoughts, judgments, goods, wives, children, honor, and life—and their relationship being that of one soul in two bodies."[12] He anticipated Romanticism because there is no foundation for the love of true friends other than the emotion of their union: "if you press me to tell you why I loved him, I feel that this cannot be expressed, except by answering: because it was he, because it was I."[13]

This intimate friendship thrives on communication between the friends. Montaigne remains indebted to the classic view of friendship but emphasizes its passionate, romantic nature in which it seeks deep communion with the other. Friendship is profoundly oriented toward the personal dimension.

Francis Bacon agreed with Montaigne both that the ancient notion of union and love simply was not strong or passionate enough for what is felt in friendship, and that the sharing of affection is friendship's primary focus, but his overall approach, even to emotion, is more rational. He carefully describes the three principal "fruits" of friendship. The first has to do with sharing affections: "The principal fruit of friendship, is the ease and discharge of the fullness and swellings of the heart, which passions of all kinds do cause and induce."[14]

The ability to share these with one's friend has the advantage of doubling the joy and halving the griefs. The second fruit relates to understanding. Through talking and through counsel, friendship is "helpful

and sovereign for the understanding . . . it maketh daylight in the understanding, out of darkness and confusion of thoughts." The third fruit
of friendship is the aid a friend can provide, because there are many
things one cannot do for oneself. Indeed, it is not enough to say, as the
ancients did, "that a friend is another himself" for "a friend is far more
than himself."[15] As well as the obvious stress on emotion, it is helpful to
note that friendship is not primarily oriented toward the development
of virtue or the common good, but at the benefits to the lives of the
friends. Michael Pakaluk notes that "Bacon is perhaps the first philosopher to conceive of the needs of friendship that is amoral, in the sense
that it is not the consequence of any goodness, natural or acquired, in
the person."[16]

The third fruit of this form of friendship is the trust that results from
disclosure. Friends share feelings, blessings, and problems, and provide
counsel, understanding, comfort, and aid in an atmosphere of mutual
trust. This is the kind of friendship of which Henri Nouwen spoke:

> When we honestly ask ourselves which person in our lives means
> the most to us, we often find that it is those who, instead of giving
> advice, solutions, or cures, have chosen rather to share our pain and
> touch our wounds with a warm and tender hand. The friend who
> can be silent with us in a moment of despair or confusion, who can
> stay with us in an hour of grief and bereavement, who can tolerate
> not knowing, not curing, not healing and face with us the reality of
> our powerlessness, that is a friend who cares.[17]

Friendship as particular and selfish

The changing emphases in friendship in the modern era have not met
with universal acceptance. There have been a number of significant
critiques in, for example, Immanuel Kant and Søren Kierkegaard. For
the Prussian philosopher Immanuel Kant (1724–1804), friendship is
morally problematic because it is so particular. It cannot be a real *good*
because it cannot be universalized. "Friendship is not universal; it is a

peculiar association of specific persons." So while one can have goodwill for all, one cannot have a special relationship with everyone or else the very essence of friendship is evacuated from it: "he who is a friend to everyone has no particular friend." Nevertheless, because moral good must be universal, desired for all, friendship cannot be more than a relative good that helps overcome the mistrust, uncertainty, and negative feelings we are prone to have in human relationship. Damning with faint praise, Kant can say that "friendship develops the minor virtues of life" but fundamentally, "friendship is not of heaven but of the earth."[18]

The reserve that Kant felt about friendship, however, pales into insignificance with the view of Søren Kierkegaard (1813–1855), who argued that friendship is essentially a selfishness that stands in sharp moral contrast to the more radical Christian notion of the love of neighbor, and even of enemies. He saw both friendship and erotic love as forms of "poetic love," which involves an essential love *of self.* The friend is, in classic terms, "another self," and friendship involves a reciprocal relationship of love that presupposes that we admire the other. This, in turn, implies that friendship is a love of self, which conflicts with the Christian love of all. "Christianity" he argued, "has thrust erotic love and friendship from the throne" and "one must rather take pains to make very clear that the praise of erotic love and friendship belong to paganism."[19]

He noted "that in [the] whole New Testament there is not found a single word about friendship in the sense in which the poet sings of it and paganism cultivated it,"[20] but there is much concerning love of neighbor. "[Poetic] love and friendship contain no ethical task"; that is, they are self-indulgent rather than anything else, whereas, self-renunciation "is Christianity's essential form."[21] Kierkegaard's focus on self-sacrifice runs counter to the modern trend toward friendship as self-fulfillment, as a way of enhancing one's life and happiness. This is a corruption of Christian faith, and he calls for existential, ethical choices marked by passion, for the aim of life is not merely to know truth but to *become* it, and to transform one's subject self. Radical love for all, rather than a preferential and ultimately self-serving care for some, is what is required. His critique of self-serving friendship is a reminder of the Christian call to reach out beyond those we like. Jesus said, "If you love those who love you, what reward will you get? Are not even the tax collectors doing that?" (Matt. 5:46 NIV).

(Post)modern friendship in philosophy and sociology

The French post-structuralist philosopher Jacques Derrida (1930–2004) shared Kierkegaard's negative assessment of modern friendship as an essentially self-serving passion.[22] For Derrida, the whole history of friendship, since the time of the ancient Greek philosophers, has been regrettable and is subject to serious critique. However, whereas Kierkegaard's intention was to stress the contrast with genuine, radical Christian love, Derrida's critique is part of his broader program of the complete deconstruction of Western metaphysical tendencies. Modern friendship, according to Derrida, has been philosophically marginalized because it has lost its broader, social, even political focus aimed at establishing democracy and justice. Instead, the hegemonic "fraternal" view of friendship in Western thought—from Greek, through Roman, Jewish, Christian, and Islamic versions—is repressive, male, heroic, and phallocentric.

He aimed to deconstruct this pervasive fraternal view of friendship that shares its logic with nationalism, sexism, and other forms of exclusion that do not welcome the other as *other*. His aim was to open friendship beyond the limits of "the canonical understanding of friendship, singularity and the quality of thought within the limits of fraternity." A friendship that does not welcome the other as other is no friendship at all. In contrast to this deficient view, friendship should be grounded in the very same principles that are the foundation of democratic politics. Hence the stress on the connection between politics and friendship. The essential principles for both are *"Liberté, Égalité, Fraternité"* (freedom, equality and fraternity)—principles which, of course, comprise the national motto of France.[23] Indeed, in the early years of the use of this slogan, *amitié (friendship)* was often used rather than *fraternité (brotherhood)*.

Simmel and the sociology of modern friendship

This shift away from the classic, Discovery model of friendship represents a new possibility for psychologists and sociologists who focus more upon the private, interior dimensions of friendship as Disclosure. Georg Simmel (1858–1918) was, along with his contemporaries Max Weber and Emile Durkheim, one of the founding fathers of sociology. His interest in social life as a set of personal exchanges constructed from play and driven by amiability, attractiveness, and warmth distinguished him from the other early researchers, who were more interested in social categories such as gender, class, and race, and also from Freud, another contemporary, whose focus was on sex.

Simmel observed that "all relationships of human beings obviously rest on their knowing something about one another."[24] This applies to business and political relationships as much as personal relationships. This means not only knowing about *what* but also knowing about *whom*, even if this knowledge is unconscious. Ideally, friendship involves a full sharing of oneself and one's possessions,[25] but this has become difficult in light of the changes that have taken place as the Western world has moved from tribal to modern society. The industrial world is a larger, more complex and diverse society that has expanded the possibilities for the individual and changed all forms of relationship. The mutual sharing of life in its totality is now not possible. The fragmentation and diversity of modern life produces "differentiated friendships," which relate to the different dimensions of a person's life, based variously on "sympathy," "intellectual community," "religious

impulses," and "common experiences." The significance of these relationships should not be diminished even though they are expressed
only in a single segment at the periphery of the person's life because
they still have their source in the center of that individual's personality. There is often no expectation that a friendship in one area will
cross over into another. This accentuates the problem of discerning the
appropriate level of disclosure—the balance of self-revelation and self-
concealment—what Simmel refers to as "a quite peculiar synthesis."[26]
This tension between concealment and revelation is at the foundation
of the "secret society." Simmel suggests that the modern person has
too much to conceal to make friendship in the ancient sense possible,
and personalities "are too peculiarly individualized for the complete
reciprocity of understanding."[27] This tension between concealment
and revelation that Simmel describes is at the heart of what I have
called the Disclosure model of friendship. In an ideal form, there is
full disclosure as a mark of friendship. Simmel's observations on the
effects of individualization, the value of a private world, the fragmentation of life and its effect on friendships, and the role of self-disclosure
versus self-reserve are illuminating. Much of it resonates with popular
perceptions of friendship in the modern world, where changes to a
more complex and fragmented way of life has led to changes in the
perceived nature and role of friendship.

Blake and Santo worked in the same office for three years. They
undertook projects together, planned how to handle difficult clients
and workers from other divisions, jointly bemoaned what seemed like
absurd demands from the head office, filled in for each other when one
of them was away, and reckoned themselves a strong team. They laughed
a lot and frequently lunched together. However, when Blake, in an off-
the-cuff comment, described Santo as his best friend, Santo realized
that he had never been to Blake's home or met his family. Moreover, he
knew nothing about Blake's life before joining the company, didn't have
a clue about what he thought about politics or what motivated him in

life, and had never shared anything of significance about his own life. He wondered, "What do I do now?"

Spencer and Pahl and changing repertoires of friendship

Some analyses of this situation, such as Robert Putnam's *Bowling Alone: The Collapse and Revival of American Community,*[28] point toward a serious decline in community relationships. But overall, empirical sociological research has not focused on micro-social networks like friendship so much as on larger network relationships including neighborhood networks, community groups, social organizations, class, gender, and race. Consequently, assumptions about friendship have generally been derived from the results of indirect studies that point to deteriorating levels of community life, increased depression, and lower levels of civic responsibility and involvement in modern society. Friendship is, therefore, seen as becoming rarer and subject to negative influences from social fragmentation and the influence of information technology and social networking, which, while increasing the frequency of contacts, tends to diminish the depth and integrity of substantial friendship. But empirical investigation of friendship itself questions some of this gloomy analysis. A qualitative assessment of friendship that allows people to map relationships in their own way, rather than requiring an assessment in terms of preexisting (and perhaps inadequate) categories, allows for real community to be discerned, functioning in revised forms. In the past, social connections were primarily face-to-face, visible, and geographically located; they are often now, because of the advent of new communication techniques, less public, less observable, and less measurable by previous methods. These community-building interactions are also less noticed because the people involved do not necessarily think about them in any methodical way. In *Rethinking Friendship: Hidden Solidarities Today,* Liz Spencer and Ray Pahl[29] investigate the situation with regard to friendship in the British context through exploratory qualitative research. They believe that friendship should be seen to exist in more diverse and positive forms than is usually the case. The process of encouraging people to map their relationships enabled them to become the significance of their own social world. They challenge the claim that people have few strong ties and introduce the idea of "friendship repertoires," which examine the nature and diversity of friendship over the life course. One of their key findings relates to the diverse nature of friendship today, its myriad forms, and the non-geographically local nature of many relationships.

> The overwhelming conclusion of our particular study, however, is that there is no single dominant kind of personal community; people live in micro-social worlds which differ enormously in their connectivity, their degree of commitment, and their pattern of reliance on given and chosen ties.[30]

While some people are clearly isolated and unhappy, with unsupportive micro-social worlds, the level should not be overstressed. Neither should there be too negative an assessment of the overall strength of community if that is based solely on measurements at the level of civic or voluntary associations, rather than at the level of informal personal relationships. The latter can be remarkably outward looking and community oriented and should not be seen as purely group or self-focused. The simplest form of friendships can be a powerful and positive influence on people.

Friendship, the image of God, and the Trinity

This short history has drawn attention to the different emphases of Discovery and Disclosure models of friendship within the Western tradition; however, as was noted at the outset, they have to be seen as approaches that are correlated through a mutual concern for a common set of themes. Although there has been a shift from friendship as a public association oriented toward the discovery of the good and of virtue toward friendship as a private relationship focused on self-disclosure, both are actually aimed at uncovering the meaning of being a person-in-relationship. A friend does what an individual cannot do for himself and, as "another self," provides a source of self-knowledge. In friendship, it is possible to find oneself; it is not possible to develop character or enhance virtue in solitude. Relationships are neither merely external to the self, nor only what the self does, but they are actually constitutive of the self through constant formation or re-formation of character. Personhood is only possible in relationship, and friendships are of essential, and not merely incidental, significance.

Liz Carmichael, in her review of the legacy of classical thought concerning friendship, observed that three ways of grounding friendship emerged. *Ontologically*, friendship can be seen as being grounded in a shared mode of being; *teleologically*, friendship is motivated by the attractiveness of the good character of a friend; and *deontologically*, friendship is an expression of virtue in being a good friend to others. "Perfect friendship" is a mutual relationship that combines all three;[31] it is a dynamic and tangible expression of what Scripture speaks of as "the image of God" in humanity, which is, itself, a reflection, or an image, of the Trinitarian "friendship" of Father, Son, and Spirit. The origin of the *imago dei* is described in Genesis: "So God created humankind in his image, in the image of God he created, them, male and female he created them" (1:27; see also 5:1–3; 9:5–6); but its full significance is found in the person of Christ, as when Romans 8:29 speaks of believers being "conformed to the image of [God's] Son."

The image is not to be understood *substantially*—as though the *imago dei* is imprinted on the person in the way that an image is impressed on a coin—but rather *dynamically* and *relationally*, with the "image" more like the kind of image one sees in a mirror. The image of Christ is to be seen in believers, and it becomes clearer as the relationship develops. The image is not a past tense but a future element, and it is formed in us in our being human in relationship. There is not one specific characteristic that makes us human; rather, God is found in us in the whole of life, and the *imago dei* is a destiny, a direction, a destination rather than simply a statement about our origin. The image of God is fulfilled in relationship to Christ, who is himself the perfect image of God, through whom others can come into friendship with God (Col. 1:15–19). In this way, in the *imago dei,* the way is open for an understanding of the human person that is grounded in friendship with Christ as the means of becoming fully human. Through friendship, Jesus draws believers into a new level of relationship—not only with himself, but also with the Father and the Spirit. In this way, his friends are able to participate in the holy friendship of God.

This connection of friendship with Trinitarian theology is also seen in Jesus' declaration of friendship, "I no longer call you servants, . . . [but] friends," which is spoken as part of a passage of teaching that is permeated with reference to the dynamic Trinitarian relationships of the Father, the Son, and the Spirit. Jesus draws the disciples into a relationship that not only involves the believer and *Jesus* ("You will abide in my love"), but also the *Father* ("As you, Father, are in me and I am in you, may they also be in us"), and the *Spirit* ("When the Advocate comes, whom I will send to you from the Father, the Spirit of truth who comes from the Father, he will testify on my behalf") (John 15:15; 15:10; 17:21; 15:26 NIV).

In short, through friendship the believer not only becomes a friend of Jesus but a friend of God, able to share in the life and relationships of God. The various biblical writers express this truth differently and with different emphases, and yet they focus on this one central, life-defining truth about union with God. John focuses on life and friendship with Jesus the incarnate Son; Paul stressed union with Christ's death and resurrection; and *Peter* speaks of the faithful becoming "participants of the divine nature" (John 6:53–57; Rom. 6:8; 2 Peter 1:4). The truth is enriched by the various approaches, and all of them point to the fact that the life of the believer and the Trinitarian relationships of Father, Son, and Spirit culminate in holy friendship, a deep union of love. It is only through friendship that the believer has life eternal—a life that is actually a shared life: communion with God.

Friendship thus exists at the center of both Christian life and theology. The love of Father, Son, and Spirit has opened up and brought about the possibility of the believer's friendship with God. Friendship with God is an expression of the free, dynamic relationships that exist in a Trinitarian understanding of divine nature. Without friendship, the concept of Trinity is sterile and pointless. Thomas Aquinas understood this and had a positive view of human friendship as a form of preparation or training for the divine relationship. He used friendship very directly as a model of relationship with God. Indeed, for Aquinas, friendship with God is the beginning of the Christian life; it is its sustaining power, and it is the ultimate goal. God, as Aquinas says, is our Chief Friend.[32] Human friendship is a reflection of the relationships of the Trinity and is the form of fellowship (*koinonia*) within the body of Christ. It is possible to agree with Aquinas when he says that "friendship is the most perfect among all things pertaining to love"[33] and with Aelred in saying that "God is friendship." Human friendship is, indeed, a preparation for a relationship with the divine. It is a mutual sharing of lives that leads to learning and growth. People are formed and transformed by friendship, particularly in learning about love and forgiveness.

If we learn, grow, and develop as persons in relationship with other people, then we do so much more in our relationship to God. Indeed, the notion of friendship as a constituting relationship applies not only to human beings but also to God. Humans are constituted as persons by this creative relationship with God, just as God is constituted as God through the mutual friendship-love of Father, Son, and Spirit. The goal of human life is nothing other than participation in friendship and love with God. Friendship, then, may well be described as the primary expression of Christian love.

The failure and the future of friendship

With this theological background and the influence of Aelred and Aquinas, the notion of friendship as a primary description of the form of divine-human relationship ought to have been a prominent theme in theological thought. The reality, however, is that it has largely been neglected. There are a number of reasons for this: (a) according to Carmichael, Thomas Aquinas's teaching on friendship ceased to be of use in most explorations of the divine-human relationship when the Council of Trent limited his use of friendship to being an explanation of justification;[34] (b) within monasticism, spiritual friendship conflicted with more ascetic forms of spirituality and presented spiritual dangers for individuals (the abuse of intimacy) and the community (through the formation of cliques); (c) the personal, preferential love of friendship sometimes appeared to be in conflict with the Christian understanding of love as *agape* that is to be offered universally and indiscriminately, rather than to a select few people one knows very closely; (d) spiritual friendship also seemed to conflict with other models of relationship with God that were more authoritarian or hierarchical in form; and (e) the loss of influence of the doctrine of the Trinity in modern theology meant that relational approaches to faith struggled to have an impact. The post-Barthian resurgence of interest in the doctrine of the Trinity, however, opened the way for more relational approaches and for friendship to find a way back to a position of some influence.[35] With Trinitarian theology now firmly entrenched in contemporary theological thought, it is not surprising that friendship has been reemerging in a variety of places.

The issues that need to be addressed in forthcoming chapters can be seen in five categories. The first area of significance, therefore, relates to friendship and the constitution and development of the Christian community. Christian principles lead inexorably toward an open form of friendship, a community open to others who are different and not necessarily simply "another self." What form of common life does genuine friendship imply? How do particular friendships fit within a whole community of friends? This is explored in chapter 6.

An understanding of open friendship also influences the ministry and mission of the church. The issues discussed in chapter 7 revolve around the way love and friendship for the community interacts with friendship for neighbor, the poor and the marginalized, those who are enemies, and at the most general level, for all. There are issues relating to specific forms of ministry and mission concerning, for example, the nature of pastoral care, relationships with other religions, engaging in evangelism, and seeking justice.

This leads to a consideration of the role of friendship as a means of enhancing public good. This is the focus of chapter 8, which notes that there has been a distinct loss of the public dimension in contemporary forms of friendship. Indeed, there is resistance to the potentially discriminatory preferences of friendship in public life. So, can friendship regain a public role? Does its preferential nature have anything to offer? Is friendship a helpful model of relationship in a society where participation is encouraged?

Chapter 9 considers the way friendship influences the "scattered" and "everyday" dimension of the Christian life, particularly given the changing repertoires of friendship in the contemporary world. How does being friends with God affect everyday life in nonreligious contexts? What connections are there with dominant friendship themes of disclosure, secrecy, pleasure, and passion? And, what role can the concept of friendship play in everyday themes and contexts, such as vocation, leisure, play, and education?

Finally, chapter 10 examines the role of friendship as a personal virtue with public significance. Can the virtue of friendship and the development of virtue through friendship be recovered in a way appropriate for today? And is it possible for individual virtues to be seen as corporate values that can enhance society as a whole through intentional lives of virtuous friendship?

Church

Transforming Friendship

6

The more we love, the better we are, and the
greater our friendships are, the dearer we are to
God; let them be as dear, and let them be as perfect,
and let them be as many as you can; there is no
danger in it; only where the restraint begins, there
begins our imperfection.

"Discourse of the Nature and Offices
of Friendship"—Jeremy Taylor

I f you have a *godsib*, then you are very fortunate! A godsib (a combination of "god" and "sibling") is a sibling by choice rather than by
birth, or a "spiritual friend" who, like a godparent, has the responsibility to build up his or her friend in faith. Although the term "gossip,"
from which godsib derives, is now used to refer to trivial or unhelpful
conversation, it was originally meant to refer to spiritually intimate
conversations that were designed to build up faith. It would be helpful
if godparents, godsibs, and gossip were active today in their original

sense; but even if that cannot be, there are other forms of holy friendship that can build believers up in faith and love.

Sworn friendships

Godsibs are simply one part of a tradition of sworn (or ritual) friendships within the church. One example is seen in the records concerning the knights Sir William Neville and Sir John Clanvowe, who were buried together after dying within days of each other in 1391 while in Constantinople. They lie buried together, face-to-face. The monks noted that after Clanvowe died, Neville suffered "such inconsolable sorrow that he never took food again and two days afterward breathed his last." Similarly, the chapel at Merton College, Oxford, has the joint tomb of clerical friends John Bloxham and John Whytton, who enjoyed a profound and publicly acknowledged friendship. Contemporary unfamiliarity with this practice has led some to confuse these friendships with sexual relationships, which they were not, although they certainly involved the formalization of a close friendship.[1]

In the Eastern Church, there is an even older celibate tradition. An eighth-century manuscript (that perhaps reflects much earlier usage) includes a prayer used when there was a desire for the recognition of a deeper, spiritual friendship. It was known as *adelphopoiesis* ("the making of brothers"), a rite that created a bond of friendship akin to that of brotherhood:.

> Forasmuch as Thou, O Lord and Ruler, art merciful and loving, who didst establish humankind after thine image and likeness, who didst deem it meet that thy holy apostles Philip and Bartholomew be united, bound unto one another not by nature but by faith and the Spirit. As Thou didst find thy holy martyrs Serge and Bacchus worthy to be united together, bless also these thy servants, N and N, joined together not by the bond of nature but by faith and in the mode of the Spirit, granting unto them peace and love and oneness of mind. Cleanse from their hearts every stain and impurity, and vouchsafe

unto them to love one another without hatred and without scandal all the days of their lives, with the aid of the Mother of God and all the saints, forasmuch as all glory is thine.[2]

It is likely that the tenth-century Patriarch Nikolas I Mysticus of Constantinople and Emperor Leo VI the Wise were made friends or spiritual brothers in this way.[3] It is difficult today to fully grasp the significance and the nuances involved in these relationships, partly because of the very different and highly individualistic approach we have to relationships, and partly because of the historical distance involved. There is no doubt that such friendships could have political dimensions and involve the role of benefactor, but the spiritual role cannot be ignored. The ritual drew, for example, upon apostolic relationships for precedent and the use of fictive kinship terminology ("brother" and "sister") in scriptural accounts of the early church to underline the importance of the relationships between believers. Adelphopoiesis was certainly *meant* to involve a particularly intimate, spiritual relationship.

The use of ritual friendship faded away, however, because of a variety of problems. In some cases, the establishment of the bond was used to create legal obligations affecting other members of the family (something which canon law eventually prohibited); there was also the problem of special friendships in larger, religious communities; and there was a fear of the misuse of the bond in forming political alliances. Ritual friendship became rare but is not completely unknown in recent times.[4] However, the idea of friendship as a spiritual discipline as in adelphopoiesis is, to put it mildly, foreign to most contemporary conceptions of friendship. The church today is dominated by popular notions of friendship as a personal and largely self-fulfilling relationship, one that only has an incidental connection to spiritual growth. It is not usually seen as an intrinsic part of the Christian life to be placed alongside prayer, corporate worship, and the reading of the Scriptures as a very specific means of lifelong spiritual growth. It even seems to conflict with the more commonly understood call for Christians to love everyone equally.

The obvious question is whether there would be any advantage in rehabilitating the concept in some form or another. A modest approach could be that of simply reminding congregations of the history and the possibilities involved in friendship. This may encourage people to pay greater attention to its spiritual potential. A more ambitious approach would be to consider whether it would be possible to reintroduce more formal commitments in some way appropriate for the present day. Although this runs counter to current perceptions of friendship as a purely private relationship, strengthening friendship through an intentional and formal focus on it, and enhancing its potential as a means of spiritual growth would be of great benefit to church and society. As Paul Wadell says, "Friendship is the crucible of the moral life, the relationship in which we come to embody the good by sharing it with friends."[5]

Covenant friendship

Sworn friendships are not the only form of Christian friendship, but they do find precedence in biblical tradition. In addition to the descriptions of friendship with God in the accounts of Moses and Abraham that were discussed earlier, there is a tradition of *covenant* friendships. This is found in, firstly, the teaching on human friendship in the wisdom literature, especially the books of Proverbs and Ecclesiastes, and also in the second-century-BC writing of Yeshua ben Eleazar ben Sira, otherwise known as Ben Sira. There are also, secondly, some influential examples of friendship, especially those of David and Jonathan, and Naomi and Ruth. These, combined with an understanding of friendship in the Graeco-Roman world, provide the background for apostolic friendships that occurred in the life of the early church. Indeed, one cannot understand the nature of the early church without understanding the friendship that was at the heart of both the holiness and the fellowship of the believers.

Wisdom literature on friendship

The Wisdom literature takes a very practical view of friendship. Ecclesiastes extols the benefit of friendship, declaring that two are always better than one (4:7–12) while Proverbs provides straightforward advice on how to maintain friendships, especially long-term ones: "Do not forsake your friend or the friend of your parent" because "some friends play at friendship but a true friend sticks closer than one's nearest kin." (27:10; 18:24). It is important, therefore, to be able to discern true friendship, and so there is advice about accepting the frank assessments of a friend and warnings against flattery: "Well meant are the wounds a friend inflicts, but profuse are the kisses of an enemy" (27:6). More comprehensive than this advice, however, are the seven pericopes on friendship found in the Wisdom of the teacher Ben Sira from around 195–175 BC. He wrote as a Hebrew with an understanding of both ancient cultures (Greek, Egyptian, and Mesopotamian) and the increasingly Hellenized society of his day. Jeremy Corley identifies four main themes concerning friendship in Ben Sira:[6] (1) the goodness of friendship (happy is the one who finds a true friend); (2) the need for caution in friendship (beware of those who are friends in name only; friendship between rich and poor is not possible; there is a need to test friends in order to discern the real friends); (3) faithfulness toward friends is important (a faithful friend is a strong shelter, beyond price); and (4) the fear of God is connected with friendship (the one who fears God will find a faithful friend; one's friends should not only be God-fearing but also wise and observing the law).

These principles are demonstrated, albeit in very different ways, in the accounts of the friendships of Naomi and Ruth, and David and Jonathan. The former is an ideal account of constant love and commitment that ends in unqualified happiness, while the latter is an example of a much more qualified kind of friendship that presents a number of serious problems in any practical application for the readers.

Ruth and Naomi

The story of Ruth and Naomi begins with Naomi and her husband, Elimelech, moving from Bethlehem to live in Moab. Their sons marry local women, one of whom is Ruth. Subsequently, both Naomi and Ruth are widowed, so Naomi determines to return to her ancestral territory of Judah. Ruth, despite Naomi's reluctance, insists on coming with her:

> "Do not press me to leave you or to turn back from following you! Where you go, I will go; where you lodge, I will lodge; your people shall be my people, and your God my God. Where you die, I will die—there will I be buried. May the LORD do thus and so to me, and more as well, if even death parts me from you!" (Ruth 1:16–17)

The goodness of friendship, the importance of fidelity, and the role of the fear of God in friendship are all amply demonstrated in this story. This account of friendship also includes a redemptive theme (through Boaz, who acts as kinsman-redeemer in marrying Ruth): the joyful birth of Obed (through whose line Christ was born) and long life for all. It has the ultimate in happy endings and is presented as a positive example of the virtue of friendship. It contrasts sharply with the closely connected account of the friendship of David and Jonathan.

David and Jonathan

The stories are similar in that both deal with the friendship of in-laws (Naomi and Ruth are mother/daughter-in-law, and David and Jonathan are brothers-in-law), and they are connected genealogically in that Ruth is, through Obed and his son, Jesse, the great-grandmother of David. But although the biblical account of David and Jonathan is (like the story of Naomi and Ruth) a story of great friendship, there is (very unlike the story of Naomi and Ruth) a large helping of duplicity, disaster, and death combined with mixed and ambiguous motives and many personal flaws.

The friendship of David and Jonathan is profound, combining strong personal affection with a sworn covenant. At a theological level, it is clearly grounded in the covenant and in the Lord's help and love (1 Sam. 18:3; 20:12–16), and it reflects the principles expounded in the Wisdom literature concerning the value of friendship. At the socio-logical and psychological level, the situation is more complex and it has been interpreted variously, including in sexual terms; but the imposition of modern sexual mores upon David and Jonathan's mutual expressions of love is misleading. More helpful are the studies of combat relation-ships and the insights of war veterans who speak of the unique nature of friendships formed in battle, especially hand-to-hand combat and the most dangerous and bloody fighting.[7] This approach provides a helpful interpretive tool for understanding certain behaviors and language both during and after war.

The descriptions of combat involving David and Jonathan are particularly graphic. They even show some evidence of a "berserker"— that is, soldiers who are frenzied or reckless in ways beyond the norm. Both participate in some extremely violent battles—Jonathan is provoc-ative and risk-taking in his behavior, while David not only slays Goliath but he also chops off his head. David also kills one hundred Philistines and cuts off their foreskins as a gift for Saul. Later, with a complete disregard of the danger, he creeps into an enemy stronghold by night in order to steal Saul's spear (1 Sam. 14:1–15; 18:27; 26:6–12). One may defend these events in the light of the overall situation, and it is possible to point to changes in standards over time with regard to appropriate behavior in battle; nonetheless, David's behavior, in particular, was regarded as extraordinary even at the time. Both David and Jonathan display the kind of heroic recklessness that leads either to death or to military citations for bravery. Their relationship can probably be best understood, at least in part, in terms of a combat friendship that is born of trauma, where comrades have their lives entirely in the hands of the other. Their friendship is sealed immediately after David's return from slaying Goliath—literally with Goliath's head in his hands—and we read that "the soul of Jonathan was bound to the soul of David" (1 Sam. 18:1).

A combat bond such as this can be particularly strong and long lasting to the point where it can create marital difficulties, as it may be perceived as an even stronger bond than marriage. As one modern-day Iraq veteran said,

> Yeah, when I got home the first time my wife didn't understand why I had to see him everyday. He's my bro and we're connected. Hard to explain, hell, no one here gets it.[8]

Moreover, the description of Jonathan's love for David ("he loved him as he loved his own life," 1 Sam. 20:17) and David's lament for the deceased Jonathan ("greatly beloved were you to me; your love to me was wonderful, passing the love of women," 2 Sam. 1:26) are comparable to that of another Iraq veteran: "I know it ain't cool, but I cry about him everyday. He was one tough S.O.B. and he ain't ever coming home. Never had a friend like that."[9]

The problem for the one reading the story of David and Jonathan—and especially for the preacher or the teacher who has to draw something out of it—is that despite the reference to covenant loyalty between David and Jonathan and their expressions of great love, it is an account of friendship that is grounded in so much violence, and it is even more problematic when this is combined with the other difficult dimensions of this relationship. These begin with a friendship that immediately involves Jonathan deceiving his father, the king, in order to protect David. The idea of an ideal friendship continues to be difficult after Jonathan's death with David's serious moral failures, including his adultery with Bathsheba and the murder of Uriah (2 Sam. 11). Nor is it easy to forget the lies to Ahimelech that led to the slaughter of his whole city (1 Sam. 21–22). Perhaps the greatest tragedy in all this was Jonathan's death, because we will never know how much David would have been helped in dealing with his impetuosity and sin if Jonathan had been able to be a genuine "friend of the king" instead of dying before David reached that position. It could all have turned out quite differently if Jonathan had followed the tradition of the king's friends in speaking firmly to David, for "well meant are the wounds a friend inflicts" (Prov. 27:6).

The most basic point to draw from this is that friendships are not only for the good and righteous, like Ruth and Naomi, but also for imperfect, fallible, sinful people. Friendships are to be found in the midst of the real, rather than an ideal, world, where there is anger, injustice, death, and despair. In the midst of this, friends like Jonathan are gifts of grace in the midst of a challenging world. They are, in short, evidence of the presence and love of the forgiving, redeeming God.

Early Christian friendship

This notion of friendship as a demonstration of love, faithfulness, forgiveness, and redemption in the midst of the real world continues in the life of the early church. That which is taught in the Old Testament Wisdom literature and demonstrated in individual relationships, such as those of Ruth and Naomi and David and Jonathan, is found in the New Testament in the friendship and fellowship life of the fledgling church, especially as recorded by Luke. The Acts of the Apostles presents an account of the early church that is, in its own way, as dramatic as the story of David and Jonathan. The situation is not idealized; the moral difficulties associated with the friendship of David and Jonathan are also seen in the life of a community that not only shared all things in common, cared for the poor, worshiped God, proclaimed the gospel, and grew in grace and numbers, but in which people deceived others, engaged in disputes, were money-loving, and were capable of great arguments. And all this took place in the midst of the drama of riots, persecution, imprisonment, execution, shipwreck, and conspiracy.

Luke's description of the life of the early Christian community takes and transforms the notion of friendship in accordance with the way of life and the teaching of Jesus and his friends. The friendship of the early believers is the implicit foundation of the fellowship of the church. Luke was very aware of both the Jewish and the Greek traditions of friendship, and he utilized them throughout his narrative. This is not only seen in the way in which he is responsible for eighteen of the twenty-nine New Testament occurrences of "friend," but more significantly, and yet less noticeably for those not immersed in the culture of his day, in his use of an existing friendship (*topos*) to demonstrate that the fellowship of "the believers" is to be grounded on a specifically Christian interpretation of friendship.

A *topos* or, one might say, a "topic" is a term used for a popularly known cluster of associated words, ideas, and phrases that relate to a single theme. These are commonplace ideas that can be evoked by the use of specific words or phrases. They are typically used to express or encourage shared values, and their effective use by writers or preachers relies upon the audience's familiarity with them. For example, in 1 Corinthians, Paul used a wisdom *topos* that served to remind his readers that divine wisdom contrasts with human wisdom, and that one cannot know divine wisdom unless it is revealed (1:20–21, 26–30; 2:6–7; also, see Dan. 2:27–28). These are themes found in other Jewish and Christian writings that he then modified in order to focus on the significance of the apparent "foolishness" of the cross that is actually true wisdom. The epistle of James relates wisdom to a *topos* of envy that relies on the shared ideas that envy produces other evils and that envy reveals a lack of wisdom. This is used to stress the need for friendship with God rather than with the world (James 3:13–4:10).

In the present situation, Luke draws on an existing and well-known understanding of the nature and responsibilities of friendship, and a number of Luke's words and phrases appear designed to elicit specific associations that would have been familiar to both Greek and Jewish readers. So when "the whole group of those who believed" are described as being "of one ... soul," Jewish readers would have recalled the friend-ship of David and Jonathan, who were described in this way (Acts 4:32; 1 Sam. 18:1). The idea of friends being *psyche mia* or "one soul" was also widely known in the Hellenistic world. Both Plato and Aristotle had referred to this as *paroimia*, a well-known saying or proverb, and it is found widely in other Greek writers[10] and in the relatively common ancient discussions of friendship. It was, at that time, an important social concept.

The evidence for Luke using a friendship *topos* as a means of teaching about the church extends further. It was well known and widely accepted that "friends have all things in common," and in Acts this becomes "*the believers* had all things in common," a phrase that would still have been completely recognizable to Luke's audience as a refer-ence to friendship modified to apply to the community of believers.[11] Other parts of the friendship *topos* include the ideas that "friends are in harmony," "friends have the same opinion," "friends are equal," "friends are partners," and "friends speak boldly and frankly." These were well-known and widely accepted qualities of good friends, and they are also the essential characteristics of the early church community as described by Luke, especially in the brief but important summaries (Acts 2:42–47; 4:32–35) that are used to emphasize the communal values that are demonstrated in the narrative as a whole.

Luke's picture of the early church both reflected and Christianized the wisdom of the times concerning friendship and the form of commu-nity. Just as friendship was seen as foundational for the polis, so it was foundational for the Christian community. But within the Christian community, friendship took on new dimensions, and in many ways it was to be distinguished from contemporary friendship. For example, while friendship in the Christian community shared the classical view, as expressed in Aristotle, that friendship is a virtue that is practiced and developed in community, it differed from Aristotle's understanding that friendship is formed by the needs of the self. For Aristotle, friendship is motivated by the presence of virtue in one who is to be another self, who is loved for his good. But ultimately, one must love oneself most of all; this is, indeed, the basis for friendship. In the Christian community, this fundamental principle is transformed by the radical nature of love of the other. Consequently, in Luke (and the rest of the New Testament) there is a new form of friendship based on the experience of Jesus Christ so that friendship is no longer based on the self, but upon the presence of God.

Luke's description of the life of the early Christian community deliberately utilizes at least four well-known principles of friendship in his depiction of the life of the early church. He used the common idea that "friends speak boldly" in the account of the creation of the community and the notion that "friends have all things in common" in his discussion of the way the community had both a common mind and common property. He also used the conviction that "friendship is equality" as the basis for justifying some new and particularly radical relationships. In *Making Room: Recovering Hospitality as a Christian Tradition,* Christine Pohl shows how friendship exercised through simple acts of hospitality is subversive and countercultural. Hospitality shown to those who are socially undervalued is very different from "more tame hospitality" that welcomes well-known and socially established people. The recognition of those not valued by society through hospitality produces small transformations that are "a witness to the larger community, which is then challenged to reassess its standards and methods of valuing."[12]

Friendship and the creation of community

The first use of friendship language, applied and modified for Christian use, is found in the way the community is formed. It was widely understood that a true friendship is to be distinguished from a false one by the honest, frank, and even bold language that takes place between real friends—compared with the flattery that is characteristic of an insincere friendship. The answer to the question posed in Plutarch's *How to Tell a Flatterer from a Friend* was that a friend will speak boldly. In Plutarch, Cicero, and others, this form of friendship stood in sharp contrast to the flattery of a false friend who is only intent on creating an atmosphere that would benefit himself. A good friend will aim at assisting in the development of the character of the other even though this may require difficult words.[13] This kind of bold speech could only be effective where there was a high level of mutual trust and was only appropriate between equals. Luke's depiction of the bold or "confident" (*parresia*) speech of the apostles (Acts 2:14, 29; 4:31) is the kind of "free speech" that was expected between friends. The Jerusalem authorities were astonished at this boldness because they expected flattery. But they, and all those who listened to the apostles, were meant to hear in the apostles' preaching the frank words of an honest friend. This is seen in Peter's Pentecost speech, where he spoke confidently and both warned and pleaded with his audience. He gave a prophetic challenge and offered forgiveness in a form of evangelism that could be construed as an offer of friendship by both the community and Christ to those who had not yet come to faith.[14]

> The community's bold speech positively expresses God's friendship to humanity, a friendship that offers promised gifts to anyone who calls on God's name, gifts of repentance and forgiveness of sins, the gift of the Holy Spirit, times of refreshing, restoration of God's Kingdom, healing, and salvation.[15]

Those who received the word became friends of Christ and the other believers. The principle is that Christian community is created through the offer of friendship. Of course, just as Luke related the life of the early Christian community to the friendship conventions of his day, so must we. In some places, there will not be the same place for the very public, bold speech that Peter engaged in. In modern, Western, secular society, the situation depends very much on the local context. What is seen as an appropriately frank but friendly speech in one place may be seen as intrusive or even offensive in another. The form that the boldness takes has to be appropriate to the context, but it should not be avoided. The Ephesian church received practical advice on the way to do this in the discussion of unity and maturity within the body of Christ (Eph. 4:1–16), which stresses the need for humility, gentleness, and patience as the essential context for that frankness which is well-known as "speaking the truth in love" (4:15). In fact, the quality of Christian friendship that is affirmed here is actually much broader than that: the present participle that is used in this verse does not relate to "speaking" other than as a logical inference from what has gone before. The word used is not really translatable except as something like "*truthing* in love." The point is that "truth" is not something only to be spoken (though that is one dimension of it), but lived in every way. The boldness of genuine friendship has to be spoken and demonstrated in life.

Of primary importance is the fact that the gospel was communicated through friendship and subsequently demonstrated in the friendship life of the community. It remains as a primary means by which the church will grow today. Indeed, it is the most normal way for the gospel to spread. Other programs and techniques are really only necessary when friendship, for one reason or another, fails. Friendship is fundamental. And it is friendship on its own terms that is important that is, not friendship as a program or a technique, but a friendship that simply seeks to love others in every way possible and that will, as a natural consequence, include the sharing of faith.

Friendship with a common mind

The second use of friendship language as a means of describing the life of the church relates to the level of sharing in the community and

derives from the way first- and second-century readers of the statement "All the *believers* were together and had everything in common"
would immediately recognize this as a modification of the well-known
conviction that "*friends* have all things in common" (Acts 2:44 NIV; 4:32;
emphasis added), especially when this is heard in the context of other
dimensions of the friendship *topos*. This friendship is demonstrated by
hospitality (breaking bread together in one another's homes) and the
sharing of possessions (no one claimed that any of their possessions
was their own), as well as by their being of one heart and soul with
each having an equal standing. Luke makes it clear that the Christian
community is a gathering of those who live as friends. Those who
came from many places, of different ethnicities and speaking different
languages (including Parthians, Medes, Elamites, Egyptians, Libyans,
and Romans), both Jews and Gentile converts were united through
meeting and eating together in one another's homes. The importance of
gathering together for meals in establishing the unity and community
of the church cannot be underestimated. Different ethnic groups in the
early church came together in friendship through hospitality. It was,
and still is, a primary way of making friends.[16] In the case of the new
Christian community, it was particularly potent because this breaking
of bread necessarily involved being aware of the continuing presence of
Jesus, the friend who united all the friends into one body. Friendship
is not only associated with what became known as a sacrament, but is
itself sacramental in that the life shared together, involving the friendship and unity of believers from all over the world, is a very present
sign of the presence of God and a foretaste of the future friendship and
fellowship of all believers in the kingdom of God.

   In the present day, the question is whether churches can be places
of genuine friendship rather than friendly churches that are primarily
institutions. Every church sees itself as friendly—partly because any
who do not have that attribute usually leave the community, and partly
because churches genuinely value and work at it. But a friendly church

is not necessarily a real community of friends. Being friendly to all and establishing an open and warm atmosphere creates one level of friendship that is valuable and important in its own right, but it does not automatically create specific friendships that function deeply and which are a primary means for building one another up in faith.

Indeed, friendliness at one level can, inadvertently, inhibit the development of real friendships by implying that friendship or fellowship only operates at a level in which all can share equally. But while it is possible to *be friendly* with many people, one can really only *be friends* with a smaller number. Deeper friendship is needed for deeper fellowship. Understanding the church as a community of friends means being friendly with all at one level and, at another level, having particular friends with relationships that involve caring in times of need, encouragement in spiritual growth and holiness, and a willingness to challenge inappropriate attitudes or any complacency in life and ministry. Being a community of friends means not being satisfied with mere friendliness, but rather it involves recognizing the importance of friendship relationships and fostering the opportunity for people to grow together in friendships that are more limited in number but deeper in relationship.

In a community of five hundred people, or one hundred or even fifty, one can be friendly to all but cannot *truly* be friends with everyone. Closer friendships are not, or at least should not be, a threat to friendliness to all. Small group ministries are a way of positively building relationships; however, from a formal point of view, training manuals and so forth usually focus on either the overall group dynamic or structured mentoring relationships. These are very useful, but teaching about the spiritual possibilities of friendships (as distinct from the utilitarian and pleasurable dimensions that are obvious to all) could lead to even greater spiritual growth.

Every form of church, large or small, has its problems. Churches that are large enough to require special buildings, rather than homes, perpetually run the risk of simply behaving like an institution. The focus is often on maintaining the unity of the larger group (which is itself important) with events and programs that bring large numbers together or that keep changing, ensuring (unintentionally) that deeper friendships have difficulty in being maintained. But whatever the size of the community, Christian fellowship is primarily developed through friendship that is itself created by lives that share together in homes and meals and in communion with Jesus.

This friendship is the focal point for spiritual growth and holiness. The early believers "devoted themselves to the apostles' teaching and to fellowship" (Acts 2:42). Together, rather than individually, they pursued the Christian life. There is nothing here similar to the modern emphasis on individualism; they shared a common life of friendship and fellowship focused on apostolic teaching. They not only shared in food and teaching but also in the presence of the Holy Spirit, which is, as James Houston puts it, "the transforming friendship" that brings a deeper quality of relationship with God the Father and the Son.[17]

Contemporary individualism also finds expression in modern congregationalism where there is a deep and widespread avoidance of any significant fellowship with Christians in other congregations that are not associated through common membership in a particular denomination. There are some notable exceptions to this and some wonderful cooperations, but they are the exception rather than the rule. A local congregation can, of course, feel a high level of connection with another congregation of the same denomination that is quite some distance away. This may mean being prepared to provide physical or monetary help at times, and it can mean speaking up when people feel the congregation or a part of the church has said or done something that seems to be inappropriate. People feel a mutual responsibility for what goes on in other parts of the denomination. It ought, however, to challenge our understanding of church when it is thought appropriate to not have any feeling about and no connection at all with a church across the street simply because it is of a different brand. Part of the justification for this isolationism is the ambiguity that exists in the use of the term "church." Many words have more than one meaning, and when they do, one has to be careful to avoid confusion. The English word "church" has at least seven related, but different meanings: (a) the body of Christ consisting of all believers ("the church universal"); (b) a particular congregation or group of believers ("there are three churches in the town"); (c) all believers in an area (Paul wrote to "the church in Rome"); (d) an international denomination ("the Lutheran church everywhere believes that . . . "); (e) a national body ("the Church of England"); (f) a building ("the church is two blocks down the road"); and (g) a gathering or service ("church is at 10:00 a.m.").

The problem is that there is a tendency to slide from one to the other within the space of a few sentences (or even words) without noticing the change. In the New Testament, *ekklesia* is the word most commonly translated "church," and it is used only to refer to definitions (a) the universal church—the body of Christ consisting of all believers; (c) the local church in an area—for example, the church of Rome; and the (g) gathering together of believers in a particular place (Matt.16:18; Eph. 1:22; 3:10; Rom. 16:1; 1 Cor. 1:2; 11:18; 14:19).

Unfortunately, these definitions often get overwhelmed by some of the others that have a denominational emphasis. This is particularly detrimental to the understanding of the church as a *universal* body of believers that exists everywhere, and of the church as all the believers in a particular *local* geographic area, as when Paul spoke of the church in Rome, Antioch, or Philippi. In Rome, and presumably in other places, there were multiple groups of believers meeting in different houses (Rom. 16:1–16), but together they were "the church in Rome." Unfortunately, today few Christians have a sense of fellowship with congregations near their own if they belong to another denomination.

My wife and I lived in one local community for nearly twenty years, and we knew people in most of the other congregations in the immediate area. I had preached in a number of them. But a time came when we decided that it would be good to visit these other communities for no other reason than that it was a friendly thing to do. And, we decided, this would not be just a once-off visit but a regular practice. We visited all the churches, not merely the ones where we felt at home, and so we went to half a dozen Catholic, Protestant, and Pentecostal congregations in churches, storefronts, and factories. We were, of course, always welcome, usually with the question, "How is it that you have come to visit us today?" The explanation that we were there for no other reason than that it was a friendly thing to do was always well received. When we went back for a second or third time, the reaction was always, "Hey, it's good to see you again! Just here for another visit?" In fact, there was only one group of people who ever expressed reservations about what we were doing. The pastors were clearly conflicted about this behavior. Although they saw that it had value, they saw potential difficulties with it and wondered what would happen if everyone did it. But the idea is not that everyone spends all their time moving around, but that a greater level of interaction could well produce new friendships and new opportunities for sharing and ministry together. It is also interesting when one responds to any question about which church one belongs to by saying, "The church of Lilydale," to which people would usually respond with a rather puzzled look, "But which one?" This allows one to say, "Oh, there is only one," and describe the various congregations, including the one that was our "home" congregation. There is only one church of Jesus Christ, and all Christians are part of it. Denominational distinctions are, as most people understand, human constructs that do not actually mark the edge of the church. But until people actually begin to behave in accordance with that belief, the life of the church will be diminished.

It is difficult to know where active friendship like this will end in practical terms, but it will be better for the church if people begin to behave like the one community that the church ought to be. This is part of a "bottom-up" form of ecumenism that is quite distinct from the more traditional "top-down" ecumenism that begins with contacts between leaders and leads to joint committees and commissions that aim to produce statements, resolve doctrinal differences, achieve a mutual recognition of ministry, and perhaps have cooperative events. There is no denying that top-down ecumenism is important, but the history of this form of ecumenical dialogue demonstrates that it is slow, difficult, and limited in effect. At the congregational level, the evidence is that people are now very willing to change denominational affiliation. Previously there was a stronger sense of identity as, say, Baptist, Methodist, or Presbyterian. If people moved to a new home in a different neighborhood there was a strong tendency to find another church of the same denomination. Today, denominational factors are far less important. People switch easily and find a church that suits their needs irrespective of denominational affiliation. The effect of this is that, individually, members tend to hold very loosely to denominational identity while, organizationally, traditional denominational patterns of inter-church relationships continue. Although many people in a congregation have a background in another denomination, there is still a tendency for congregations to have minimal connections. There is a need for greater levels of fellowship and cooperation and bottom-up ecumenism that begins a journey with simple friendship. It is difficult to know exactly what would happen if more and more people were actively engaged in relating across congregational boundaries and if Christians were, locally, more engaged. But unlike top-down forms of ecumenism that usually begin with a specific aim in mind—a statement, a series of meetings, a declaration—friendship does not set out an agenda in advance. It simply waits to see what will happen. Its power stems, at least in part, from this flexibility and the ability to respond as the relationship develops.

Friendship with common property

The conception of friendship expressed in Acts whereby the believers were united in one body was no abstract notion. In their particular situation, there was an immediate development from common *mind* to common *property*. "No one claimed private ownership of any possessions, but everything they owned was held in common" (Acts 4:32). The fact that believers would sell property "and distribute the proceeds to all, as any had need" (Acts 2:45) is found in both of Luke's brief summaries of the life of the early community. The sharing of the early church was radical and equitable, yet voluntary. The non-obligatory nature of the sharing is emphasized in the account of Ananias and Sapphira, whose sin was not in giving only a part of the proceeds of the sale of their property to the apostles for distribution to the poor but in the lie by which they claimed to have given all. Peter was clear that the proceeds were always theirs to do with as they saw fit. The proceeds of the sales were laid at the apostles' feet, not for their use or out of a sense of obligation to them, but simply because they were seen as being appropriately responsible for its distribution, a task that became so onerous that they called for the selection of seven others of good standing to take over this work.

The practical friendship involved in caring for those in need extended as the church spread (Acts 5:1–11; 6:1–7; 11:29; Rom. 15:26–27; 1 Cor. 16:1–4). While commentators often note that this is illustrative of Graeco-Roman philosophy and Plato's ideal community as described in his *Laws*, it is even more illustrative of the presence of the kingdom of God. This is a point made by the claim that "there was not a needy person among them" which is reminiscent of the eschatological promise to Israel, "There will, however, be no one in need among you, because the LORD is sure to bless you in the land that the LORD your God is giving you as a possession to occupy" (Acts 4:34; Deut. 15:4); it is also found in Jesus' announcement of the presence of the kingdom, which Luke recorded earlier in his gospel, "The Spirit of the Lord is upon me, because he has anointed me to bring good news to the poor . . ." (Luke 4:18–19). Indeed, all the elements of the promise from Isaiah 61 that Jesus proclaims (good news for the poor, release to the captives, recovery of sight to the blind, and freedom for the oppressed) are found demonstrated in the life of the early church. This good news is realized through sharing that comes from friendship. Clement of Alexandria commented on this in his *Exhortation to the Heathen,*

> [L]et us commit ourselves to God, loving the Lord God, and regarding this as our business all our life long. And if what belongs to friends be reckoned common property, and man be the friend of God—for through the mediation of the Word has he been made the friend of God—then accordingly all things become man's, because all things are God's, and the common property of both the friends, God and man.[18]

This practice of radical sharing was not, however, followed everywhere, although the principles of generosity and equity remained as important principles for the church. This form of complete sharing of all possessions is easier in certain circumstances, such as between a smaller number of people equally committed to one another and a common vision, as in marriage, a close friendship of a few people, or a clearly defined religious order. It is more difficult within broader and more diverse communities.

In Acts, Luke describes the complex interaction between ideas and their actual expression in the life of the community. This is not, as noted above, idealized; it includes reference to moral failures and the realities of life. This, however, does not negate the importance of the various principles for a healthy church that Luke expounds, including the principle of equality among friends—a principle that stands in sharp contrast to both contemporary consumerism and modern individualism. Their immediate reaction on being united together in Christ was to see their responsibilities to the needy among them. This was not, initially at least, a program of care for others *outside* the community. This was a community of believers that *included* the poor.

Contemporary Western churches often—though by no means always—understand the responsibility of caring for those in need on the premise that they are outside the church. There are many places where caring for the poor is done as a part of outreach with little said or done within the community, either because it consists entirely of the materially well-off or because of the denial or avoidance of the somewhat embarrassing needs of those who are not. In many places, churches are socioeconomically stratified so that they no longer represent the poor, and the principle of equity and radical sharing by the community of faith is lost. This is not only to the disadvantage of those who could be helped materially but also to those who could grow in faith through the gift of generosity. Working "with" the poor is very different from working "for" the poor. The early church faced the issue of "the needy *among them*" rather than "the needy over there," and so the concept of friendship came to the fore, compared with the more institutional and professional modes of caring that are generally involved in caring for the needy in other places. One example of a community that had to focus on the poor within is the early Methodist movement. John Wesley stressed the need to follow the apostle Paul's injunction to "work for the good of all, *and especially for those of the family of faith*" (Gal. 6:10; emphasis added). He was not addressing well-off congregations considering the nature of ministry to those outside the church, but a movement that had gained traction among the poor of his day. Care, charity, and compassion were not so much specific actions that were to be performed by Christians on behalf of others so much as they were a way of life for a community called by God to scriptural holiness. What Richard Heitzenrater says about Wesley's view of the Christian life being primarily about being a certain kind of person rather than about doing certain activities[19] could be refined so one would say that, for Wesley, the Christian life is defined by being a certain kind of community. He saw the importance of that preferential friendship for those nearby, without in any way minimizing the importance of caring for others. Genuine care does not stop with the Christian community, but it does start there. The first epistle of John points out that one cannot love God whom one has not seen if one cannot love one's brother whom one has seen (4:20). So, too, one cannot care for those in the wider community if one cannot care for those who are closest to home. Students consistently find that one of the most challenging aspects of a course that I teach relates to a practical ministry exercise that follows on from course material related to the notion of ministering with (not just "to") the poor who are among you (rather than being "out there"). It challenges assumptions concerning the nature of the church and ministry and their own relationships with others. Working with the poor who are at a distance is often considerably less challenging to one's view of genuinely Christian friendship!

Friendship and equality

A fourth use of friendship language for describing the life of the early church is based on a development of the Graeco-Roman proverb that "friendship is equality." At the time of the birth of the church, it was well known that Aristotle had concluded that while it was possible to be friends with a slave in a certain sense—in terms of common humanity—there cannot be genuine, full friendship between a free man and a slave because of the inequality in the situation. While the Christian view of friendship agreed with the notion that friendship demands equality, it was much more radical in that it argued that a common faith in Jesus Christ provided the basis for the equality that is needed for genuine friendship between slave and free (Rom. 8:15; 1 Cor. 7:22; Gal. 3:28; Philem. 16). The notion of friends having a common mind and common wealth based on a common faith inevitably led to the general principle of equality within the community of friends. Paul's discussion in 2 Corinthians 8–9 of the rationale behind Christian generosity and the sharing of material goods is based on this principle and echoes the proverbial need for equality between friends: "It is a question of a fair balance . . . in order that there may be a fair balance . . . 'The one who had much did not have too much, and the one who had little did not have too little'" (2 Cor. 8:13–15). This is not the radical sharing of the first friends in Jerusalem, but it still embodied the principle of equality; it also extended beyond the material and involved a reappraisal of distinctions of all areas of social status. As Benjamin Jowett expressed it much later in his sermon on friendship:

> Christian friendship is different to that of the ancients "For it is not merely the friendship of equals, but of unequals; the love of the weak and those who can make no return, like the love of God towards the unthankful and the evil . . . It is not a friendship of one or two, but of many. Again, it proceeds from a different rule— 'love your enemies'." It is founded on that charity which "beareth all things, believeth all things, hopeth all things, endureth all things" nothing short of this is the Christian ideal which is set before us in the Gospel. And here and there may be found a person who has been inspired to carry it out in practice.[20]

The declaration in Galatians 3:28 that for the baptized, the friends of Christ, "there is no longer *Jew or Greek*, there is no longer *slave or free*, there is no longer *male and female*" (emphasis added) has been called the Magna Carta of Humanity,[21] a fundamental statement of equality before God. There is no doubt that Paul's primary focus is to assert that the salvation Christ brings is equally applicable to all people, but this is a salvation that is both personal and social in nature, and these three couplets cover the most essential human relationships and have racial, cultural, and sexual implications. These specific relationships reflect the three blessings that appear at the beginning of Jewish morning prayer: "Blessed be He that did not make me a Gentile; blessed be He that did not make me a brutish [i.e., an ignorant peasant or slave]; blessed be He that did not make me a woman."[22] There is no evidence that this particular prayer was recited as early as the first century, but the thought it expresses certainly extends back to that period. In fact, it is similar in concept to a sixth-century-BC saying attributed to the Greek philosopher

Thales, who said he was glad that he had been born a human and not a beast, a man and not a woman, and a Greek and not a barbarian.

Paul's declaration brought cultural and ethnic unity. The Jew-Greek distinction was a deep-seated division of the first century, and the most obvious effect of this declaration was that Christian Jews could no longer regard themselves as superior in any way to Gentile believers or require Gentiles to embrace Jewish law. Jewish and Gentile believers could, and should, worship together, and the priesthood that had been for Jews alone was now open to all believers. The declaration also challenged the prevailing attitudes toward slavery. It was a revolutionary step to suggest that the lowest of the low in social terms could become a son or daughter of God. Elsewhere Paul required that if there was a slave and his master in the church, their Christian status as friends and brothers should take precedence over social status (Philem. 15–16; Eph. 5:21; 6:5–9).

In both the first and the twenty-first centuries, friendship, social equality, and community well-being are closely and inextricably linked. Research shows that friendships are protective of good health and well-being, while inequality and status differences are harmful. As inequality increases, the strength of community life declines. For some years now, studies have shown apparently unusual results, as when people with friends are demonstrably less likely to catch a cold. Indeed, the more friends they have, the more resistant they are. And physical wounds heal faster if people have good relationships with their intimate partners. But more recent research has gone further and has accumulated data and research findings from around the world and from every area of life (social relationships and dysfunctionality, mental health, drug use, physical health, life expectancy, obesity, educational performance, violence, criminality, and social mobility) and concludes that less equal societies are less healthy in every respect.[23]

Consequently, friendship, which is either indicative of a less stratified society or which actually bridges gaps in stratified societies, creates a healthier society for everyone. The greatest stresses in a society do not arise from external threats but from internal tensions between members of the same society when there is inequality, competition, and a sense of less control. In such situations, levels of health and well-being decline. Consequently, social integration and friendship are important determinants of a population's physical, emotional, and social health.

In the developed world, the level of equity within a society is a more important determinant of well-being than the overall level of wealth. This is not only observable when comparing developed nations but also when comparing the fifty US states. All areas of social well-being improve with greater levels of social equity, rather than with overall wealth. And what is really important to note is that greater levels of equity benefit everybody, not just the poor. For example, greater inequity means that even the well-off have shorter lives, and greater equity leads to greater well-being for all. As the British researchers Richard Wilkinson and Kate Pickett say, "the benefits of greater equality spread right across society, improving health for everyone—not just those at the bottom. In other words, at almost any level of income, it is better to live in a more equal place."[24]

It is the church's calling to exhibit in its own life the friendship and equality of which the Scripture speaks. Whether it is possible for the church to transform society into a more equitable mode of being will depend upon numerous factors, many of which are not within the church's control. But in any event, focusing upon these values in its own life and providing a model of the possibilities may well be the best way of influencing wider society toward the greater equality that is the hallmark of friendship.

The spiritual formation of the church

The material above shows that Luke's adaptation of the contemporary philosophy of friendship was critical in his depiction of the formation and the life of the early Christian community. It was used to demonstrate the common attitude and the common life that they shared and the radical equality that was the basis for justifying new and radical relationships. The point is clearly made that the apostles were friends in Christ. They shared a messianic friendship that exhibited the qualities of friendship admired in Ruth and Naomi, David and Jonathan, and the "friends of God" tradition of Abraham and Moses. Mutual commitment, a common mind, and a shared life were characteristic of the community as a whole and were frequently illustrated in particular friendships, such as those of Peter and John, Paul and Barnabas, and Paul and Silas. One of the important dimensions of this friendship was a commitment to the holiness of the community. Sin was not tolerated (as in the case of Ananias and Sapphira), growth was encouraged (as in Barnabas's support for John Mark and Paul's mentoring of Timothy), and they were prepared to speak frankly with one another (Acts 15:2, 39).

The arguments do not (primarily at least) illustrate bad temper, and they are not indications of a loss of friendship; they are demonstrations of the honesty that good friends have with one another: they were concerned about spiritual growth. This very honest friendship was important for spiritual growth. It stands in contrast to the modern insistence that one "do your own thing" or "be your own person," which, more often than not, is very poor advice and a spiritually unhelpful approach to life. True friendship involves challenging one's friends to be *more* than what human nature expects them to be. Holy friendship goes beyond "unconditional acceptance" and "tolerance" to call for change and transformation. As it has been said, "the perfect friend is one who knows the worst about you, and loves you just the same." Friendship accepts that friends are imperfect and does not reject them because of it. Holy friendship is not modern tolerance because it does not accept that transformation cannot take place. When, in the classic film *The African Queen*, Charlie Allnut (Humphrey Bogart) defends his gin drinking to his new friend (and sometime antagonist and future wife), Methodist missionary Rose Sayer (Katherine Hepburn), he declares it to be simply human nature to drink in this way. But Rose's challenging response is, "Human nature is what we are called to rise above!" At the heart of friendship is the ability to make demands on friends precisely because these demands are seen to be for the other's own good. Some see any such expectations as demanding and decidedly unfriendly, but the call to a higher standard of life is really the best way to honor and bless one's friends.

The potential for friendship to enhance our spiritual life is particularly important in the light of the current need for the spiritual formation of the congregation to be the primary task of the church. Jürgen Moltmann describes the maturation of the congregation as the unfinished work of the Reformation that restored the prominence of the notion of the church as the priesthood of all believers. This is to be worked out in the life of a community that is neither fundamentally hierarchical, nor authoritarian in form (the medieval ecclesial model that was being opposed) or individualistic in approach (as it often became under the ruinous influence of the modern era). The life of the church involves both freedom and community, and thus he concludes that "the concept of friendship is the best way of expressing the liberating relationship with God, and the fellowship of men and women in the spirit of freedom."

This is an affirmation of Hegel's view that friendship is "the concrete concept of freedom."[25] Friendship can only emerge in the context of freedom, and in turn, it nurtures the freedom of both the friend and the community. So when "the parent-child relation comes to an end, when the master-serving connection is abolished and when privileges based on sexual position are removed, then what is truly human emerges and remains; and that is friendship."[26]

Holiness and friendship

Holy friendship, whether it exists in a formal mode as a sworn, public relationship or in its more contemporary informal mode, can be a means for strengthening the church. It has the advantage of being a universal relationship, accessible to all, as it functions separately from the presence of specific gifts or abilities. And while it may exist in almost ideal forms, as with Ruth and Naomi, it can also be found, perhaps even more importantly, in less-than-perfect lives and relationships. Christian friendship does not come about because people are perfect; rather, it is the means by which people can be drawn toward perfection. It is a valuable means of mutual discipleship. Friends can powerfully and intentionally mediate the grace and love of Jesus Christ, enhance the work of ministry, and extend their friend's understanding of the possibilities that can be achieved. Christian holiness is more a corporate than an individual pursuit. My holiness depends—as everyone's does—not only on me but also on the life, teaching, and example of those around me. And I, likewise, bear a responsibility for those close to me. We are what we can be as Christians with our friends in Christ. It is they who can build us up, challenge our failures, and mediate grace and forgiveness. Life together is a holy friendship with others and with Christ.

Friendship is an essential, but presently underestimated, means of grace whereby congregations and individuals can be formed into the image of Jesus Christ. For Thomas Aquinas, friendship was *the primary* calling of the disciples. He described a triple calling of the apostles, with the first being a calling to "friendship and faith," the second call was to evangelism, and the third to their apostleship.[27] However, it was the call to friendship—with Jesus in particular, but also to a communal life with others—that was the foundation for the others. It was in eating, living, traveling, and ministering together as friends that they were formed as evangelists and apostles.

It is appropriate to refer to friendship as nothing less than a means of grace. This is a term often reserved for those activities that develop the spiritual life of believers, especially participation in the sacraments, prayer, and the reading of Scripture. But friendship also deserves to be seen in this light because it is central, rather than peripheral, to the formation of believers in community. Friendship needs to be seen not only as a significant relationship that enhances and gives meaning to human life, but also as a means by which people are enabled to reach full salvation—the ultimate spiritual destiny that is given to humanity by God. It is to be oriented toward life with God.

This eschatological orientation is seen in the writing of John Wesley, a man particularly focused on measuring everything by the extent to which it contributed to holiness. For Wesley, everything had to contribute to finding "the way to heaven." All pursuits have to be assessed in this way, and not only do those activities and attitudes that detract from holiness have to be rejected, but so does anything that is good in itself but does not positively contribute to greater holiness. That, ironically, can include human friendship itself if it is not specifically focused upon developing holiness. For Wesley, friendship was not a private relationship oriented toward enhancing the joy and happiness of this present life; it was to be a means of grace for growth toward God, and therefore, friendship was not to be confused with what we might call niceness. The measure of the quality of a friendship is not to be measured by anything other than the extent to which it brings individuals and the community to God. Friendship, like all the other means of grace, had, among its other dimensions, the function of making individuals and the community accountable for their actions. Wesley commended one of his correspondents who had attempted to correct what he perceived to be some of Wesley's mistakes: "I am exceedingly obliged by the pains you have taken to point out what you think to be mistakes . . . for what is friendship, if I am to account him my enemy who endeavors to open my eyes or amend my heart?"[28]

Indeed, he noted to another correspondent that it is the "painful offices" of correction and reproof that best demonstrate "the sincerity of friendship."[29] There are obvious implications here for those who hold friendship to be simply an intimate relationship oriented toward mutual satisfaction: friendship is to be more substantial than this. Of course, the danger in applying Wesley's teaching is that of the tendency to offer advice rather than to receive it, which is likely to be a case of paying attention to the speck in another's eye while ignoring the log in one's own. As Wesley shows, this difficult dimension of friendship must first be applied to oneself, but eventually it is something that has to be mutually recognized and practiced in order to build up the whole community.

The reason for this corrective function in friendship is, positively expressed, that the purpose of friendship lies in its ability to lead people to know and love God. The purpose of friendship does not lie in itself or in satisfying oneself or in serving another. It lies in loving God. Some of Wesley's specific advice about when to withdraw from friendship with those who are not contributing to one's edification may seem over-particular (and this is something on which he varied over time), and perhaps friendships with unbelievers could be viewed more positively (though he always stressed the need to love them), but his fundamental point is valid—that the ultimate goal is not friendship *per se* but salvation. This is why friendship with the *godly* could be as dangerous as friendship with the ungodly, if its pleasures detracted from a focus on the true source of happiness—friendship with God.

His advice, therefore, is to cultivate friendships that contribute positively to holiness. Friendship is really nothing other than a way of describing the growing Christian life. Indeed, he argued, only Christians can really have friends, since "wicked people are, it seems, incapable of friendship"[30]—at least of friendship anything like the way Wesley envisaged it, as an important part of fellowship and the outworking of divine grace.

However, says Wesley, this does not mean only loving Christians, as it is important not to confuse friendship with love. Believers should certainly love their friends, but he also stressed the importance of loving all people, even, as Jason Vickers points out, in exactly the same manner: "Love friends and enemies as thy own soul. And, let thy love be long-suffering, and patient towards all men. Let it be kind, soft, benign: inspiring thee with the most amiable sweetness, and the most fervent affection."[31]

Friendship is not simply love, for that is owed to all. Friendship is more particular; it is an important means to holiness. Friends are guides on the way to heaven. Indeed, the final lesson to learn from Wesley is to avoid friendships that do not contribute to holiness. He gave his followers clear instructions on the need to avoid friendship with the ungodly, saying, "[Scripture] clearly requires us to keep at a distance, as far as practicable, from all ungodly men."[32] One may relate to the ungodly in terms of routine business, but undue connections are to be avoided, and so, too, is anything that may lead one to "slide into conformity to the world" or lead to a diminishing of religious duties.

The idea of friendship as a spiritual discipline as in *adelphopoiesis*, or as a means of grace in Wesleyan thinking is, to put it mildly, foreign to contemporary conceptions of friendship. The obvious question is whether there would be any possibility, any advantage, in rehabilitating the concept in some form or another. A modest approach could be that simply reminding congregations of the history and the possibilities involved in friendship may encourage people to pay greater attention to its spiritual potential. A more ambitious approach would be to consider whether it would be possible to reintroduce more formal commitments in some way appropriate for the present day. That, however, runs most counter to current perceptions of friendship. Nonetheless, just as the church has been very concerned for many years to focus on, teach about, and encourage growth in the spiritual dimensions of marriage and family, it could do something similar for friendship to develop its potential as a means of spiritual growth, resulting in a benefit to both church and society and a challenge to the more self-focused forms of friendship that prevail today.

Ministry

What a Friend We Have in Jesus

7

> As the representatives of Christ
> we appeal to you to accept the offer
> of friendship that God is making to you.
>
> 2 CORINTHIANS 5:20, TRANS. WILLIAM BARCLAY

One of the best-known definitions of Christian ministry is found in 2 Corinthians 5:18–20, where the apostle Paul refers to the ministry of reconciliation that is part of the new creation in Christ. The central concept of reconciliation, expressed by various forms of *katallage,* appears four times in three verses as Paul shows how God's work of reconciliation in Christ leads to a ministry of reconciliation for all believers: "God ... reconciled us ... In Christ God was reconciling the world ... entrusting the message of reconciliation to us ... we entreat you to be reconciled to God."

Properly understood, *katallage* refers to the process of "making friends," and the intent of the passage is to emphasize the way the death of Christ has actually transformed enemies into friends. Unfortunately, few translations express the full extent of the way relationships are transformed because "reconciliation" in modern thought has taken on a largely negative connotation as the removal of enmity, rather than being a positive creation of friendship between those who were formerly enemies. John Fitzgerald notes that very few modern translations convey to readers "the idea that reconciliation implies not simply the termination of hatred and hostility but also the establishment or restoration of friendship, and thus the inception or return of affection."[1] One translation which does exactly that, and which thus puts the full, positive meaning of reconciliation into this well-known passage, is that of William Barclay:

> And the whole process is due to the action of God, who through Christ *turned our enmity to himself into friendship*, and who gave us the task of helping others *to accept that friendship*. The fact is that God was acting in Christ to turn the world's enmity to himself into friendship, that he was not holding men's sins against them, and that he placed upon us the privilege of taking to men who are hostile to him *the offer of his friendship*. We are therefore Christ's ambassadors. It is as if God was making his appeal to you through us. As the representatives of Christ we appeal to you to *accept the offer of friendship* that God is making to you.[2]

For Paul, reconciliation was not merely the removal of a barrier that exists between people; it was the process of making friends. As this passage shows, he was keen to stress this idea, noting (a) that Christ had turned his enmity into friendship, (b) that in fact he has turned the world's enmity into friendship, (c) that he has given to his own friends the privilege of making known this offer of friendship to others, and (d) that the Corinthians should be sure to become friends with God. Few biblical passages stress the important role of friendship as much as this.

This chapter explores the implications of ministry being understood in terms of friendship. Friendship mediates the grace of God and is the concrete form of salvation. The relationship between friendship and pastoral ministry, church leadership, and professionalism is also discussed. Friendship plays an ongoing role in Christian ministry and mission through to death and eternal friendship with God and other friends.

Friendship as the meaning of reconciliation

Unfortunately, although the formal English definition of reconciliation is "to restore to friendship after an estrangement," common usage tends toward understanding it merely as the removal of a barrier that returns a relationship to a more neutral standing, rather than turning it into friendship. According to this attenuated view of reconciliation, forgiveness does not automatically mean friendship. An example of this is found in the use of the word in the South African *Truth and Reconciliation Commission* that sought to deal with the effects of the apartheid era. Perpetrators of injustice and their victims were brought together for restorative, rather than simply punitive, justice, but reconciliation here did not require, and could not compel, friendship. The Commission itself

> highlighted the potentially dangerous confusion between a religious, indeed Christian, understanding of reconciliation, more typically applied to interpersonal relationships, and the more limited, political notion of reconciliation applicable to a democratic society.[3]

But Paul's point is that Christian reconciliation is not merely the process of dealing with a problem; it has a positive dimension that goes beyond the idea of overcoming sin and dealing with enmity, to actually stressing that this produces a new, warm relationship with God. The idea of a "new creation" is shown to be grounded in a "new relationship." When a war between nations comes to an end and an armistice is signed, it does not mean that the previously warring nations are now suddenly friends; it merely means that hostilities have ceased. But when Christ's sacrifice brings enmity to an end between God and anyone at all, it immediately involves the creation of a new relationship. *God's grace is not a grudging dismissal of a set of awkward problems but the start of a beautiful friendship!* Consequently, Paul was enthusiastic about this conception of the ministry that God has given to believers as a ministry of friendship. In these few verses he repeatedly makes the point that God not only called us into friendship with him, but that he gave us the task, the privilege, of helping others accept the offer of friendship that God is making to all. The Christian message is not just that you can be released and forgiven, but that you can have a friendship with God.

The centrality of friendship for Paul's theology can be expressed in two statements. The first is that being a friend of Jesus and taking the friendship of Jesus to others *is* Christian ministry, and one that is a privilege. And the second is that friendship with Jesus is not the means by which one achieves salvation—*it is* salvation. This critical point is frequently misunderstood. It is popularly thought of in this way: that a relationship with Jesus is important as the means to achieving eternal life (or "salvation"), but the reality is that the relationship—a friendship—with Jesus *is exactly* what eternal life or salvation actually is. There is *nothing more* beyond friendship with Christ. Certainly, the form of friendship changes as either death comes or this world ends and we transition to a new, resurrection life. The fundamental nature of the relationship, however, stays the same—we are friends with Jesus and live in his presence. There is a danger that "having a relationship with Jesus" or "accepting Jesus into your life" can be seen as the means to an end—to avoid hell and enter heaven—but *the relationship* is what God wants with us.

As friends of Christ, offering his friendship to others, it is important to understand that friendship is both the *means* of communication and the *message* that is proclaimed. Marshall McLuhan's dictum that the medium is the message applies here. A message about friendship can only really be communicated through a friendship, and so one communicates the message about God's friendship by being a friend. Of course, any friendship that leads to an offer of friendship with God needs to be a genuine friendship and not a purely utilitarian relationship with no other motive than conversion. Evangelism is by no means incompatible with friendship, which wants the best for others in every possible way. Maxie Dunnam said, "How you speak is vitally important. A loving spirit is essential. Do not take shortcuts, presenting a formula or a plan to win another, without taking the trouble and the time to make friends. Unfeeling invasion of the personal privacy of another will set up a barrier for any sharing of Christ." However, there is no escaping the role friendship plays. "If you want a formula, here is the best one I know: make a friend; be a friend; win the friend for Christ."[4] The aim is not to objectify people or to manipulate friendship; the simple fact is that one cannot really talk about a relationship with God until one has a relationship with the person. And wanting others to become friends with God is never inappropriate—it is simply a case of wanting the very best for one's friends. Paul understood this and, in 1 Thessalonians 2, discussed his own motives in his ministry of friendship in Thessalonica. Paul disclaimed any deceit, trickery, or flattery (the sure sign of a pseudo-friend) but claimed that he had been gentle and caring; indeed, it was precisely because he cared "so deeply" for them that he was "determined to share . . . not only the gospel of God but also our own selves" (1 Thess. 2:3–8). This is real friendship. Many others, since Paul, have been willing to give their lives for the sake of friendship that derives from faithfulness to the gospel. Philip Haillie's *Lest Innocent Blood Be Shed* recounts how, during World War II, the French village of Le Chambon-sur-Lignon led by pastors Andre Trocme and Edouard Theis collaborated to save hundreds of Jews who lived in the village. Simple village folk—men, women, and children—performed heroic tasks to save their fellow villagers, knowing that anyone caught hiding Jews was subject to arrest and even death. After the book was published and their heroism was widely known, Mme. Barraud, one of the surviving villagers, observed, "What's the big deal? Mr. Hallie acts as if we did something extraordinary. We did the only decent thing." One does not have to be as famous or well known as the apostle Paul to be gripped by deep, caring, self-giving friendship.[5]

Friendship as the formation of the Christian

This friendship with Christ, which is the totality of salvation, is the central fact of the Christian life, and it is a possibility for everyone. The New Testament speaks of Jesus having some special friendships, such as those Jesus had with the Twelve, with "the beloved disciple" and with Mary, Martha, and Lazarus (John 11:1–16; 20:2; Luke 10:38–41). But while these were historically unique and unrepeatable relationships, genuine friendship with Jesus is possible for all. It is the privilege of every follower of Christ and the defining characteristic of being a believer. No one today needs to regret not having lived when Jesus walked on earth in order to be able to be close to him and to know his friendship, to feel the warmth of his love, and to experience the richness of his grace, because such a close friendship is available to all believers even now. Indeed, the special friendships that Jesus had with Peter, John, Mary, Martha, and Thomas should not be seen as unique, set apart, or different, but rather as patterns or examples of the kind of friendship all followers of Jesus can have. There is no limit to the closeness of the friendship we can have with Jesus other than the limitations we place upon it. Friendship with Jesus is the power of the gospel. Believers are not called to a set of religious behaviors, to a creed, to a code of ethics, or to an ecclesiastical system, but to love and follow a person. This is not limited to a few, but it is the gift of God for all.

This friendship, like all true friendships, is transformative. It is inevitable that friends become like those with whom they live closely and whom they appreciate, admire, and love. And so, as we live in friendship with Christ, we are transformed into his likeness. Friendship is the means by which believers are clothed with the new self and conformed to the image of Christ. Through friendship, we are made like our friend Jesus (Col. 1:15; 3:10–11). Those who are asked to describe the people who have been of most help in their Christian growth will commonly describe someone who has been a friend to them. The person may have been a colleague, a family member, a pastor, an older person they knew, or someone else, but it is likely that the impact came about not because of the *role* the individual had but because they had a *relationship* which was that of a friend.

I regularly give the students in my ethics classes an exercise that asks them to write a brief account of the person who has most influenced them for good in terms of morality and holiness of life. This informal survey shows that for these students there are three main categories of influential people: parents, pastors, and friends. The inclusion of parents is no surprise given the role parents have in bringing up and modeling right behavior for children. What is significant is that when one examines the role pastors and other Christian leaders are described as having in influencing the students, it is relatively rare to read about ministry gifts and abilities, such as good teaching and preaching, or biblical knowledge or professional attitude. Nor is there, initially at least, much reference to the presence of general moral qualities such as honesty, humility, peacefulness, truthfulness, and so forth. These are, indeed, often the qualities that are learned; but what almost everyone is more concerned to stress in explaining the influence these people have had are the personal and relational qualities that have been expressed. Again and again one hears that they were "more like a friend," they were "interested in my life," "we were genuine with one another," "they spent hours sharing their lives," and "she demonstrated this to me in her life." It is these friendship qualities that impress people and open them up to learn about the right way to live. Ministry without friendship is minimized in its effect.

In the eighteenth century, the poet Elizabeth Barrett Browning got to know the author, clergyman, and reformer Charles Kingsley. She greatly admired his Christian demeanor and asked him, "What is the secret of your life? Tell me, that I may make mine beautiful too." Kingsley's well-known reply began "I had a friend."[6] The real-life accounts of personal influence that I have accumulated indicate that this principle still applies. So many of them begin, "I have a friend" or "The person who has influenced my ethical life most is my dearest friend, Mary" or "First of all is my friend Max, who continually challenges me to live by the convictions I talk about."

Christian friendship is to be transformative. It is a loving ministry that transforms us into the image of our friend Jesus, and enables us to be friends and reflectors of Christ's character to others. Christ's kingdom is not won by war. It does not come by force. Evil is not overcome by sheer power. The moral life is not achieved by anything other than friendship with Christ, and this is most often mediated by friendship within the Christian community. Eberhard Bethge was Dietrich Bonhoeffer's friend and close companion with whom, for many years, he prayed and worshiped daily. They were each other's confessor, and they discussed theology, the Christian life, music, the arts, and politics. Bonhoeffer reflected on their friendship,

> That the two of us could be connected for five years by work and friendship is, I believe, a rather extraordinary joy for a human life. To have a person who understands one both objectively and personally, and whom one experiences in both respects as a faithful helper and adviser—that is truly a great deal. And you have always been both things for me. You have also patiently withstood the severe tests of such a friendship, particularly with regard to my violent temper (which I too abhor in myself and of which you have fortunately repeatedly and openly reminded me), and have not allowed yourself to be made bitter by it. For this I must be particularly grateful to you. In countless questions you have decisively helped me by your greater clarity and simplicity of thought and judgment, and I know from experience that your prayer for me is a real power.[7]

One of the most important aspects of ministry through friendship is the way in which it involves a mutual give-and-take relationship. Those engaged in giving ministry are partners with those receiving it, and it is frequently the case that both parties are enriched by the relationship. This is the great discovery of much ministry—that it is equally a blessing to the one helping. This is actually well known as a basic principle of life, that one of the best ways to avoid depression, to lift one's spirits, and to enhance well-being is to help someone else. Altruism is good for you, and the truth of this mutuality is reflected and stressed in friendship terminology. Frank Woggan's discussion of ministry includes the observation that

> friendship mediates the reality of God's grace and presence in our lives and in the lives of those who we care for. It is not a romantic affair, but it is a calling, which finds guidance in the open and creative friendships that Jesus lived . . . It risks mutuality and acknowledges the potential for change both in oneself and the other.[8]

Mutuality and grace are both intrinsic to friendship. Some time ago, my wife and I befriended an emotional young woman who was causing a disturbance on a local bus. Abbie—as we came to know her—had Tourette's syndrome, a disorder that exhibited itself in the form of constant and uncontrollable body movements that meant arms and legs would suddenly thrash around and cause her to stumble, drop things, or strike others. She also had equally uncontrollable swearing so that every sentence was littered with @#$% and $#@ and constantly with *&%$##@. Frequently depressed, she often appeared threatening and dangerous, and when cheerful and exuberant, she seemed crazy or drunk. The very loud swearing always created high levels of public attention and disapproval. Abbie had been particularly rowdy on the bus because it was no longer possible for her to live at home, and after a long argument with her parents, she had left for good. Now she had nowhere to stay and no one she could call on for help. It was obvious that without friends she would be homeless and would psychologically deteriorate. So we invited her to live with us for a while, although we soon got an idea of the effect of her obsessive swearing and uncontrollable tics. During the first meal, a full bowl of beetroot in juice was passed to her, and it was immediately tossed over her head as an uncontrollable tic affected her. It is nothing short of amazing how far a bowl of bright-red beetroot juice can spread over walls, carpet, and people! It was also an education for our children and all our visitors about the pointlessness of swearing with literally every sentence having two, three, or more bad words in every sentence! This is just about the most socially alienating condition one can have, and without friends life is impossible. But with friends everything is manageable, and she became more stable and was able to be helped into a better and more permanent situation. Professional help was important, but without friendship, it would not have happened.

Sometime after she had left us, she saw me while I was walking down the town main street. She ran up to me with her arms thrashing around while swearing loudly and cheerfully. People looked on disapprovingly and moved away to allow this apparently crazy or possibly intoxicated women to get through. This was another potent reminder of the need for friends who would accept her as she was and help her become what she could be. Obviously, we did not have the solution to the Tourette's syndrome, but the worst problems can be handled if one has friends to help. And when care is undertaken within the context of friendship, there are few limits on who gains from it. I am not sure that it was Abbie who was helped the most. It was a blessing to us to have someone so exuberant, who worked so hard to overcome her difficulties, and who demonstrated courage in the face of great adversity. A ministry of friendship brings blessings to all concerned.

Reframing Christian ministry in terms of friendship does not do away with the imagery or the activities involved with the more common understanding of ministry as service or servanthood. But it does bring into play other motifs and emphases. First, in friendship the ministry is decidedly mutual. Friends minister to each other and gladly accept the help of friends. Ministry understood entirely in terms of service can become tiring, as one's self-perception is always as a servant, even though one may also be served by others. Always being a servant can be very tiring and liable to neurotic distortions where people can find it hard to accept the ministry of others ("*I* am to be a servant, not the one being served!"). The imagery of friendship is also very good for people's well-being. A conception of ministry as friendship also opposes any view of ministry that is authoritarian, controlling, or one-sided.

Secondly, this is also, obviously, a very intimate form of ministry. Friends, unlike servants, know the inner life of the other, and friendship is a better expression of the fundamental commandment to "love one another." Friendship ministry cannot be done by proxy or at a distance. It is based on a personal relationship and, most importantly, models the form of relationship that God has with us in Christ.

Finally, friendship ministry is also individualized to the specific context and the situation of the people involved. Servanthood can be subject to external expectations and obligations as when, as we saw earlier, it was connected with leadership and, consequently, professionalized. This ongoing process of professionalization has influenced the way ministry has been understood and expressed within the life of the church. Cultural pressures affirming professionalization have stressed this model while, conversely, friendship has rarely been seen as the fundamental meaning of the ministry of reconciliation. This is a feature of ministry that needs to be relearned by the church, by pastors, and by all those engaged in ministry.

In doing so, it is important to avoid any simplistic suggestion that an idealized understanding of friendship will suddenly transform the entire life of the contemporary church; nonetheless, it is possible to pursue a more modest proposal—that friendship is a theme that needs to be discussed more in pastoral theology because it has the potential to enhance the life and ministry of the church in a postmodern era. It is possible to demonstrate ways in which a ministry interpreted in terms of friendship can be faithful to biblical principles, spiritually satisfying, relevant to contemporary church, and a corrective to secular trends in ministry. The aim ought simply to be to recover what has been lost in terms of the understanding of friendship compared with, say,

the thinking of Aelred of Rievaulx. In contemporary Western ecclesio-
logical thought, friendship has not been able to play its full role because
of, first, a lack of appreciation of the place friendship plays in divine and
human relationships, and second, because of cultural presuppositions
concerning friendship as a purely private relationship and ministry as a
professional vocation.

Friendship and professionalism in ministry

Although law and medicine had been referred to as professions for
some centuries, it was in the mid- to late-nineteenth century that the
foundations for a particularly modern view of a profession were established. In 1886, the prominent Episcopalian clergyman and author
Phillips Brooks delivered a public lecture at Harvard University, and
the title of his address expressed the idea that he wished to propose,
that of "The Ministry as a Profession." He nominated a number of
elements that made it a profession: it was a specialized calling, by
which the minister sought to earn a living by the exercise of his skills,
and by which he seeks both to make himself (or, later, herself) the best
person he can be, and to do good to others. Brooks was articulating a
view that had been developing for some years. In his review of the shift
in the perception of ministry, Donald Scott argues that in the latter
part of the nineteenth century,

> the clergy had become a profession, a coherent, self-conscious occu-
> pational body, organized and defined by a set of institutions, which
> were outside lay or public control, which controlled the special
> learning needed to become a clergyman, and which possessed the
> power to determine who could enter the clerical ranks.[9]

According to Brooks, a professional ministry would be beneficial
for both church and society because, he argued, "leadership is the great
want of this day and in the ministry this want is most apt to be supplied."
Ministers were to become leaders, not only within the church but within

wider society as well. The aim was for ministers to be civic leaders of many movements for charity, temperance, civil reform, and for settling social questions. Naturally, this would require a different and broader form of training and education, beginning with the introduction of the humanities into the theological curriculum. If one now leaps forward a hundred years, one finds that Brooks's vision has become reality in almost every respect. Although pastors perhaps do not have the high level of civic influence Brooks envisaged, the ordained ministry has nonetheless become one of the helping professions, deeply involved in resolving new social issues, exercising civic leadership, and being appropriately skilled, educated, and remunerated. There are many beneficial results of this. This professionalization has produced new approaches to ministry, brought about higher levels of competence in ministry skills, increased training and education, and developed leadership abilities. It has also developed ethical standards and codes of conduct. But the success of this transformation of ministry has not been without cost. It has altered both the nature of ministry and the role of the pastor. This has to be said with some reserve because the situation is mixed, with a number of perceptions of ministry and minister coexisting within the church. But it is certainly possible to see Brooks's vision implemented in the main—with ministry generally being perceived as a helping profession and the minister as a social leader.

While the new, measurable leadership and ministry skills and activities that were developed were valuable in raising standards and extending the breadth of ministry, they also produced a more ambiguous benefit by providing a professional level of credibility and social status to ministers who had been suffering a loss of faith in their vocation and the traditional forms of pastoral ministry. In a working culture that increasingly stressed efficiency and strongly focused on management by objectives and outcomes, many ministers suffered an identity crisis due to the intangibility of the "outcomes" involved in the traditional ministries of preaching, prayer, and pastoral care. Consequently, many were glad to adopt a new attitude along with the new skills that were offered. Practical skills rather than prayerfulness became the measure of a minister. There was an emphasis on the notion of a career as well as a calling, on contracts rather than covenants, on management rather than ministry, and on salaries rather than stipends (with pay increases based on qualifications, experience, and position). Professionalization and the development of ministry as leadership—as so eloquently articulated by Philips Brooks—has displaced, or at least rivaled, other approaches to ministry. And the main issue is not so much the introduction of new skills but the dominance of a new attitude that conflicts with the notion of ministry as friendship that was demonstrated by Jesus. Some, such as William Willimon and Stanley Hauerwas, have protested at these changes, arguing that they are a deviation from the original focus of ministry. Service is an authentic, Christian manner of life; but, they argued, it is "practical atheism" to believe that the church is sustained by services it provides.[10] David Wells goes as far as arguing that "professionalization produces a culture—a way of looking at life that is at odds with the view ministers need to have if they serve Christ and his people."[11] Some understanding of the significance of this change in attitude can be seen in an examination of the way Jesus exercised his ministry.

Friendship in the ministry of Jesus

It was true of Jesus, as the proverb says, that "a man is known by the company he keeps," for Jesus was widely known for his association with those who were socially outcast. Indeed, the teachers of the law could not comprehend this and demanded to know of his disciples, "Why does he eat with tax collectors and sinners?" (Mark 2:16; see also Luke 5:30; 15:2). It was considered such unusual behavior for a man of God that he probably became more well known as the "friend of tax collectors and sinners" (Matt. 11:19; Luke 7:34) than as a prophet or a teacher. Jesus did not merely treat the sinners, the unclean, and the outcast as objects of mercy and compassion; he treated them as human beings, as real people, and even as friends, and in the eyes of his enemies, this was the worst sin of all. Ultimately, Jesus was not condemned so much for being an unorthodox teacher or social activist as for being a friend to sinners. It was this that they found most offensive. Perhaps it would have been easier for the scribes and Pharisees to understand his manner of dealing with sinners if he had related to them, to use an anachronistic term, in a purely "professional capacity." The Pharisees also came into contact with poor and outcast people and would sometimes have related to them with charity and kindness, for they were teachers and leaders who knew what the law said, and they sought zealously to obey it. They were religiously committed people, and it is wrong to assume that they never engaged in any kind or charitable deeds. Indeed, they are not condemned by Jesus for a complete absence of such actions or because they were the worst of all people, but because they considered themselves among the best and relied on their actions to save them. The same can be true today, and it shows up whenever generous actions, such as giving to a local charity, have a double motive—doing good for someone else and absolving the giver from any actual, personal involvement. Of course, no one can be involved in every good or useful ministry, and no one else can possibly know when charity or even certain forms of involvement are being used as defenses against personal commitment, but everyone can, and should, examine their own motives. Our friend Jesus wants us to share ourselves (and not only our money) with him and his other friends—especially the socially alienated and oppressed.

The real problem for the Pharisees—and also potentially for us—was not sin but self-righteousness and the failure to understand grace. They could have understood a ministry that offered the services of education, liturgy, counsel, or charity, but they could not understand the grace of friendship. They would not refuse the obligations of the law, for they understood religious duty all too well. But they would refuse to associate or eat with "sinners" (and therefore with Jesus), for they did not, they could not, they would not understand grace or friendship that goes beyond all that is required by law and duty. Our context today may be different, but the implications are the same. Friendship goes beyond what is expected of a servant; it exceeds the requirements of the law; it is more than charity can give; and it challenges a purely "professional" view of ministry. Jesus' friendship-based ministry was central to both the way he lived with the disciples and his mission to others, so there is no surprise that it was taken up as a model for ministry in the theology of Paul.

Friendship and pastoral care

Friendship shifts the ministry emphasis considerably. First, when relating to someone, there is more of a focus on *personhood* than upon the presence of a *problem*. When ministry is seen in terms of friendship, it is a mutual relationship between two persons who are friends rather than the resolution of a problem by one person on behalf of the other. As far as the role of the minister is concerned, the emphasis falls upon *being a friend* rather than achieving certain outcomes. And as far as the other is concerned, the emphasis falls upon him or her as a person rather than a problem. The emphasis is on the relationship rather than on achieving certain outcomes. Of course, professional people may well be friendly, but the measure of their work is the result rather than the relationship. In friendship, however, the outcomes are secondary to the relationship itself, and this is fundamental for ministry as well. As Wayne Oates said in his discussion in *The Christian Pastor,* the first level of pastoral care is friendship. So much of the time, what is needed in pastoral care is provided by friendship. Oates defined five levels of pastoral care: friendship, comfort, confession, teaching, and counseling and psychotherapy. All these can be used to move people toward spiritual growth, but he observes that friendship is the "indis-pensable necessity for all other deeper levels of pastoral work."[12]

Pastoral friendship has, however, been resisted. Many pastors will be aware of the tradition that insists that pastors ought not be particular friends with any of the people within their care. I well remember being somewhat astonished, but at the same time challenged, at the exhorta-tion of a senior minister to the cohort of ministry candidates to which I belonged, to the effect that, "You cannot be friends with anyone in your church." This emerged out of the pastoral concern that special friend-ships can inhibit the need for pastors to relate well to all of their people, and has been intensified by the expectation that a professional relation-ship should not be in conflict with other forms of relationship. But, of course, pastors need friends just as much as anyone does, and friendship is not always to be denied when people work together. Care must be taken to ensure that such friendships do not damage other relationships within the congregation, and it is appropriate for codes of ethics to limit certain forms of relationships to avoid power or sexual abuses. But Christ's own example of friendship and ministry indicates that the two are not incompatible. This is seen, most obviously, in the relationship Jesus had with the Twelve—especially with some of the Twelve, including James, John, Peter, and Andrew. He set an example of leading by friendship, and this is possible because friendships are inherently influential, whether for good or ill. The level of influence increases as a friendship deepens. The closer people become, the more they will listen to, trust, and respect what is said. If leadership is about influence, then close friendships have the greatest potential for significant leadership. This kind of leadership will function without any precise program being involved. It will change people in every area of life. To put it simply, "People who get along best in life and deal with uncertainties and trials and tribulations have friends."[13]

It is a tragedy if people believe that the requirements of a code of professional ethics means that pastoral ministry has to end the kind of open, caring, friend-based relationships that are a fulfillment of the command to love one another. If friendship comes into conflict with a specialized form of professional relationship, then it may be necessary, if one is to remain a pastor, to give up the specialization—which others can provide—rather than the possibility of pastoral and spiritual friendships. Early in my ministry, after a course of training, I spent a year working part-time in a church-based marriage counseling center. It was to be a part of my pastoral ministry, but I soon found that dealing with serious and difficult relationship matters could become all-consuming and actually conflict with my pastoral role to people as a couple and a family. Therefore, I limited the kind of issues I would deal with and made sure that I remained as a pastor and a spiritual friend rather than as a professional trying to sort out the details of people's relationship problems. Similarly, because there was a desperate need, I trained as an honorary probation officer. It was, again, to be an adjunct role to my pastoral ministry, particularly in the local community where our church ministered. My first responsibility was to be the probation officer for a young man released from prison after serving his time for manslaughter—slashing someone with a broken bottle; the victim then died from the loss of blood. Surely, I thought, dealing with situations like this is, like working with the most difficult marriage conflicts, the kind of real ministry in which a pastor should be involved. It is, indeed, an important ministry; but I found that there were not only inhibitions in relating to this man because of professional responsibilities, but also conflicts in relating to local families in the town as both pastor and probation officer. So it was time to give that role away as well. The point is not that one form of ministry is more important than another, but that for pastoral ministry, it is necessary to begin and maintain the most fundamental relationship of spiritual and pastoral friendship.

When friendship and leadership merge, then the greatest possibilities can be realized. Malcolm Messner undertook a study of friendship and leadership in the church and concluded that the vast majority of people surveyed believed that in their own situations "friendship with leaders made the leadership more effective."[14] Being able to get close to leaders not only provided inspiration, but also enabled them to model their own behavior on that of the other leader. The research showed that not only was there strong support for the idea that it is possible to be both a leader and a friend, but respect for the leader grew as people came closer. Conversely, leadership without relationship was considered weak. It was clear that people were looking for approachable and caring leaders who would walk beside them and care for them. Indeed, their influence increased along with the level of their care. This kind of very positive assessment of the relationship between leadership and friendship requires relational and emotional maturity and an understanding of the various roles and responsibilities that people hold. It also needs clear communication and, most significantly of all, a willingness to take the risk of friendship—the risk of disappointment and loss. Because of these risks, some avoid friendship altogether, but those who accept it frequently find a blessing that is beyond comparison.

Friendship in leadership

Without friendship in leadership, institutionalism will inevitably dominate, the joy of leadership will diminish, and the ability to experience transformative change will be reduced. Messner concludes that leadership needs to be enhanced by intentional friendships that follow the example of Christ. He hopes they will understand that they cannot be best friends to everyone, but they should nonetheless look for people with whom they can develop strong friendships. By doing so, "they will not only be more effective and influential, but also more satisfied as people." He recommends "that Christian leaders at all levels, follow the example of Jesus by setting the goal of intentionally developing friendships with twelve people, and even closer friendships with two or three.

By doing so, they will have a deep and lasting impact that otherwise will not be realized."[15]

This issue is not new. The English bishop and popular writer of his day, Jeremy Taylor (1613–1667), wrote a *Discourse of the Nature and Offices of Friendship* in order to respond to the question, "How far a dear and perfect friendship is authorized by the principles of Christianity?" The answer, he argued, was that friendships should really "be as universal as our conversation." That is, the Christian should treat everyone they have contact with as their dearest friend, and the only limitation on universal friendship is the limitation that we, as finite and sinful people, place upon it. Consequently,

> the more we love, the better we are, and the greater our friendships are, the dearer we are to God; let them be as dear, and let them be as perfect, and let them be as many as you can; there is no danger in it; *only where the restraint begins, there begins our imperfection*; it is not ill that you entertain brave friendships and worthy societies: it were well if you could love, and if you could benefit all mankind; for I conceive that is the sum of all friendship.[16]

He understood rightly that there should be no limitation placed on messianic friendship, neither refraining from special friendships nor from treating everyone we possibly can, in every way that is within our power, as dear, close, and spiritual friends, just as Jesus did when he told his new friends, "Everything that I learned from my Father I have made known to you" (John 15:15 NIV). The minister should adopt this open, honest, and revealing form of friendship in all of his dealings with other Christians and not merely with those with whom he is particularly close. In so doing he will reflect the openness of Jesus, who, after his arrest, declared to the high priest, "I have spoken openly to the world. I always taught in synagogues or at the temple . . . I said nothing in secret . . . Ask those who heard me. Surely they know what I said" (John 18:20–21 NIV). This open speech was replicated in the early preaching of the church, and it should be the same today. Preacher and professor Gail O'Day describes preaching as an act of friendship in ministry:

> At least one possible function for preaching is to be a friend in one's preaching. Note carefully that I did not say that one possible function is to be friendly in one's sermon. There is plenty of friendliness in much of the church's preaching—jokes, chatter, anecdotes told simply to make a congregation smile or to get them on one's good side, tangential personal asides—but friendliness is not the same thing as gospel friendship.

Being a gospel friend means speaking plainly, frankly, and honestly. It means telling the truth, the whole truth, and nothing but the truth. A failure to do this can happen in a number of ways. Flatterers say what they believe people want to hear said about them in order to advance their own position by being well thought of; deceivers preach doctrines that people would like to be true in order to gain more adherents to their way of thinking (2 Tim. 4:3); far more common than either of these are the well-meaning, measured sermons of those whose friendship is not fully formed. They tend to think that friendship depends on kind words and gentle encouragement, and there is not enough to challenge or extend the believers. It is important to note that Jesus told his disciples some very hard things about being ready to die. The Great Commission specifies that disciples are to be taught everything (rather than some select teachings), and the apostle Paul chided the Corinthians that despite their immaturity they needed to receive the "solid food" of his difficult teaching that critiqued their willingness to listen to, and boast about, foolish teachers (1 Cor. 1–3). In short, preaching as a friend in the tradition of the ancient world means almost the opposite of what it means according to contemporary thought. It is not a lightweight, personal sharing that is always "friendly"; it means making an open, honest assessment of the situation and applying spiritual lessons in order to build up that which is good and to challenge that which is not helpful.

Friendship with the marginalized

Friendships with those who are like us are a normal part of life, but Christian friendship reaches out, in particular, to those *who are different* and *those who are marginalized*. In contemporary Western society this can include those who suffer poor mental health. A local church men's group went camping for a weekend, and Jim asked Bill if he would like to come. Jim offered to provide Bill transport and help with his tent and food because, although Bill lived independently, his life-skills were limited, especially in a new environment. Each year he would spend a week in a residential care home, where he was helped and assessed. He attended church every Sunday and during the week was keen to attend the community care program, where he took on the job of making cups of tea for people. He enjoyed the weekend away, although Jim found sharing a tent with him to be difficult. On Sunday morning, just before the service of worship around the campfire began, Bill had to visit the bush-toilet, and as it was a take-your-own-paper situation, he asked Jim for a roll of paper and then went off. He returned while the worship service was in progress and, as he would have done at any other time, walked straight through the middle of the circle to get to his seat, only pausing on the way to hand the remainder of the toilet roll back to Jim, who was, at the time, in the center of the circle, delivering a short communion address while standing beside the log that held the elements for communion. Without either of them commenting, the paper was handed over, Bill took his seat, and Jim continued the prayer of thanksgiving with Bible in one hand and toilet paper in the other. Somehow this was not disturbing to the sense of worship; indeed, it seemed to be a sacramental act in itself, and the sense of God's presence was very much felt as the bread and the cup were shared.

Many churches are open and more than willing to share with those who are disabled or who have mental health or social problems, even when their behavior is unpredictable or not socially helpful. That is very commendable, but the significance of this care is undervalued when it is seen as an act of simple service rather than as a sacramental act that reveals the character of God. It is a pity if such actions are seen *only* as a ministry of care that benefits the individual concerned rather than as an essential, sacramental dimension of genuine fellowship that enhances the life of the whole church.

It cannot be anything other than sacramentally significant when, in describing the Last Supper, the Gospel of John recounts how Jesus washed the disciples' feet at the precise point in the narrative where all the other Gospels have Jesus and the disciples sharing in the bread and the wine (Matt. 26:26–30; Mark 14:22–25; Luke 22:14–23; John 13:1–12.). Readers of this in the early church who were familiar with any of the Synoptic Gospels and who, subsequently, read John's gospel (probably the last gospel written) would have been expecting nothing other than to hear Jesus' words of institution. To have his act of service substitute for them is a way of pointing to the sacramental significance of service.

In *Resurrecting the Person,* John Swinton argues that friendship is not peripheral but should take center stage in the church's care of people with mental health problems. This stands in contrast to the dominant medical model that controls the field of mental health care. As a specialist in psychiatry and learning disability, Swinton does not want to diminish the scientific and medical dimension, but he does want to broaden the perception of what is involved in mental health and bring pastoral care and messianic friendship to the fore.

A purely medical model has the tendency to individualize the problem and draw attention away from the socio-relational dimension of the person. It can also be depersonalizing if the focus falls upon the *problem* rather than the *person*. This, in turn, can lead to social stigmatization and the exclusion of people because they are primarily identified as problem people. Medical practitioners are often the first to recognize this, and it is important to emphasize the tremendous results achieved through scientific medicine. But the fact remains that individuals are not constituted by their problems but by their relationships with others in community, and these have to become a part of any valid model of care for people.

Unfortunately, many people with mental health problems are deprived of friendships. It is not unusual for all of their relationships to be with people who are paid to medicate, watch, assess, and to a significant extent, control their lives. It is hard for those of us who have healthy, free, mutual relationships to imagine what it would do to us if we did not have any of them at all. The depersonalization and alienation of people with mental health problems restricts their ability to grow, develop, enjoy, laugh, relax, share, be trusted and loved, and participate meaningfully in their community. An absence of friends makes it difficult to develop self-respect, a sense of worth, and social confidence; it leads to loneliness, despair, and depression. The positive aspect of this is that simple friendship has a great potential for enhancing the mental health care of people with mental health problems. While medical researchers may devote themselves to the biological dimension of the person, the role of the church lies in creating a community that will nurture relationships and enable people to grow to wholeness. As Swinton says, "The priority of friends is the personhood of the other and not the illness."[17]

This requires a radical form of friendship because it goes beyond the natural tendency of people to make friends with those who are like them and with whom they feel an affinity. However, befriending people with mental health issues should *not* be seen just as an act of charity or service, because then it loses something of the character of a genuine friendship and becomes, for a person with a mental health problem, more like yet another relationship that is based on obligation and responsibility—albeit in this case, not a paid one. Of course, it may be difficult or impossible to begin in this way; and if, initially, the only motive is that of service, then that is the place to begin. It may well, however, be possible to follow the example of Jesus and move from being simply a servant to being a friend. At that point, it becomes clear that the benefit in the relationship is mutual and that the friendship enhances the community as a whole. Caring for "the poor" in this way is not simply an act of charity but an expression of the true nature of the church. Friendship with those living with mental health problems or who are marginalized in some other way is not an option for the church; rather, it is a primary mark of the identity and faithfulness of a church that is seeking to demonstrate messianic friendship every day, in every way, to everyone.

Friendship building in the church

Messianic friendship follows the example of Jesus and the teaching of Paul, and therefore challenges contemporary cultural understandings of friendship. And because it is an essential dimension of Christian relationships and Christian ministry, it needs to be intentionally taught and encouraged within churches. Yet Christian education ministries within the church have only rarely focused on the role friendship plays in personal and communal development. Indeed, sometimes friendship groups have been treated as cliques and as inhibitors of progress toward a healthy community life. They have also been ignored or disempowered because they are seen as *competitors* to institutionally devised groupings that are usually based on gender, age, or the needs of an educator or a program. Friendship, in this view, is not seen as a ministry and should not conflict with more specifically religious activities. An additional issue is that natural friendship groups that are fluid and varied in form do not easily fit into educational programs that are predicated on other systems of order and relationship. Consequently, friendship has not been given great attention in Christian education.

Some educators and programs focus on the individual (discussing developmental stages, learning styles, and individual characteristics), while others focus on the community as a whole (with a stress on

congregational development, social theory, the processes of encultura-
tion, and the importance of worship life). But friendship groups link
the individual and the community as a whole and are an ideal grouping
for bringing about lasting change in people. Children, for example, gain
a significant sense of order and authority from their relationships with
adults, but it is their relationship with friends that is the major source
for the development of many characteristics, such as sensitivity, self-
understanding, and interpersonal cooperation. Consequently, there is
great merit in the proposal of educationalist David Shields for "friendship renewal" as both a goal and the means of educational activity. It
needs to be a *goal* because friendship

> opens us to a realm of freedom and creativity. We cannot make
> a friend fit a schedule or talk to us through a script. Friendship
> calls us out from our frantic search for meaning through work. It
> challenges the unidimensional, product orientation within us by its
> demands of time, attention and noninstrumentality.[18]

Moreover, friendships formed across "lines of structural enemy-
hood" such as race and social standing, provide a powerful force for
change. Even though it is not usually possible to be personal friends
with many of those who are on the other side of social divides, just one
or two such friendships can teach much, dismiss stereotypes, and build
compassion and a desire for justice. Shields notes that

> neither the individual nor the community are efficacious contexts
> within which to promote fundamental change. If we focus on the
> individual, we fail to provide a supportive context for sustaining
> critical growth and change . . . without support, the individual
> often conforms or burns out. On the other hand, when we focus
> on the congregation, we quickly get bogged down by institutional
> inertia, entropy, and active resistance . . . To unite continuity and
> change, a small group of gospel-creators, not a large crowd of
> gospel-consumers, is needed. The friendship group provides an ideal
> context for God's promise to take hold.[19]

Friendship groups have many advantages. They are self-determining and directing, are small enough and flexible enough to adapt readily to new ideas, and have power to influence the larger collectives of which they are a part far more effectively than the isolated individual.

It is also helpful if friendship is a *means* of education, both utilizing existing friendship groups and creating new ones that can last far longer than classes based on other criteria. This means creating a new educational methodology that will involve teaching about the depth and the possibilities inherent in messianic friendships in contrast to the lightweight notion of friendship that is prominent in contemporary thought. It will be important to deepen relationships, to encourage new friendships, and to develop learning along friendship lines. As no ready-made program for this exists, it will be experimental, and it can, to some extent, be considered supplemental to other educational methodologies, rather than as a replacement; however, it will require the end of certain attitudes. There should be no undercutting of this deeper notion of friendship by assuming that all church-related groups will come to an end, or that friendships best operate on the basis of age, gender, ethnicity, or social standing. Indeed, friendships across social boundaries should be encouraged.

The suggestion that the revitalization of the church will come through a renewal of friendship should not be taken as implying that genuine, Christian friendship is unknown or not encouraged in existing forms of church life. There is no doubt that many healthy spiritual friendships exist, and current church practices, especially small group programs, foster friendship throughout the church. The issue is that a greater level of attention to this dimension of life will greatly enhance the life and ministry of the church. There are three aspects of the situation that need attention. The first is that there is a need for a new and deeper understanding of the spiritual depth and significance of holy friendships. Messianic friendship is not merely a church-based version of secular friendship; rather, it is a different form of relationship based and modeled on friendship with Jesus. It is open and caring in form, seeks the good of the other, and aims at coming closer to God in Christ Jesus through a mutual relationship of love.

Secondly, there needs to be a more deliberate attempt to develop an educational methodology that intentionally enhances the spiritual, discipling, sacramental, and missional dimensions of friendship. It is possible to develop programs that help people develop relationships like this. There is a sense in which friendship can be taught. Although friendship itself is a dynamic relationship that cannot be conjured up on demand, most experts agree that the skills and attitudes that lead to friendship can be taught. It is, in part, a matter of the will; and just as Jesus taught that love can be *commanded* (John 13:34), so, too, can friendship. It is possible to choose self-disclosure over independence and trust ahead of doubt. The approach to friendship found in Dale Carnegie's famous *How to Win Friends and Influence People* may have inappropriately located friendship within the sphere of good business techniques (and the same mistake must be avoided with regard to evangelism); nonetheless, it did very effectively demonstrate to many, many people that friendship skills could be taught.[20]

Finally, there is a need to ensure that there is a close connection between friendship and the mission and ministry of the church. While many friendships do originate within church circles, not all of them understand the significance or the potential that they have for personal spiritual growth, for enhancing the life and fellowship of the church, and for creating teams of like-minded and mutually committed and supportive teams for ministry and mission. The first essential need of almost any group of people called together for a specific task is to create a commonality of thought and attitude and to form a community of friendship and mutual trust. Yet these are often already present in friendship groups and can provide a secure foundation for outreach. Messianic friendship is, of course, not inward looking, but is constantly seeking to extend the circle of friendship in every direction.

PART IV
Friendship as Public Good

Theology

Public Friendship

8

> Friendship seems to hold states together,
> and lawmakers care more for it than for justice.
>
> ARISTOTLE

It is surprising, but true, that if your friend's friend (whom you have never met) puts on weight, then it is more likely that you will too. The benefits—and the disadvantages—of friendship are extremely pervasive. This is true at all levels of society—personal, social, and even international. At the *personal* level, health researchers Nicholas Christakis and James Fowler have, through their research into friendship and social networks, reminded us of the influence that friends have. Their work gained considerable publicity when it was shown that if your friend's friend puts on weight, then you are more likely to do so as well. They demonstrated this and many other effects through their examination of the influence of the social networks of 12,067 people.[1] Their research began with the observation that obese people tend to be friends with other obese people, while thin people tend to be friends with other thin people. Their work showed, however, that the connection is *causal*, so that if someone becomes more obese, then his or her friends are also more likely to become more obese. And beyond that, there are even more extensive chains of influence concerning many forms of behavior, so that there is an influence on, for example, a person's sexual practices and the incidence of back pain, based on the actions of his friend's friend's friend (who is unknown to him). The influence through chains of friendship is very significant. The fact that friendship has this power may seem obvious, but it does not detract from the importance of demonstrating it statistically. The fact is that friends are good or, unfortunately, sometimes bad for you. It is also a reminder of the responsibility involved in being a friend.

At the *public* level, it is not hard to see the benefits of friendship. Society would struggle to deal with sickness—even where there is a public health system—without friends who help sick and disabled people. Friendship helps maintain the volunteer networks that do so much good. Friendship has economic benefits as friends encourage one another in business, and the trust that is a part of friendship is influential in that it provides an example of the trust that is essential to commercial transactions. The values of integrity, honesty, and fidelity that are intrinsic to friendship have provided a model for many legal principles, providing, for example, precedent for contract law and "duty of care" responsibilities. Friendship is also vital in countering social division; it only needs a couple of people to establish a friendship across a social divide to create a healthier relationship that influences many people.

At the *international* level, personal friendship provides a standard of relationship that nations aspire to. Jiang Zemin and Vladimir Putin signed a twenty-year "Treaty of Good-Neighborliness and Friendly Cooperation Between the People's Republic of China and the Russian Federation." The treaty outlines the actions that are to be the basis for peaceful relations and economic cooperation. Idealistic? Perhaps. Will it be fulfilled? Maybe. But the key idea is that friendship is something they aspire to. The hope of friendship becomes even more important when it is not actually present. It creates an environment, a sense of hope that is important for a society to have.

Some form of friendship is often important in the creation and maintenance of national identity. Friendship can contribute significantly toward social unity and cohesiveness, and can be particularly important if it is perceived to be a central part of the national character. The concept was fundamental in the establishment of the United States. Article 3 of the Articles of Confederation (1777), which specified how the various states were to join together to become the United States of America, describes the original motivation for political union as a desire "to secure and perpetuate mutual friendship and intercourse among the people of the different states of this union."

Across the Pacific Ocean, friendship was not a part of the motivation for the establishment of the convict colony that became Australia, but the country outlived its inauspicious beginnings and developed a strong ethos of friendship as part of the national identity. It is referred to as "mateship" and it became so influential that prime minister John Howard sponsored an attempt to have the term added to a preamble to the national constitution that would describe the national character: "Australians are free to be proud of their country and heritage, free to realize themselves as individuals, and free to pursue their hopes and ideals. We value excellence as well as fairness, independence as dearly as mateship." Although Australian culture is, in many respects, moving away from the bush and military cultures that created the concept of mateship, it obviously remains a highly valued quality for many people. It embodies the ideas of egalitarianism and loyalty, courage, and teamwork. It is often seen as opposed to elitism and authoritarianism and somewhat larrikin.[2] However, the proposal did not gain widespread support for various reasons. It is a male-orientated term that has some negative connotations, and while putting it into the national constitution would be high recognition of a national characteristic, it also seems somewhat contrary to its intrinsic antiauthoritarianism. In order not to affect other, more important, matters that were part of the referendum, Prime Minister Howard regretfully dropped the concept that he said had "a hallowed place" in the Australian lexicon.[3]

These situations illustrate the way friendship exists as a part of the social fabric, as an important quality for individuals and communities and, as an ideal, for nations. A specifically Christian understanding of friendship has the potential to enhance the quality of social interaction and lead people toward a deeper understanding of the gospel. The remainder of this chapter discusses the principal characteristics of friendship understood as a fundamental principle of the Christian approach to community life, a flexible and contextual approach that focuses attention on the everyday actions and the character of friends more than on specific forms of social structure. It makes a difference to all levels of social life if the Christian approach to friendship with God is intentionally extended to being "friends of God in church and culture," with Christian virtue as its primary content and friendship as the principal vehicle by which virtue is formed.

Friendship in secular society

Before outlining the way civic friendship can actually operate in modern society, it is first of all necessary to briefly defend the principle that faith-based thinking and action has a legitimate role in contemporary secular society. It is frequently claimed that the notion of a secular society necessarily rules out religious involvement in the public arena. If that is the case, then not only is Christian civic friendship ruled out, but so, too, are numerous other Christian and religious approaches to contemporary society. After asserting the appropriateness of the principle of interaction, the next step is to provide a typology of existing models of the relationship as a foundation for describing the workings of a friendship model.

The situation is variously expressed in terms of Christ and culture; faith and society; church and state; sacred and secular; and in terms of two cities, two kingdoms, two citizenships, and two governments. These dualities are not all equivalent terms. They have their own nuances and deal with different (though overlapping) concerns, focused variously on, for example, the role of the church or the responsibility of individual Christians. Or they may focus on either the present age or the eschatological future. All of them, however, deal with a dual form of life and the question of their relationship. While some approaches posit a complete discontinuity between the two, others challenge the popular notion that "secular" and "sacred" are to be understood as polar opposites so that anything sacred or religious is excluded from the realm of the secular, and vice versa. Many assume that because modern, Western societies are typically described as "secular" societies in which no religious viewpoint is officially established, the public arena is to be kept clear of any religious matter. The general principle is that the two do not mix, and so religion is relegated to the realm of private life and opinion. Indeed, it is not uncommon for Christians and other religious people to agree with various forms of this demarcation, often because it does, to some extent, preserve religious faith from external criticism by having it as a personal opinion rather than a fact of public life. This, however, is to misunderstand the nature of a secular society. The corollary to "secular" (Latin: *saeculum*) is not "sacred" (Latin: *sacrare*) but "eternal." That is, the *secular* has to do with *this world* (or "generation" or "age") in distinction to the *eternal* (which is the eschatological future of God). The secular realm is neither the eternal realm nor a realm devoid of spiritual or sacred meaning. It is a world with its own autonomy, and it provides an arena within which *all* views can be aired and debated. It is not controlled by religion but is a legitimate sphere for Christian activity. The opposite of sacred is profane, and within this secular age the sacred and the profane are engaged in a dialogue (or perhaps more realistically a deadly struggle) while, from a Christian point of view, awaiting the future eternal state.

When the distinction between the secular and the profane is not recognized, it is usually assumed that the secular should not contain the sacred ("keep religion out of the public arena"). It is thought that only with the absence of the religious is there a neutral, objective space, without realizing that, in fact, this approach unfairly preferences those operating with a nonreligious, profane worldview or philosophy that contains as many presuppositions as any religious view does. It is necessary to reject this form of "hard secularism" that requires the complete removal of faith from the public arena and to reaffirm the legitimacy of a secularity (or "soft secularism") that allows faith to engage non-faith and other faiths on shared ground without seeking to dominate it. It is essential that a civil society be able to seek consensus and to identify differences between worldviews.

This approach affirms the legitimacy of all models that seek a dynamic interaction between faith and the public realm. This includes seeing Christian friendship and Christian virtue as qualities suitable for the public realm. That is, they are not only personal qualities but also qualities and behaviors that can be commended for society as a whole. This inevitably creates a degree of vulnerability, as it not only opens Christian theory to public scrutiny and analysis, but it also challenges Christians to live themselves according to the highest ideals of friendship. The advantage is that it also creates an evangelical opportunity for the gospel to transform lives and social structures.

A faith-and-society typology

The aim at this point is to create a typology of approaches to the relationship of faith and society. This typology does not aim to define all historical positions so much as to characterize the different approaches in order to be able to assess them. The notion of civic friendship as a model of social engagement will be best understood by comparison with other approaches. The most widely known example of this kind of typological approach is H. R. Niebuhr's *Christ and Culture*, in which he outlines five models of *the relationship* between Christ and culture: Christ against culture; Christ of culture; Christ and culture in paradox; Christ above culture; and Christ the transformer of culture.[4] The following typology, however, consists of eleven models, and it focuses on the various *roles* Christians play in relation to society as a whole.

The first, and oldest, model of relationship between church and society sees Christians as *aliens in a foreign land*. It involves the church existing as an unwanted religious movement (opposed by Jews) and as a new and illegal sect (restricted and persecuted by Romans). Christians live with legal uncertainty, as vulnerable as aliens in a foreign country or as captives in enemy territory. It is possible for there to be a mixture of both acceptance of the role of government and resistance to it (compare Romans 13 and Revelation 13) because the real focus is on that which is central, which cannot be challenged by earthly authority—the church's participation in the life of the kingdom of God, a citizenship in heaven (Phil. 3:20; Heb. 11:8–10). This position at the bottom of the social order, unloved and even oppressed, is not something to be hated; it is, according to the well-known passage from *The Epistle to Diognetus* (c. second century AD), an "illustrious position" that has been assigned by God. It is not part of the Christian vocation to seek to climb the social ladder. Despite this, Christians are to actively seek the good of the society that oppresses them. Christians are to do as the Jewish exiles did in their "Babylonian captivity" and seek the welfare of the place where they are settled—the place of their enemies. For in doing so, they find their own good (Jer. 29:7).

The second model for society involves being *rulers in Christendom* and refers to the situation where the church has taken on an official, established role in society to the point where the distinction between the two is almost nonexistent. This idea is associated with the emperor Constantine (c. 272—337), who made Christianity the official religion of the empire, and was also very influenced by the work of Eusebius of Caesarea (c. 260—340) who connected Hellenistic ideas of divine kingship with a Christian monotheism, which itself modeled a political autocracy with one supreme earthly emperor as the image or representative of God, chosen to protect the people. This created a symbiotic relationship with no sharp distinction between the individual and society or between the church and the state. The term "Christendom" is used extremely broadly. It encompasses the Eastern version (Byzantinism), which extended in various forms for a thousand years, and occurs in the West in much later times in such things as Erastianism (named after Thomas Erastus [1524–1583], a Swiss theologian who argued that the sins of Christians should be punished by the state). The term is also used for all sorts of other forms of relationships at different times in very different political contexts, including, for instance, so-called Christendom of the left (with funding and welfare dependent upon the government) and of the right (moral enforcement is dependent upon the government).

The most famous book on the relationship of church to society is Augustine of Hippo's *The City of God*, which was developed within the context of Christianity being the official religion of an empire that was collapsing. The sacking of Rome by the Visigoths in AD 410 left Romans wondering whether this was a punishment for turning away from pagan gods to Christianity. Augustine spoke of the contrast between the city of man and the City of God that would ultimately triumph. Christians are *residents of two cities,* and Christians, Augustine argued, should be concerned with spiritual matters rather than earthly politics, an idea that helped develop the idea of the separation of church and state. He, therefore, offered little in the way of advice about involvement in political life, but he did argue that God cannot be ignored in society. The concept is used in various ways: some use it to argue for the need for a secular realm within society, where religion is restricted; others argue that although Augustine did not want a theocracy, neither did he envisage a place without God, and that it would be anachronistic to turn Augustine into a modern liberal. There are, however, certainly elements of his thinking that can be used in a theological defense of a secular, pluralist state.

It should be no surprise that the Reformation brought with it elements of a new form of relationship between church and society, with Christians being *reformers of the world*. There were elements of the Reformation that tended toward a continuation of theocratic social control (including using Scripture to provide a detailed basis for laws, establishing official churches, and supporting Christian principles by military means). However, there were other aspects of Reformation principles (including the role of individual conscience and the concept of Christian freedom) that led to an understanding of a more dynamic relationship between church and society, one neither as fixed as Christendom nor as divided as the two kingdoms. In terms of Niebuhr's typology, this is the "Christ the transformer of culture" model. It argues that God's will is for all, but it is combined with a recognition that many aspects of Christian life need to be taken voluntarily rather than by legislation or force. But it may well disrupt the status quo. As Catherine Booth (1829–1890), cofounder of the Salvation Army, observed, "There is no improving the future without disturbing the present." It is the church, rather than the state, that is to bring about change in the world through example, persuasion, and active involvement.

There are other heirs of the Reformation who are less certain that the Christian role is to seek to change the culture rather than to under-stand that the church is a culture in itself—one whose primary purpose is to live, according to our fourth model, as *models of an alternative life*. The church may be small or even oppressed, but it is seen as having a legitimate place, and by living as the church, it influences the world. As Stanley Hauerwas says, "The primary social task of the church is to be itself."[5] This approach, of simply living as the church, has been described as isolating or even anticultural ("Christ against culture" according to Niebuhr's typology), and that may be so for some expressions of this approach, but it by no means represents the views of all. Others see the work of establishing Christian community as a profoundly helpful activity for the whole of society. What the church is called to be is no different from what the whole of society is called to be, but the problem is that society is simply not able to live as God's community because most people do not have faith. The first step, then, has to do with changing people's hearts, rather than the world, and a most effective argument for this is for the church to demonstrate in its own life the implications of being Christian. There are a number of variations (including evangelical Anabaptism and post-liberal narrative theology) and different views on the degree of isolation from the community, but all interpretations of this view see the church as a culture, a community in itself.

The sixth model is represented by Dutch journalist, theologian, politician, and prime minister Abraham Kuyper (1837–1920), who wrote various works on politics and faith and developed the notion of "sphere sovereignty." Kuyper famously said, "No single piece of our mental world is to be hermetically sealed off from the rest, and there is not a square inch in the whole domain of our human existence over which Christ, who is Sovereign over *all*, does not cry: 'Mine!'"[6] Kuyper argued for the doctrine of *common grace* as the basis for Christian involvement in the created world, and that God built principles of life into creation that can be discovered through experience. This means that although church and state are to remain separate, the individual Christian can share with the nonbeliever in discovering these principles, the good of which can be apparent to all. Christians are, therefore, to be *workers in all spheres of life*. Kuyper avoids any vertical or hierarchical view of the structure of society in which government dominates. He stresses a more horizontal concept that reduces the overall role of the state and enhances the role of people in the various spheres of life (arts, education, trade, business, etc.) to determine their own structures and controls according to their particular needs. This model argues for Christian involvement in every sphere of life. It has a distinctive approach to the way society should operate, and links Christian with non-Christians in the pursuit of the common good on the basis of principles of life that are built into society.

Modern Catholicism's approach to the relationship between church and world reflects the principle that "grace perfects nature." That is, there is a continuity that involves neither a separation of church and world nor their identification. The church seeks to perfect the world, that is, to lift it up to operate according to Christian standards, and Christians are *agents of change working from above*. This involves a theology of the fundamental goodness of creation, the universality of God's concerns, and the continuity between reason and revelation, nature and grace, this world and the kingdom. Niebuhr calls it "Christ above Culture." Catholic social teaching relates biblical principles (having to do with the value of the person, the needs of justice, etc.) to principles of natural law and philosophical concepts (common good, subsidiarity, human rights, etc.). The concept of subsidiarity refers to the primary purpose of the state, which is to assist all the other dimensions of social life (families, schools, businesses, charities, hospitals, etc.) in fulfilling their goals. A recognition of this concept should, therefore, prevent injustices and promote equity.

An eighth model involves seeing Christians as *agents of change working from within* society. This is related to Niebuhr's Christ *of* culture, and it is most effective when it occurs when the values of church and the culture are closely related. This model is thus related to the notion of Christendom, but the very different political contexts and the different approaches to the implementation of values mean that it is best seen as a different approach. Those who adopt this approach may be optimistic about society (with the church largely conforming to existing social beliefs and norms, as per liberalism) or more pessimistic (and thus requiring change, as per Niebuhr), but this view is always characterized by both an immanentist view of God at work in the world and significant levels of cultural assimilation. It often diminishes super-naturalism in favor of a purely rational approach to faith, minimizes the demands of radical love in favor of justice, and normalizes the radical Jesus into being nothing other than a good teacher.

The model that describes Christians as *priests of a Christian culture* is sometimes referred to as "the new Christendom," and it involves a resurgence of the search for a society that is explicitly Christian based. This model varies from strong forms that involve a confessionally founded society based on Christian creeds through to more moderate forms where society is simply widely understood to be based on specific Christian values. This includes Christian Reconstruction and Christian Heritage movements and proposals for an established faith (as in the UK) in either strong form (preferencing Christian faith) or as a pluralist, liberal democratic society specifically founded on Christian principles. In the latter case, it is argued that it is precisely and only Christian principles that establish the framework for tolerance and a "secular" democracy where all views are permitted. The failure to understand the role of Christ and "evangelical liberty" in creating such a society ulti-mately leads to the "liberal tyranny" of the late-modern age. This view argues that it must be recognized that the Christian faith has formed contemporary Western society, and that just as it is foolish to climb up a ladder onto a roof and then kick away the ladder and pretend you got up there without one, so it is foolish to ignore the origin of the prin-ciples that have formed our society today.

According to the tenth approach, Christians are nothing other than *citizens of a pluralist culture.* The church functions as part of a secular, pluralist, and morally diverse community that is, as far as is pragmati-cally possible, neutral in its public convictions. The liberal society that is intrinsic to Western culture is predicated on human freedom, equality, and natural rights. It allows freedom to individuals and involves the recognition of moral diversity, pluralism, and pragmatism. It is not only possible to argue for such a society on the basis of pragmatic consensus, but also on the basis that there is an overlapping consensus of ideas, a common set of minimal values, which emerge from the various world-views. In this context the Christian aims to persuade others of the value of his or her beliefs and lifestyle while protecting the rights and responsibilities of those who think very differently. As Karl Barth emphasized, in the modern liberal state, no appeal can be made to the word or spirit of God in the running of its affairs.[7] This leads to the principal criticism of this approach that because the state has to be neutral between conceptions of the good, there is therefore a moral, conceptual void at the center of the state. The civil community is spiritually blind. However, it can be argued that this is not a rejection of faith; rather, it is an acceptance of the right to believe or not believe, and the opportunity for the communication of the faith of Jesus Christ remains.

The ten models presented in this typology so far have expressed the relationship of church and society in terms of various roles: alien, ruler, resident, reformer, model, worker, agent of change, priest, and citizen; and the intention is now to add friend to that list. The final model, and obviously one that is advocated here, is that of *being friends with the world*. A typology is, of course, a formal construct, and the real situation in any particular context is likely to involve a mixture of models, but a friendship model is particularly amenable to being added to other approaches. Usually, despite overlaps, the models do not merge together. It is difficult, for example, to combine the role of the social reformer with that of the alien in a foreign land, the ruler in Christendom with the citizen of a pluralist society, or the priest of a Christian culture with the worker in every sphere of life. They are not always conceptually contradictory, but they are certainly different. But friendship, by its very nature, coincides happily with other roles. This model has no claims on exclusivity; it can permeate other approaches while presenting itself as an authentic model in its own right. Much has already been done to demonstrate the value of friendship in numerous contexts, and more will be done in that regard in the following material, but before doing

that, one further biblical example—set against its classical background
of the political influence of biblical principles—will be helpful.

Public friendship in classical thought

The public dimension of friendship, with its focus on self-knowledge
and moral transformation, was a major theme in Graeco-Roman ethical
thinking and the philosophy of public life. For Cicero, the whole of
society is dependent upon friendship, for "if the mutual love of friends
were to be removed from the world, there is no single house, no single
state that would go on existing";[8] Plutarch's concern to distinguish true
friends from flatterers is important because friendship is ethically and
politically vital to society;[9] and Aristotle devoted two out of ten books
in the *Nicomachean Ethics* to friendship because it was the relationship
on which democratic society depended. Of his three forms of friendship
(based on utility, pleasure, and virtue), it was the last, which was perfect
friendship, that was needed for the city. He argued, "Friendship seems
to hold states together, and lawgivers care more for it than for justice."[10]

Good lawmakers prefer greater friendship ahead of more laws
because justice will only exist where there is already a positive association based on the equality, trust, and fellowship that friendship brings.
Justice is thus dependent on friendship, and the rule of law will be
less required where people behave to each other as friends.[11] Aristotle
understood there to be three possible forms of political constitution:
monarchy (with the most common distortion of it being tyranny);
aristocracy (with its major distortion being oligarchy); and timocracy
(which is the rule of the majority of those with property rights, and its
major distortion is democracy, which, he conceded was only a slight
distortion of the ideal).[12] Each form required friendship because they
all have to exhibit justice in their operation. In a monarchy, for instance,
a form of friendship exists between a king and his subjects, and this
means that he confers benefits on his subjects. However, if there is no

friendship, then he will become a tyrant rather than a good king.[13] This kind of friendship is neither exactly the same as the modern concept of personal friendship nor completely different. In the Graeco-Roman context, even personal friendships have an important role in character development and the common good.

However, in the present day, the divide between the public and the private has removed friendship from public discourse. This has had several effects on public life. First, there is a tendency to stress the making of a law rather than relying on the goodwill of friendship to resolve difficulties, leading to a more legalistic and law-heavy form of government; and second, with the absence of friendships as the glue of public discourse, political parties have become the dominant form of relationship. These may involve friendships, but it is certainly not assumed that they are essential to it. Those who are not friends, and who may even be enemies, and people with very different values are expected to work in association on policies that the party as a whole has agreed on. In summary, it may be said that the classical model can contribute to political theory today; however, the biblical model, while aligned with this less-privatized approach, is also much more radical. A clear biblical example of this is found in Paul's dealing with Philemon.

Friendship and the end of slavery

Paul wrote to Philemon, a believer in Colossae, about one of his slaves, Onesimus, who had apparently run away. Onesimus met Paul, became a Christian, and was now willing to return to Philemon. Paul wrote to deal with the difficulties of this situation, as a slave who committed the crime of running away was potentially subject to a death sentence. Slavery in the Roman world was widespread, and the forms of public and domestic slavery varied from those who were trusted servants who worked alongside their masters to those whose lives were considered worthless and subject to the cruelest tyranny. It was as contrary to human dignity then as it is now, although that was not universally recognized. Within the Christian culture, slavery was clearly undergoing a significant change because of the teaching of Jesus, who on the one hand took on the role of a servant (to the initial distress of the disciples), while on the other hand he discharged the disciples from slavery to God and made them his friends. Slavery thus became a meaningless institution as far as faith was concerned. Paul wrote "to Philemon our dear friend" and spoke of his love and constant prayers for him (Philem. 1). Having established a foundation of fellowship, Paul said, "Though I am bold enough in Christ to command you to do your duty, yet I would rather appeal to you on the basis of love" (vv. 8–9). He could have required Philemon to release Onesimus on the basis of Paul's authority and Christian responsibility, but instead he appealed to him out of friendship and love both for himself and Onesimus. The appeal was based on Christian friendship. It began with the friendship between Paul and Onesimus that led Paul to appeal to Philemon as a friend and to consider the implications of the friendship in Christ that there was between Philemon and Onesimus. This friendship in Christ overrode all other roles and relationships and called for equality rather than slavery.

Paul has been criticized for supporting slavery, but this charge only makes sense for someone who is fixed within another of the models of the relationship between faith and culture. If, for instance, one can only see real change taking place through activism that leads to new laws, then one will not understand the more radical and fundamentally subversive approach grounded on Christian friendship.

A more contemporary example of the way friendship can override other roles is seen in the story of Kenyan teenagers Hussan and Mohammed, who arrived in Australia as stowaways on a boat. They were denied the refugee status that they sought, and were to be deported. But Caroline and Debbie, lawyers working in an organization helping refugees, argued that they had not been adequately defended, and after some hours of high drama, obtained a court order requiring a review of their case while the teenagers were actually in the air on their way out of the country. In order not to inconvenience other passengers on the plane with a return to an Australian airport, an agreement was reached with the airline and the government that the plane could continue and the boys would be able to return on another flight. The legal struggle continued as the documentation the government agreed to provide to enable their return on the next flight back to Australia expired while they were in midair so that, once again, they landed without any more rights than that of someone claiming refugee status. In the succeeding months, they were assisted by Debbie, Caroline, and other lawyers, but Debbie decided that they needed something more than justice; they needed friendship. When the opportunity came, she took them into her own home and cared for them. Her personal involvement meant that it was difficult to have the objectivity of being their lawyer. She commented, "The objectivity that we're all taught to bring to our jobs is really tested in this area, and I don't think it's a bad thing to lose it sometimes because, if you don't lose it sometimes, you're not a human being."[14] She was right to think that she could give far more in friendship. Legal help was still needed, but friendship was primary.

A friendship model of public engagement

A friendship model of public engagement can work with other models. It also has integrity as an approach in its own right. The form of friendship described here is messianic friendship, a fuller form of friendship that can function as a principle of social life along with egalitarianism, justice, integrity, and the other social principles that are more readily recognized as such. An approach to the relationship of faith and society model based on the notion of public friendship may well be described as *Friends of God in life, church and culture,* and it has the following seven characteristics.

First, it is a person-centered relational approach that focuses attention on the simple, though profound, everyday actions of friendship, and on the character and the virtue of those involved. An example of a closely related approach is the relational strategy espoused by Michael Schluter and the Jubilee Centre in the United Kingdom.[15] It is a coherent and wide-ranging social agenda that is presented as a biblical alternative to capitalism, socialism, and other ideologies. Whether dealing with nationhood, government, family, economics, or justice, the focus is always on the quality of the relationships rather than, say, merely the economic implications.

Second, this friendship is a principle that applies to all areas of life, including the personal, the ecclesial, and the public. As shown in earlier chapters, it is not only a way of describing interpersonal relationships, but also of characterizing a healthy relationship with God and the fellowship and ministry of the church. It also functions as a guide for social relationships in wider society and can contribute significant insights into a wide range of social issues, including structural policies (such as the nature of liberty and the role of law and politics), as well as to specific issues (such as work, business, leisure, play, the arts, infra-structure planning, health policy, family and community life, and financial and economic issues). In some other models, the focus only falls on certain fundamental issues, such as the nature of liberty, the role of law, and political structures. The principle of friendship has something to contribute to issues in every area of public life.

The third aspect of public friendship is that it is able to unite personal and social identities. The underlying tension in contemporary Western society is a struggle between the public and the personal. We are private people who happen to live in groups. We are individuals who develop communities based more on the rights of each separate member than on our obligations to the whole. Friendship is a relationship that bridges individual and social realms, and it runs counter to the individualism of contemporary society. It locates personal identity in a relational context. The person is not merely an individual but a person-in-relationship, and that relationship exists in the positive, life-enhancing form of friendship.

Fourth, public friendship—like friendship in general—has a high degree of flexibility of form. It is a model of relationship between faith and society that is contextually flexible, able to accommodate and to supplement other approaches. It is less interested in achieving a specific form of social structure than in building certain attitudes and relationships. This stands as a corrective to those who see only one Christian approach to culture, such as, for example, some of those who fall into the "Rulers in Christendom" model and who continually want to make laws for all people based on Christian principles. Sometimes that is, indeed, very appropriate, but at other times it is contrary to the principles of a free society (which is, itself, predicated on Christian principles). A friendship model can take a different approach that affirms Christian values without being overly controlling.

Fifth, all genuine friendship is based on grace, and grace is, indeed, the theoretical presupposition and the practical foundation of public friendship. Prevenient grace provides the foundation for the relationship between the Christian community and the world; it is this that enables people to do good, serve individuals and society as a whole, and lead people toward friendship with Christ.

Sixth, this approach to the world has Christian virtue as its primary content, and friendship is the principal vehicle by which virtue is formed. The virtues include "the fruit of the Spirit" (love, joy, peace, patience, kindness, goodness, faithfulness, gentleness, and self-control) and other biblical virtues, including faith, hope, service, and grace. These are to be applied as *values* for a society as well as *virtues* for individuals.

Finally, whatever precise form it adopts, public friendship tends to avoid domineering, hierarchical, or authoritarian attitudes. It is, by nature, egalitarian and affirming (though frank and open) in form. It is sometimes assumed that the "prophetic approach" is the best way of relating to society. This involves the denunciation of those cultural behaviors and policies that are perceived to be socially damaging and declarations of the changes that are needed. There is no doubt that this "prophetic" approach can be effective, particularly when it includes a good rational argument, and as a strong "top-down" approach, it seems to have greater potential than a "bottom-up" friendship strategy. In reality, both approaches are needed. For example, the prophetic approach certainly achieved a great deal—but not everything—in the US civil rights movement of the 1960s. The prophetic approach to speaking out combined with nonviolent resistance contributed much to the legislative and social changes that were so badly needed, but the elimination of official segregation does not automatically produce new relationships. The reality is that long-established segregation and personal attitudes and relationships do not easily change. Despite the large-scale political and civil changes, black and white churches continued with little or no dialogue among pastors or congregations. This is where the Christian organization Mission Mississippi and the simple notion of friendship come in.

With the aim of "changing Mississippi one relationship at a time," Mission Mississippi challenges people in African American and white churches to undertake one-on-one, individual friendships. Mississippi was, of course, at the heart of the civil rights movement because of its history of racial division, its reactionary attitudes, and the state's resistance to federal desegregation rulings. But social prophets and civil movements are better at bringing justice than at developing love and can do more for civil rights than for creating personal friendships. Mission Mississippi aims at very intentional friendship making where people are asked, typically at a prayer breakfast, to sit down and begin conversations of understanding. This is not rapid work; it has been a continuing ministry for twenty years. People come from different traditions, with different attitudes, experiences, and expectations, and with very different concerns about the way power and justice function in social relationships. However, with prayer and a desire to develop a friendship, change takes place. And while it starts with individuals intentionally establishing personal relationships, it does not stop there. The experience of the Mission is that as Christ-centered, reconciling friendships develop, all parties come to see the need to address broader issues of injustice and poverty. Phil Reed of Voice of Calvary Ministries says, "When you develop this kind of friendship, then it [poverty] is no longer a statistic. This is my friend that can't find a decent job, that doesn't have a decent place to stay . . . It is not a statistic anymore; it is my friend. And so, *it all starts with friendships*."[16]

In this way, friendship making becomes a means for broad-based social development. Some aspects of society may only change by a prophetic ministry, but more people's hearts are changed by messianic friendship.

Public friendship as Christian love

The strategic principles noted above provide the agenda for a Christian understanding of friendship as a public good. It would, however, be possible to raise two questions about the value of this approach. The first question asks whether it would not be easier to leave friendship aside and simply say that the guiding principle is "to love one another." After all, is friendship really anything other than this? And the second is to ask whether friendship (or love, for that matter) is actually a "model" or an "approach." Is it not just a much more general attitude that lacks the precision necessary for a model?

In response to both questions, it is true that treating friendship as a public strategy is, in one sense, nothing other than a reaffirmation of the command to love one another, but it is that love orientation presented in a particular way that provides people with guidance as to what it actually means to love one another. The call to love has to be explained and to point toward friendship as a concrete expression of love. Everyone is

familiar with the basic concept of friendship and understands that it is
a close and intimate relationship based on a particular attitude of love
and affection that is necessarily expressed in specific, caring actions. It is
also understood that it is an open-ended and fluid relationship with few
specific rules as to the way it is conducted. This understanding of friendship is, almost inevitably, understood to function in the private world, but
it can be developed and can become a relationship that is offered more
widely and also utilized in ecclesial and public domains. The point is that
everyone understands something of the nature of friendship, and consequently, it provides concrete guidance in terms of attitude and behavior.
Moreover, the content and significance of friendship can be extended to
incorporate spiritual, messianic dimensions. As it does, it takes on the
character of a specific approach or model of relationship between faith
and culture, one that is open in terms of precise form—never based on
law and obligation, but always on grace and freedom.

The final evidence for friendship as a public good and as a coherent
strategy is the way it is seen expressed in the life and ministry of
Jesus. Friendship was, in his life with disciples and "tax collectors and
sinners," a guiding social principle and a fundamental expression of
love. The objection of the Pharisees and scribes to his friendship with
sinners arose out of a fear that this meant a revolution in social structures (Matt. 9:11; Mark 2:16; Luke 5:30). Jesus' friendship implied the
end of existing authoritarian power structures and degrading social
relationships, and had messianic significance as an anticipation of the
heavenly banquet and the eschatological life to come (Matt. 22:2–9).
The friendship of Jesus speaks of a community life that has love and
friendship as the primary form of relationship—a form of relationship
that is not domineering, hierarchical, authoritarian, or founded upon
class or caste. Such a society is not necessarily structureless, anarchic,
or without responsibility and authority. Nor does it imply the absence
of social groupings that are larger than can involve a few close friends.
It will be a society permeated with friendship at every level, with

leadership aimed at community rather than at control, and any social organizations or groups oriented toward building community and the common good rather than divisiveness or group interest.

Friendship, partiality, and justice

It has been suggested that the notion of friendship as a public good is problematic because of an inner conflict that only exists when it functions in the public arena. While friendship is good and appropriate for private relationships, it seems to be antithetical and damaging to the responsibilities of citizenship. Friendship necessarily involves, it seems, a preference for certain people and preferential actions on their behalf. One does things for friends that one may not do for others. In distinction to this, public service of any kind necessarily involves just the opposite—it requires impartiality and personal neutrality so that all actions are undertaken without any preference for one's friends. Friendship in the public arena appears as favoritism, and public actions that give preference to friends appear to be a throwback to a feudal or monarchical form of government where privilege is dispensed to existing friends and in order to make friends of certain others. It is the kind of action seen in some despotic states where "friends" who receive preference are "cronies," and "friendship" becomes "corruption." In a just society, the citizen's responsibility lies in protecting and working with the institutions of government to promote mutually beneficial projects for all, and not only for family or friends. In his study on friendship, Gilbert Meilaender proffers this critique as a fundamental reason why civic friendship is an incoherent ideal:

> The fellow-citizen bond, precisely because it *must* concern itself with justice, is not a personal bond . . . Nor should we be too quick to bemoan this. If human beings are as prone to sin as Christian belief suggests, it is probably important that political authority be impersonal . . . [Friendship] conflicts with the necessary political

good of justice and the impersonality which justice requires. Finally, I want to suggest, hesitantly but firmly, that a Christian ethic *ought to recognize the ideal of civic friendship as essentially pagan, an example of inordinate and idolatrous love.*[17]

Meilaender had no doubts about the importance of friendship-love, but argued that it could operate only in the personal sphere of life and not in the political realm. Friendship is important, but one should not seek from it more than it can give. Personal friendship-love and impersonal, egalitarian justice simply operate in different spheres according to different principles, and there is not even sufficient contact to determine a hierarchy of operation or a priority of one over the other. Meilaender says, "There may be no way to stipulate in advance when one's obligations as a citizen take precedence over one's loyalties as a friend."[18]

The conflict Meilaender comments on is expressed in E. M. Forster's (1879–1970) well-known aphorism "If I had to choose between betraying my country and betraying my friend, I hope I should have the guts to betray my country."[19] Of course, the aphorism is predicated on a distinction between two worlds, where personal friendship and national politics are fundamentally separated. Nonetheless, there has to be an acceptance that it is impossible to ignore the potential conflict between personal and preferential friendship and impersonal and egalitarian justice. Even though this problem is not fatal to the fundamental principle of civic friendship, it does require a commitment to uncovering and resolving such potential conflicts. It has to be conceded that when certain forms of friendship are combined with politics, it can lead to tyranny through collusion, conspiracy, and corruption. But ultimately, a society without friendship is even more likely to become corrupt and unloving. True friendship is more important than citizenship. For a society to become a community, it *requires* friendship.

Moreover, in Aristotelian terms, the potential conflict between the implications of friendship and the obligations of citizenship primarily relate to friendship as described in only the first two of Aristotle's three forms of friendship—where friendship is based on utility or pleasure, rather than virtue. Both of these motives call for civic responsibility and privilege to be transmuted into preferential action for oneself or for one's friends. But Aristotle's third form of perfect friendship, founded on virtue and seeking the common good, contains within it principles that are at least as altruistic as any impersonal form of social justice. Without denying the possibility of such a conflict at any time (for life will inevitably produce situations that have no good outcome), conflicts emerge most commonly when friendship is understood in terms of pleasure or utility.

The benefits of friendship understood in terms of virtue are, however, easily overlooked in a society, such as the present one, which is dominated by utilitarian individualism. In that situation, there is inevitably a difficulty in recognizing, as a form of friendship, this more idealistic common moral commitment to the good of society as a whole. The benefits of social justice and equity could not exist unless grounded in friendship. In short, civic friendship remains as a coherent and potentially useful principle for modern society.

Friendship in public life

A friendship approach to public engagement is a constant reminder that politics and laws cannot do everything that needs to be done for the common good. Laws and political action can restrain evil more easily than they can create that which is good. *Friendship does precisely what politics cannot.* Aristotle argued that good lawmakers pay more attention to friendship than to justice because laws are limited in what they can achieve. Laws coerce people to act as citizens, but friends go beyond what is required by law. Friendship is more than citizenship, although it cannot be said that it is everything, or that parties, policies, and laws are not needed. But it is friendship that makes it clear what politics should aim at.

The inherent danger associated with what may be referred to as "the seduction of politics" has long been recognized, though not always well handled. John Henry Newman pointed out that "many pursuits, in themselves honest and right, are nevertheless to be engaged in with caution, lest they seduce us." Those that deserve to be treated with special caution are those that seek people's social and political well-being. "The sciences, for instance, of good government, acquiring wealth, of preventing and relieving war, and the like" he argued, are "especially dangerous; for fixing, as they do, our exertions on this world as an end, they go far to persuade us that they have no other end."[20] Jacques Ellul argued that, regrettably, in contemporary culture,

> [p]olitics is the only serious activity. The fate of humanity depends on politics, and classic philosophical or religious truth takes on meaning only as it is incarnated in political action. Christians are typical in this connection. They rush to the defense of political religion, and assert that Christianity is meaningful only in terms of political commitment. In truth, it is their religious mentality that plays this trick on them. As Christianity collapses as a religion, they look about them in bewilderment, unconsciously of course, hoping to recover where the religious is to be incarnated in their time. Since they are religious, they are drawn automatically into the political sphere like iron filings to a magnet.[21]

While it needs to be remembered that the church has a mission within this present world, it is possible to focus on the present world to the neglect of the future kingdom. "Worldliness" is usually associated with sinful activities, but what is possibly a greater danger arises when the apparently good things, including politics and community service, become ends in themselves. It is an example of the principle that "the good is the enemy of the best." It is useful to remember that expecting a political party or a national government to transform a society is like expecting a football team to win a state election. It is not going to happen because they are actually playing a different game. Friendship, as an expression of Christian love, does what politics cannot and refocuses our attention on relationships. Politics and public life are necessary and important, but they need friendship as both a guiding principle for community life in the present and as a goal for the future.

One would think that implementing a friendship approach to public engagement would not be controversial, especially among Christians, but it can be. When I was director of public theology for the Australian Evangelical Alliance, and therefore responsible for public policy, it was decided, in the light of various controversies over international war and terrorism and local cultural disputes, to put out a public statement on Christian relationships with Muslims. The statement was headed, "Making friends with Muslims," and it proposed that Australian Christians should at that time make a particular effort to intentionally befriend Muslims. The paper also discussed an extensive range of material dealing with various aspects of both the local and the international situation; but after noting that in Australia, as in other places, Christians and Muslims had shown that it was possible to live and work together peacefully, it suggested that Christians ought to "do as Jesus said and love Muslims as much as they love Christians ('love your neighbor as yourself')." If anything, I thought the statement was too obvious and innocuous, but that only showed how naïve I was. It was soon clear that for many Christians the appropriate response to the problems was, in some sense, to fight back (even though the ones affected by this were not necessarily the ones who were the problem), to resist Islam in every way and only work to show them to be wrong, and to remove them from Australian society if possible. The statement was described by a number of Christian workers as "appeasement" and "weakness." There were, however, any number of conversations that I subsequently had where those who objected to the direction of the paper could be seen to be visibly conflicted trying to relate the primary stress of the statement on the obviously biblical "love for neighbor" (and even enemy), which yet was not what they wanted because it did not seem to deal with their fears of "the other." Of course, what was needed was a recognition that, as 1 John 4:18 says, "perfect love casts out fear." And perhaps that could become "perfect friendship casts out fear." Messianic friendship has a place in public life; it counters the fear of "the other," points to the importance of relationships, expresses Christian love in concrete form, and ultimately, offers the possibility of friendship with God in Christ.

The possibilities are illustrated in the story of Jerzy Kluger (1921–2011), a Polish Jew who, through simple friendship, helped bring about a significant improvement in Catholic-Jewish relationships after centuries of anti-Semitism. In the 1920s, he was a young boy in the same town as Karol Wojtyla—later Pope John Paul II—and the two became life-long friends. They met in primary school, played soccer in the streets, and did homework together. They remained close friends throughout their lives. Wojtyla's very first audience as pope was with Kluger and his family. He asked Kluger to help begin a diplomatic effort that led to the Vatican recognizing the state of Israel. Subsequently, he became the first pope to visit a synagogue; he also visited the Auschwitz death camp, and later issued an official act of repentance for the Catholic Church's failure to do more to stop the Holocaust. Kluger was credited with much in this, but he explained his role simply by saying, "I was a friend. We had friendly conversations, and friendly relationships which one way or another helped these developments. That's all."[22]

The next step

This chapter has begun to show how friendship can be seen not only as a personal relationship but also a public good, even in a secular, pluralist society. Christian friendship works with most of the typical models of social engagement, but also has its own place as an approach in its own right. It has been shown to influence the form of social structures and is as important as other civic concepts, such as freedom and justice. The next two chapters continue this theme of the public relevance of friendship, but with their own perspectives.

In contrast with this present chapter's structural approach and its conception of the "gathered church," chapter 9 examines the public role of friendship from a common, everyday, "bottom-up" point of view, and it works with a conception of the church as "scattered" throughout the community. It shows how civic friendship crosses national, social, economic, and status boundaries, and works with the marginalized.

Then, chapter 10 looks specifically at the development of virtue. Personal holy friendships encourage and build one another up in faith and virtue, and the question addressed concerns the way civic virtue can benefit society. It particularly looks at the connection between individual virtues and social values. After examining the personal and social implications of holy friendship, it concludes with an examination of the implications of holy friendship for God, and the role it plays in the destiny of the world.

Mission

Friendship and the Scattered Church

9

> "Go therefore and make friends of all nations."
>
> The Great Commission (adapted)

At the famous Edinburgh Missionary Conference (a consultation held at the start of the twentieth century that continues to influence global mission strategy today), Bishop V. Samuel Azariah of South India applauded the heroic and self-denying labors of missionaries, but famously appealed to those delegates who came from sending countries for something he considered to be even more important than either missionaries or money: "You have given your goods to feed the poor. You have given your bodies to be burned. We also ask for love. *Give us friends!*"[1]

Azariah understood friendship as a concrete expression of the love that is the dynamic power of the gospel that changes the world. It is central to both the life and the mission of the church, so it was not enough for there to be a mission that changed social structures, converted people, healed bodies, and relieved poverty if there was no

real friendship between missionaries and those to whom they ministered. It was counterproductive if they offered the gift of the gospel of
reconciliation while themselves remaining separated from the people
to whom they ministered. It was not enough if the missionaries were
influential leaders, evangelists, agents of change, and social reformers,
but were not actually *friends* with the people of the church.

There are many factors, good and ill, that can inhibit friendships
and keep ministers and missionaries apart from those to whom they
minister: cultural differences, the conviction that the church or the individual should be allowed to develop uniquely, a desire not to become
too emotionally involved, feelings of superiority, a sense of propriety
and position, and the desire to retain control can all play a part. But
the gospel cannot flourish in situations where people stand apart from
real, genuine friendship and fellowship. Evangelism, social change, or
church growth without love and friendship is superficial. One may have
an abundance of gifts, strategies, and resources, but without friendship,
they are noisy gongs and clanging cymbals.

And it has always been this way. The book of Acts is the story
of groups of friends, like the Twelve, Paul and Silas, Barnabas and
John Mark, and Silas and Timothy, who traveled and labored together
sharing the gospel and establishing communities of faith. The friendships they established along the way are sometimes recorded at the
end of various epistles along with warm greetings and holy kisses
(Rom. 16; 1 Cor. 16; Phil. 4; Col. 4). James Miller puts it all down to
friendship.

> Ever since the day of Pentecost this wonderful friendship of Jesus
> has been spreading wherever the gospel has gone. It has given to the
> world its Christian homes . . . it has built hospitals and asylums, and
> established charitable institutions of all kinds in every place . . . The
> friendship of Jesus, left in the hearts of his apostles, as his legacy to
> the world, has wrought marvelously; and its ministry and influence
> will extend until everything unlovely shall cease from earth, and the
> love of God shall pervade all life.[2]

In terms of the models discussed in the previous chapter, the earliest Christians could only see themselves as a marginalized group, little more than *aliens* in a foreign country. But soon they had more of a social role and could be described as *residents* of two cities before, eventually, through association with the power of the empire, becoming *rulers* in Christendom. But the dynamic power of the gospel is love, and this is primarily expressed in all of the actions and attitudes that are part and parcel of being *friends*.

The missionary dimension of friendship can be developed further by an examination of one of the best-known instructions given by the Lord Jesus to his friends, a passage known as the Great Commission (Matt. 28:18–20).

The Great Commission: go therefore and make friends of all nations

When one considers everything in the life of the church in relationship to friendship, it is tempting to rephrase the Great Commission in that way: "Go therefore and make *friends* of all nations, baptizing them in the name of the Father and of the Son and of the Holy Spirit, and teaching them to obey everything that I have commanded you" (Matt. 28:19–20).

In a general sense, this is appropriate, as Jesus' disciples are certainly his friends, and it does effectively make the point that the mission the church is engaged in is really nothing other than to take the friendship of Jesus to the world. This, in turn, fits very well with the notion that a "making-friends mission" is the responsibility of the *whole* church and not merely some people. Unfortunately, there are many who still perceive the missionary responsibility of the church as being limited to some people specifically appointed to that task, such as missionaries and pastors.

There are two aspects of the Great Commission that are misunderstood that actually contribute to this more limited way of thinking. The first is that the focus on mission as "disciple-making" is seen as a very intellectual responsibility that requires the one who does it to be highly trained, like pastors and others with degrees in theology and ministry, not least because the disciples have to be taught "everything" that Jesus commanded. This is obviously a job for a specialist. The second is that the Great Commission has a stress on "going" in order to do this, so it seems that one needs to be a cross-cultural missionary in order to be able to fulfill it. And that, too, is obviously a job for someone specially trained for it.

Of course, neither of these two perceptions is at all valid. Mission is as much about staying right where you are and being a friend as it is about going to another place to teach disciples. This can be shown in the following way.

The first point to make is that the "going" aspect of the Great Commission can be stressed too much. Yes, there is always a dimension of going in mission, but it should not be interpreted as the primary point. The main instruction—which is found in the sentence's main verb—is to "make disciples," and the instruction to go is a participle (literally, "going") that is subordinate to the main verb. It could be translated "make disciples as you go, baptizing them . . . teaching them." But irrespective of what one does with the actual translation, the main, indispensable activity is *making disciples*. This disciple-making mission is not only undertaken when one literally goes from one place to another. It can, and ought to be, fulfilled in every place, by those who have stayed as well as those who have gone to another culture or country. This, in the modern world, really eliminates the picture of mission as involving some "sending" and some "receiving" nations—the kind of picture envisaged at Edinburgh. This is the universalization of mission with disciple-making taking place everywhere. This, of course, is not a new idea at all. But because of the way many people think, it is something that has to be continually restated.

The second point is that the disciple-making focus of mission should not be interpreted in too intellectual a manner, even though the new disciples have to be taught everything that Jesus commanded. There is a tendency to see this teaching as the responsibility of some, such as pastors and others with degrees in theology and ministry—and not others. A disciple in Jesus' day was one who followed a teacher in order to learn. Jesus is often described as "teacher" and "rabbi" (e.g., Matt. 8:19; 9:11; John 1:49; 4:31), but he clearly established his own form of relationship with the Twelve, one that was not bound by convention. For example, he was quite unconventional in that he took the initiative to call certain people to be his disciples, and he called them not once, but twice. After their initial call *to follow him* (Matt. 4:18–20; Luke 5:1–11) and after spending time with them, he called them again—this time *to be his friends* (John 15:12–15). Because by this time, having followed him around and having spent time with him, they knew everything that Jesus had himself heard from his Father (John 15:15). They had learned what they needed by being with him and by being his friend. The point is that Christian discipleship involves an ongoing association—a friendship—with Jesus Christ. There is a real sense in which "disciple-making" takes place through friendship, and this is something that everyone can do in one way or another. Friends teach one another very much. One does not need to have a degree in ministry to be a friend who can both learn from, and teach, a friend.

In short, the mission of the church is the call for the friends of Jesus to help others learn to become friends of Jesus. And although the going ought not to be stressed too much, neither should it be ignored. It expresses the dynamic sense of the friend-making mission—that it is not an activity that happens accidentally or inevitably. One should approach it intentionally, and it may require effort. It will certainly involve being guided and led by the Holy Spirit, and one must be attentive to that. But making friends for Christ is something that can happen everywhere and it is something in which every Christian can be engaged.

Friendship in the church

Unfortunately, friendship like this—that intentionally sets out to cross whatever boundaries have to be crossed in order to make friends with others—is not automatically part of the life of every church. It is a fact of life that virtually every congregation will perceive itself as being "a friendly church," but this can be a judgment made on the basis of a fairly superficial understanding of friendliness rather than in terms of a more radical form of open, transforming, messianic, missionary friendship. Are, for example, US church members more likely than nonchurch people to have friendships that go beyond their own social grouping? Churches do teach about the importance of ministry with the poor, the needy, and the marginalized, but is there any evidence that this results in personal contact and friendships with people in other social groups?

Robert Wuthnow's research indicates that there is, in fact, not a strong relationship between the churches' teaching and actual practice. He asked whether, taking into account demographics and all the variables of context, US church members were more or less likely to be friends with certain representative categories of people, including manual workers, persons on welfare, African Americans, and Hispanics. Positively, he noted (a) that there are congregations that attract diverse memberships and do well in befriending across status boundaries; (b) that there is a positive relationship between religious participation and friendship with manual workers; and (c) that where higher levels of volunteering is present, the likelihood of friendships that transcend status distinctions is higher. However, there was no evidence of, overall, a positive relationship between religious participation and the other categories, so it is not clear that religious involvement itself encourages people to live out its teaching on befriending those who are different. This is probably because the positive teaching of the church has to counter certain sociological factors that can lead to churches being stratified materially, socially, politically, and ethnically. The neighborhood nature of many churches promotes stratification, and the voluntary aspect of participation in church life combined with the general tendency to choose friends who are similar makes it difficult to achieve church communities with strong friendships that transcend the full range of the community's social groups. This reinforces the need for there to be a focus on the development of Christian friendship that will overcome these inhibiting factors. Without that, the life and mission of the church will not be able to be fulfilled.

The scattered church

If the friends of Jesus are to be offering his friendship to the world, then this has implications for the way the friends perceive themselves in relationship to the world. Notwithstanding the ambiguity about the meaning of "church" (as noted in chapter 6), there is generally today a strong emphasis on the gathered nature of the church. There is less of a sense of the existence and life of the church at other times when it is scattered—not gathered together. It is as though the church comes into existence when people gather together, and it almost seems to go out of existence at other times. There is a need today for a stronger sense of the scattered church and the importance of the life and ministry of the people of God when they are in the world.

The dual nature of the church as both gathered and scattered can be seen in two important descriptions of the church found in 1 Peter. First, in 1 Peter 2:9 there is the well-known description of the church as a *gathered* community: "But you are a chosen race, a royal priesthood, a holy nation, God's own people." There is a stress here on the way believers come together to constitute the church, a view that is supported by related material about being stones built together into a spiritual house (2:4–5). The emphasis is on the gathered church.

The other, less-commented-upon description is found at the beginning of the epistle, where the church is described as a *scattered* community: Peter addresses "God's elect, strangers in the world, scattered [*diaspora*] throughout Pontus, Galatia, Cappadocia, Asia and Bithynia" (1:1–2 NIV). This image of the church that stresses scattering needs to be taken as seriously as the other images that stress gathering, but at present, the practical emphasis of the life of the modern church is very much weighted toward understanding, teaching, and encouraging the church to be a congregation.

The description of the church as *diaspora* can be taken in two ways. The first takes it as an actual description of a fledgling church that is thinly scattered through the empire. It describes the reality that while some of the Christians who made up the *diaspora* of the early church would have had a community of other believers with whom they could meet, others would have had a much lonelier time of it. And even where Christians were gathered in communities, there was far less chance of it being able to act as the kind of comprehensive social group, meeting every social and spiritual need that is found in modern congregations. The second approach takes this description as a prescriptive image of the way the church should see itself—an image of the scattered church that complements the many other images of the gathered church (body, vine, flock, people, and so forth) that are found in the Scripture.

The implications of this for the mission of the church are considerable. This image presents a picture of a church that genuinely permeates society (rather than gathering in its own social groups), is found in every place (and not concentrated in Bible belts), and is distributed in every social group and stratum. The emphasis lies on the *spread* of the believers rather than upon the *size* of individual communities. It is certainly a challenge to hold both images—gathered and scattered—together within one community, and so congregations tend to perceive themselves primarily as either a "gathered" community or as a "scattered" one. But there is no doubt that the gathered church mentality dominates at present.

Churches that are strongly gathered in orientation, where the social structure is complex and the programs of the church strong and well-run, need to consider the following: (a) that believers are not unfaithful or lacking in commitment if they are not always at the center of church life or not thoroughly involved in all appropriate church programs; (b) that a stress on the church running its own programs can alienate people from community-based programs and events where church members might be able to be even more effective witnesses than through church-organized programs; and (c) that the greater their success in providing programs and activities, the less chance there is that the members will have any nonchurch friends at all. This problem of the lack of friendships outside the church is a very real one. The US Congregational Life Survey demonstrates that the longer people worship at a church, the more bonds they develop with other members both inside and outside church activities, and the less contact they have with non-church members.[3]

Where the church is perceived to be a scattered church, it is likely that the believers will be more involved with the culture outside the church and more likely to have a greater number of friendships and other social relationships with non-Christians. It is possible that a church that is noticeably a scattered church might ultimately be more influential than a church that has a higher level of corporate cultural significance and social status, but which is largely gathered together in its own social groupings with many members who simply have no significant friendships outside the church.

Of course, the description of congregations in terms of gathered and scattered is typological, and churches will, in fact, be some mixture of both. The scattered church, which cannot exist without a gathered dimension, has advantages in terms of missionary friendships—those that exist outside the church and which draw people toward friendship with Christ. But gathered churches can also learn to recognize the scattered dimension that does exist in most churches, but which is fundamentally ignored because it appears to run counter to the idea of a gathered church. This is the area of life that involves the majority of people's lives and interests, yet is all too rarely left unaddressed by church teaching. There is, one might say, a gap between Sunday and Monday.

The gap between Sunday and Monday

Until I had an after-church conversation with Gary, I never knew one could have an occupation as loss adjuster let alone what losses one could adjust. I found out that such a person is an independent assessor of the losses incurred by an insured business after, say, a fire has occurred. Insurance covers the business for physical losses and for loss of income while out of business. Calculating the costs involved in the loss of stock, buildings, the depreciation on unused machinery, and the (seasonally adjusted) loss of future business is a complex matter. But what was really difficult, as Gary explained it, was the tension that can emerge between trying to do what is right not only by the business owner and the insurer, but sometimes the police (a loss adjuster may find a motive for a fire that is not accidental) and one's own employer (the contracted loss-adjustment company that wants a good result that will bring in more business). I asked whether church teaching had ever helped him deal with this, and while he generously referred to the importance of basic teaching about honesty and integrity, there was nothing that really addressed his situation. I can also confidently say that in my own time as a pastor, I never addressed the issues associated with loss adjustment myself. While I fully understand the practical difficulties preachers face in relating their preaching to the world of work, the fact is that unless the church finds more and better ways of helping people relate faith to work and business, we will perpetuate a dangerous division of sacred and secular worlds.

For many people their strongest and most meaningful relationships outside the family occur at work. These relationships with colleagues or coworkers may not extend beyond working hours, and they may not consciously be distinguished as "friendships" because that term is generally reserved for personal relationships that exist independently of work. In this view, colleagues may become friends, but a collegial relationship itself is not generally characterized as friendship. But if one applies a classic rather than a purely contemporary approach to friendship, then it becomes obvious that collegiality at work includes a significant aspect of friendship that is often not found in personal relationships. That is, these work relationships not only involve large amounts of time (often more than almost any other relationship), and develop significant levels of closeness and sharing, but they also function in an environment where people are engaged together on a project that is being undertaken for the common good. The value that workers attribute to these relationships for themselves can be measured by the way in which, in terms of remaining with an employer, they are frequently rated as being more important than significant salary increases.

These friendships, which can be very positive friendships "in the world," have to be distinguished from the friendship "with the world" James warned against when he wrote, "Do you not know that friendship with the world is enmity with God?" (James 4:4). The friendship with the world to which he was referring is clearly identified in the epistle as the pursuit of selfish pleasure, a life of unspirituality, wrong speech, and a lack of care for the weak (1:27; 3:6, 15; 4:4.). This is illustrated in Abraham (the "friend of God"), who was not isolated from the world but who was commended for his righteousness in relating to it (2:23). One can be a friend *in* the world and a friend *to* the world without being friends *with the values* of the world.

Being a friend to the world preeminently means offering the friendship of Christ to the world. This is where the mission of the church needs to take place, and to return to the point about the scattered dimension of the church, it is a world Christians already inhabit as they relate to work colleagues and others they relate to in the wider community from Monday to Saturday. Unfortunately, despite the fact that the wider community, the workplace, and community organizations are the right and proper location for our greatest ministry, this is often underplayed in favor of a stress on the ministry a person can exercise for an hour or two a week within the structures of a local church. It seems that the church is reluctant to stress the role of this wider ministry, as though a focus on the scattered church would lead to a diminution of the life of the gathered church. In fact, the reverse is the case. The gathered church can find its true purpose—a full life of worship and mission—when it turns its attention to the huge potential ministry its members have at those times when they are not in church.

A group of Christians together can demonstrate the community dimension of the church, but a community without mission becomes a ghetto, and too much separation between workplace and worship is one sign of this happening. Gathering together as church *is* very important, but we need to recover a notion of the scattered church and intentionally address the activities of Christians outside the church building. Many Christians feel that their work lives are marginalized from their church life, and others have never been challenged to consider in any depth the missional implications of what they do from Monday to Saturday—whether it is carpentry, cleaning, cardiology, or caring for children. All too few churches recognize either the significance of the work or the value of the friendships that exist at work when considering the missional responsibilities of the church. There is a tendency to create new programs and structures rather than finding ways of enhancing mission through existing structures and friendships. A number of factors lead to this.

First, there is the widespread dichotomy of faith and work that locates them in different—private and public—domains. Second, there is uncertainty about how participation in a secular society affects the role faith can play in the workplace, and this tends to lead to inaction. Third, there is the institutional pressure that leads to churches creating their own programs that can be more easily controlled. This is related to a busyness factor, with many pastors so tied up in church programs and the myriad internal church tasks that need to be done, that issues that extend outside the life of the gathered congregation easily get left behind. Two fundamental principles involved in developing a focus on the scattered church are, first, making good use of the specific knowledge and experiences of the people who work in a particular area, and second devising church programs that are oriented toward helping people engage right where they are (rather than creating a ministry that draws them away from that). People should be encouraged to pray for their work, their colleagues, and for the exercise of a ministry within that context. The aim is not just evangelism; it is also to determine what contribution Christians can play in the work itself. People should learn to think biblically about their work and its social value as it contributes toward the common good. Sermons and Bible studies can focus on this, and groups of people can be commissioned to minister within specific contexts.

Finally, and perhaps partly as a consequence of the foregoing issues, there has also been a widespread loss of the sense of Christian vocation. The existing stress on the church as a gathered community has diminished the church's corporate perception of the value of mission by the scattered Christian community. Consequently, the next section will focus on the nature of the church and the vocation of Christians. There is a need for a renewal of Christian vocation both in *extent*—understanding it as relating to everyday life—and in *expression*—as a particular way of being a friend.

Understanding vocation as friendship

We live in a "post-vocational" world where there has been a shift away from seeing work as a vocation, that is, as a calling from God and a way of contributing to the common good. Work is generally seen simply as a means of making money and providing what one needs for family and self in order to live well and engage in personal recreational activities. Christians are certainly aware of the responsibilities of discipleship, but the concept of work as a calling, a vocation, is not common. After outlining how calling can be understood, the main point is to demonstrate the way in which vocation can best be understood in terms of a call to friendship with Christ. This restores a profoundly personal dimension to calling and counteracts the common emphasis on calling being understood in terms of work and "doing things for God" rather than relationship and "being a friend of God."

Vocation and occupation

To have a "calling" from God is the *same* as having a vocation (ex *vocatio*, which is Latin for "calling"), but the terms have often been used differently. This came about as society moved toward being more socially mobile and less rigidly structured. Previously, people had their statuses and occupations largely fixed at birth and had no real option other than to continue within their given stations in life—whether as peasant, noble, or king. But social, economic, and political factors were changing this; social mobility was increasing, and the Reformers found themselves speaking about a person's daily work at a time of considerable change. They utilized the notion of "calling" so that (ultimately, at least, in a developed form) it theologically legitimized the idea of personal choice while, at the same time, affirming God's role in this dimension of life. Thus, every person's work could be an expression of his or her Christian commitment, and God was vitally interested in it all. The Reformers, notably Luther and Calvin, stressed the religious nature of *all* work, not only the specifically religious, so that, according to their general mode of thought, one's calling or vocation could involve being a plumber or a pastor, a musician or a missionary, an accountant, a carpenter, a teacher or dentist.

But distinctions began to emerge, at least in some contexts, between calling and vocation. For some, a calling became a specifically religious vocation (pastor, priest, missionary, or religious). Certain other occupations could be a *vocation* but not a calling. This distinction is seen in the way the question, "Do you have a calling?" is taken as an inquiry about whether one is to enter "the ministry" of the church or not. Of course, it implies that others do *not* have a calling, although they may be considered—somewhat inconsistently—to have a vocation. The immediate problem is that there is a basic division in the spiritual value attributed to particular forms of work.

A degree of elitism also crept into the situation and continued the process of making distinctions where there ought to be none, so that only certain occupations could be considered a vocation. These were the professions that were no longer considered (by some at least) as a calling. Originally the professions (a work through which one "professed" one's faith) included only divinity, medicine, and law; but if the religious vocation becomes a separate calling, then that leaves, according to one view, the other professions defining the meaning of a vocation. However, with the advent of technology and specialization, the professions expanded to include other specialized bodies of knowledge. Although none of these professions are, according to the Reformation theology, any more religiously beneficial than farming, baking, cleaning, or laboring they have been seen by many as socially and, ultimately, spiritually, more significant. So the distinction between profession (loosely identified with a vocation) and occupation (non-professional "work") emerged.

This means that it becomes possible to distinguish between calling, vocation, profession, and occupation/work, but these distinctions produce some theologically unhelpful results. It means that calling absorbs the spiritual dimension of life so that occupation, profession, and often vocation tend to become secular concepts. And if the idea of God's call is limited to specifically religious occupations, then it implies that others do not have a call to do whatever it is that they do. This means that for most people their occupation is "a choosing" rather than a calling, and this leaves them with the concept of "careerism"—a view that expects people to seek what suits them best and to maximize financial success, security, and personal satisfaction with little or no reference to God.

Finally, there is the less-commented-upon effect that because only religious callings (which, in practice, primarily function within the gathered community) are fully spiritual, there is a tendency to focus on calling in terms of the gathered (rather than the scattered) life of the church in such a way as to exclude the majority of church members. Those who are called to a ministry within the church exercise spiritual gifts (they are, indeed, taken as evidence of a call from God), but those who do not have a call are not, generally at least, seen as exercising spiritual gifts in their life as part of the scattered church. They may exercise spiritual gifts as part of their ministry *within* the gathered life of the church, but spiritual gifting is, by and large, alienated from their professions or their occupations and the larger part of their lives that is spent as part of the scattered church.

What is required in response to this is not only a reaffirmation of the notion of calling for all people, but also a demonstration of the way the concept of a calling is revitalized when it is understood in terms of a calling to friendship with Christ and his friends. This, then, has significant implications for one's understanding of the exercise of spiritual gifts in the life of the scattered church.

Called to friendship

It is possible to see three stages in God's call. The first is the universal call to humanity to live and share in community, working harmoniously and creatively in the world that God has given us. The second is the call to be transformed by Christ, baptized, and commissioned to Christlike character and service. This is connected with the Great Commission, and it means making disciples of all, and teaching them to obey "everything" that Jesus commanded (Matt. 28:19–20). The third and most individually specific call is the calling each person has to his or her own particular ministry, work, family, and social roles and tasks. As the apostle Paul said, "Let each of you live the life that the Lord has assigned, to which God called you" (1 Cor. 7:17).

It is vitally important to understand Christian calling as a life to which we are called, rather than primarily as specific activities of some kind. Christ calls us to a relationship—a friendship—with him and with his other friends. This is the primary focus. Every person, every relationship, and every friendship is unique and important. These relationships certainly include different activities, including the exercise of various gifts and ministries and other occupations, but it is a mistake to turn what is secondary into what is primary. The gifts and occupations we engage in contribute to the relationship that is building between us and Christ and other friends of Christ—but it is the *relationship* that is primary. The problem of reversing the order is that it means that when it comes to considering one's call, many people struggle to determine precisely what it is, because they are trying to focus on some occupation or gifting that will define the nature of their calling when they should be focusing primarily on the nature of their relationship with Christ. Occupations and gifting are not unimportant, and they are expressions of the relationship to which Christians are called, but they are not to be equated with it. Gifting and occupation can change over time, according to circumstances, and can adapt as the individual matures and as God leads him or her.

One can certainly be called to a specific task as part of one's overall calling (and that will be discussed in the next section), but the fundamental call is to belong to Christ. Christians need to have a strong sense of this belonging before all else. This is illustrated in the descriptions of those called to be bishops and deacons in Ephesus, as described in 1 Timothy. In both cases, the focus falls upon the nature of the person rather than the gifts he exercises. A bishop is to have various qualities (including being above reproach, married only once, temperate, sensible, respectable, hospitable, gentle, a good parent, and humble) that seem to be far more prominent in Paul's thinking than the ability that is mentioned—being an apt teacher. And for deacons to serve, they need *qualities* rather than *abilities*: to be serious, not double-tongued; sober, not greedy; faithful and blameless (1 Tim. 3:1–13). That is, as regards our calling, it is who we are in relationship to God and others that counts. The proper end and purpose of being called is nothing other than entering into a relationship—a friendship—with Christ and his friends.

Friendship, spiritual gifts, and the scattered church

Though the concept of calling relates primarily to belonging to Christ, a secondary dimension involves a calling to the specific gifts of the Spirit that will function in a person's life. Unfortunately, the exercise of these gifts is often limited to operating within the life of the gathered church and thus seen as irrelevant to the life of the scattered church. This comes about as a result of the general tendency to focus on the church as gathered rather than as scattered, and also as a result of the emphasis placed on those gifts exercised by the ordained ministry and full-time Christian workers. The contemporary emphasis on the role of spiritual gifts through teaching, personal gift inventories, and so forth, has been very positive, but this wider awareness of the presence of the gifts of the Spirit has not affected the way the focus largely falls upon the role of the gifts within the life of the gathered community.

This is mainly because, whether intentional or not, the prime example for the exercise of spiritual gifts is that of pastors, priests, and other full-time workers—who function almost exclusively within the life of the gathered church. There is, of course, nothing intrinsically wrong with a person's gifting becoming his full-time occupation as a leader of the community life of a congregation, as is the case with priests and pastors, but it should be noted that, in New Testament terms, this is a somewhat abnormal situation. The apostle Paul (who, ironically, is usually taken as the main New Testament source for teaching on the gifts of the Spirit), for instance, insisted on supporting himself in his ministry through tent making (Acts 18:3). Again, it must be stressed that it is not wrong for the church to develop full-time ministry, and it is a good and useful thing to commission or ordain appropriate and gifted people as pastor, minister, priest, or deacon. Indeed, some of these ministries (at least in the way they are structured today) cannot, by their very nature, be exercised adequately without a public call and the recognition of the church community. But none of this provides a standard by which the exercise of all gifts should be measured. It is not the norm that a person's gifting leads to a calling to work in a full-time, remunerated position within the life of the community. Yet I would suggest that this is, implicitly, seen as the case.

On relating gift and occupation

The first effect of this is that churches are inhibited in helping people recognize God's calling on their lives. When the concept of calling is either limited to, or modeled by, the kind of calling a pastor receives, then it becomes very difficult for other people to recognize God's call on their lives. Consequently, churches tend not to commission other people to ministries in ways that would be appropriate for them. A congregation could well commission people to the exercise of their gifts and ministries (service, caring, teaching, healing, and so forth) within their occupations. And if a church does this, it definitely must *not* imitate the world and forget the calling of the unemployed, of parents, caretakers for the disabled, and the retired. They, too, are all called by God to minister with Christ Jesus. A call is not something reserved for ministers and missionaries. To assume this is to deprive the rest of the church of understanding their own calling to belong to Jesus Christ and minister with him.

So does this mean that the church should commission people to ministries of butchery and banking? That may sometimes be useful, but that is not what logically emerges from a discussion of the gifting of all believers. There is a very important distinction to make here. What the church should do is recognize in some way or another, whether formally or not, the gifts that people exercise *within* their occupations of butchery, banking, and, equally important, in homemaking, retirement, and unemployment. Note that it is a rare thing for gifting and occupation to be the same thing: it is generally only true in the case of ordained ministers. The essential dimension to be recognized is the spiritual gifting, which is universal among Christians, rather than just the occupation where these gifts could be used.

The distinction being made here is often blurred in popular teaching as, for example, when a preacher, speaking about spiritual gifts, noted that while some people were given the gift of being an apostle, a prophet, a pastor, or an evangelist, others were given the gift of being a teacher, a carpenter, an accountant, or a secretary. The point stressed was that each person should appreciate and use the gift that God has given him or her, and that no one should expect to have somebody else's gift. While there is some truth in the fundamental message, it also perpetuates an unhelpful misunderstanding. When the apostle Paul listed being an apostle, an evangelist, a pastor, a helper, or one who works miracles among the gifts of the Spirit, he *could* well have included occupations such as tent making, farming, carpentry, fishing, or shop-keeping. But he did not—because each of these is a different type of activity: an occupation. Spiritual gifts are specifically given for building people up, but they do not operate in a vacuum, and it is very possible for them to function within the person's occupation. As well as a gift or gifts, everyone has an occupation—the place where they spend much of their week. This can be a paid position, retirement, parenting, or even recovering from a long and serious illness.

Friendship and the scattered church

Spiritual gifts are limited if they are only seen as operative within the four walls of a church building or within the period of time in which we engage in church activities. God wants his people to be ministers all the time, and every Christian needs to consider how his gifting applies within his whole life. There are many ways that people can exercise their gifting of being pastors, apostles, prophets, healers, helpers, or workers of miracles in their workplaces, homes, or community organizations. The term *pastor*, for example, is not an exclusive designation (as though one person taking the title excludes others from sharing in the ministry). In all likelihood, the person usually called "pastor" in a church is completely unable to exercise that ministry in the workplace. Yet people need that kind of care, and they will only receive it if those Christians who share in that gift exercise it in the context of their daily lives. Some will teach within the confines of the gathered church. But others are gifted to be teachers of spiritual things in everyday life, through friendship and the myriad social interactions that take place down the street and in homes, offices, and workshops. And the only apostle that many people will come into contact with will be a Christian who is their friend, who lives next door, or who works on the same production line. God is at work in the world, and he calls us to befriend the world and share our gifts and our love.

Called to friendship

This approach also explains how a person's calling remains even when his or her occupation is taken away. A person's calling should be seen as living the life that the Lord has called you to (1 Cor. 7:17), which includes a life of holiness, exercising gifts and ministries, and fulfilling family and social responsibilities. But if it is simply equated with a particular occupation (whether being the pastor of a church or a dentist), then when this is taken away, God's calling has, apparently, finished. If vocation is nothing other than a career or a job, then retrenchment is not only a blow to one's identity but also to one's service to God, and retirement becomes a permanent loss of vocation and a sign of ever-increasing uselessness. But when calling is seen more broadly, then even an involuntary and perhaps unwelcome change of occupation is none-theless still an opportunity for the individual to be employed for God and a time to demonstrate character and exercise one's spiritual gifts. This is all possible because our calling is primarily to friendship with God in Jesus Christ, and to offering this friendship to others. Friendship is the concrete expression of the love that has to be the context within which all ministry is offered (1 Cor. 13:1–13). The Lausanne II Manila Manifesto notes that "witness takes place, by women and men, not only through the local church . . . but through friendships, in the home and at work . . . Our first responsibility is to witness to those who are already our friends, relatives, neighbors, and colleagues."

When witness is understood within the context of a genuine friend-ship, it becomes very clear that it is not just speaking gospel words, and not even just ministering to someone in word and deed, but it is engaging in a mutual relationship, living with a person, and receiving as well as caring and sharing. Messianic friendship of this kind is under-taken out of love. It is not aimed at manipulating the other, and it is not merely a utilitarian strategy. It is a genuine, reciprocal relationship that reflects the friendship offered to all by Jesus.

In short, the first challenge for a missionary church is to intention-ally focus on friendship as the basic means of mission. The second is to bring much more attention to the scattered dimension of the life of the church. The third is to help people understand their gifting and the role their occupations play in their lives and the way the two are related in terms of their call to be friends with Christ.

Virtue

Holy Friendship

10

Wesley viewed service to God and the pursuit of
holiness as the primary,
if not sole purpose of friendship.

JASON VICKERS[1]

Elizabeth was confined to home, so Janet, as many ministers
would do, visited her as a part of her pastoral responsibilities. She went to serve Elizabeth but discovered a relationship
that was deeper than that of either serving or even being served. She
observed, "The fact that Elizabeth was eighty-nine and confined to her
home and I was a thirty-nine-year-old with a hectic lifestyle—were
irrelevant. Elizabeth offered me the gift of holy friendship."[2]

Together Janet and Elizabeth engaged in spiritual conversation
and shared silences, they provided personal support and advice to one
another, and each benefited from the other's wisdom and understanding.
The distinction between servant and the one being served disappeared
and was replaced by the reciprocity and mutuality of friendship. While
Janet had offered service, she had discovered friendship. If we only ever

have a servant attitude, then we will miss most of what others can offer to us that can enrich and bless our spiritual lives.

There are a number of lessons in this encounter. Friendship can change our perception of "a problem" ministry. Janet's view of ministry with older, homebound adults changed as her friendship with Elizabeth developed. Images of "obligation" and "problems" were replaced with "friendship" and "gift." The relationship challenged the very common, impersonal, and disembodied notion of "old person." "How easy it is," she observes, "for us to visualize aging itself as pathological, a troubling concept we'd rather not think about"; but "what if ministry with home-bound older adults were a matter of developing friendship rather than tedious obligation?"[3] This involves a new perspective and is not just a matter of a moment, but a way of relating. It is important not to idealize friendship with older people, or any other ministry, but a shift from "problem" to "person" will always bring people closer together.

But the greater lesson concerns friendship itself, notably that it is a *reciprocal* relationship that changes both parties in the relationship, and that it can emerge in the most *unexpected* places. There are a number of factors that can lead us to overlook friendships with those who are different from us. There is the natural tendency to relate to those close to us, there is a general social expectation that we make friends with those who are like us, and there is sometimes a desire to be encouraged in our own spiritual life by those who are on a similar spiritual journey. This can limit the range of friendships we have, and it means that Christians tend to make friends with other Christians who are, socially, very similar to themselves. Indeed, the most common form of friendship within the church is not "holy friendship" as such, but rather a form of social friendship, much as the whole of Western society practices it. Holy friendship means sharing one's spiritual life with another, with Jesus as a mutual friend. This is the kind of friendship about which Paul spoke in his letter to the Philippians. This epistle is nothing if not a profound and challenging letter about the way Christians should live in the world as friends of one another (and not with envy or rivalry), as friends of God in Christ (who is our chief friend), and as those whose lives take the friendship of Christ to the world (a form of citizenship of heaven that determines how friendship is shown in the world today). The Philippians, Paul suggests, should follow his own example as he has demonstrated the virtues of true friendship (sharing with Christ in all things, especially suffering).

This chapter will, with reference to Paul's teaching, continue the theme of public friendship. The possibility of public friendship, as outlined in chapters 8 and 9, showed how it functioned from the point of view of the scattered church. The focus in this chapter is specifically on the development of virtue in holy friendships. It will consider the following:

1. Holy friendship as a virtuous relationship between individuals with Jesus involved. In this section, we see that it is a holy relationship that, through mutual encouragement and example, enhances virtue, transforms character, and forms people into the image of Christ.
2. Holy friendship as a form of social holiness. This section shows that the virtues that individuals develop can become the values that a society lives by. Thus, it is a relationship that can influence society and build the common good.

Holy Friendship and the family

It has been argued that in Philippians Paul utilized an existing rhetorical form for letters that were specifically written when one was not able to be personally present yet wanted to maintain or develop a friendship. Scholars have recognized the presence of this particular epistolary form and have classified Philippians as "a letter of friendship."[4] John White, for instance, analyzed 117 ancient letters and categorized them as letters of introduction and recommendation; letters of petition;

and family letters, out of which grew "cultivated letters of friendship." Others have argued that Philippians is better understood as a letter written to *family* rather than to *friends* because Paul used a sibling metaphor and aimed to create an atmosphere of family in his writing. But perhaps the choice of one or other is unnecessary and the distinction between the two approaches can be too finely drawn. The people to whom he was writing were really friends that Paul wanted to become a fictive or metaphoric family. The point is that friends are to be as close as family and to take on the qualities of a family. So it is both a letter of friendship and a family letter. The concept of "family friends" is well understood as those friends who hold a special place, with particular privileges in the life of a whole family rather than simply an individual. Paul used family language and the well-known classical friendship *topos* throughout the letter, especially in chapters 1, 2, and 4, to warn a church filled with envy and rivalry against pride and self-centered attitudes. He encouraged them to come together as friends in the Lord and, through doing that, to take on the nature of Christ Jesus (Phil. 1:15; 2:1–11; 4:2–3). The friendship motif is seen in the way he reminds them that friends rejoice together in their friendship (Phil. 1:4, 7, 25; 2:2, 17–18, 28–29; 4:1, 4, 10) for, as Aristotle says, "It is characteristic of a friend to rejoice for no other reason than because the other is rejoicing."[5] It is also noted, as in classical terms, that friends are of "one soul" and "in one spirit"[6] and that, as Cicero argued, friends "think the same thing" (Phil. 2:2; 4:2) and friends constitute a community (Phil. 1:5, 7; 2:2; 3:10; 4:14–15). The unity of friends is also seen in Paul's repeated use of the prefix *syn*, which stresses the nature of friends sharing in all things, especially joyfulness and struggle. The end result is, as Johnson says, that "no Greek reader could have missed Paul was talking about friendship."[7]

The classic understanding of friendship was, according to Aristotle, seen in three forms of friendship, and the epistle to the Philippians relates to, but modifies, each of them. In classical thought, there was utilitarian friendship, which probably would not be called friendship today, as it is focused on the way someone can be useful in business or social affairs. Then there was the friendship of pleasure, where people share in enjoyable activities or discourse; and finally there was the perfect friendship of virtue, in which friends develop virtue in the other and both seek the common good. Such friendship, especially the friendship of virtue, is marked by five characteristics: *goodness* (in perfect friendship there is a search for the common good that all may benefit from the relationship); *trust* ("it is among good men that trust . . . and all the other things that are demanded in true friendship are found"[8]); *equality* (whether in mutual pleasure or in developing virtue), *respect* (for the other in their own right, rather than only as the means to a personal end); and *justice* (both justice and friendship are actually "concerned with the same objects." The proverb, "what friends have is common property," expresses the fundamental truth that friendship involves justice in community).[9] By employing friendship terminology, Paul was implicitly affirming these virtues, which are important aspects of Christian friendship, but his purpose in writing about friendship was not to simply repeat well-known concepts. The Philippians did not fully describe Christian friendship, and Paul intended to show them the reason for this. He was intent on demonstrating to them a yet higher view, and in doing so, he also points us toward a more spiritual understanding of the way friendship operates between Christians. This is shown in the way he modified each of the three classic forms of friendship:

1. In discussing friendships of *utility*, he proposed a different approach to sharing material possessions.
2. In terms of friendships of *pleasure*, he offered a different perspective on the joy of friendship.
3. When it came to friendships of *virtue*, he proposed an even more extravagant list of virtues for true friends and a different way of

actualizing them. This transformation of virtue (and the changes to pleasure and utility) are outlined in the next three sections.

Holy friendship: being together in Christ

It is possible to observe Paul's transformation of the classical view of *a friendship of utility* by noting that when reading Philippians one cannot help but be struck by the apparent tangle that Paul got himself in when thanking the Philippians for their gifts to him. They had sent him, via Epaphroditus, gifts at a time when he was in "distress" (4:14), and while appreciative of this, he made it sound like an extremely qualified sort of thank-you. He expressed his appreciation for their gift not just once or twice, but three times. Each time he qualified his appreciation, as he was quite insistent (a) that he really did not need it, (b) that he was perfectly content without it, and (c) that he had not sought it (4:10–18), all of which sounds a little less than grateful to modern ears. But it was important to Paul that he clearly differentiated his understanding of the basis of their friendship in Christ from the friendship of utility described by Aristotle in which one is friends with those who are useful to you in one way or another. Paul was clear that usefulness was not the basis of his friendship with the Philippians. He was not writing to them because they had helped in the past and he was looking for further help in the future, and he was not writing because he owed them anything in return. And so he walked a difficult line between gratefulness and independence. Paul had a double lesson that he wanted the Philippians (and us) to understand: first, that Christian friendship is grounded on a relationship with God in Christ, and second, that the believer's life and strength come from God rather than from any other friend.

It is this view of the relative importance of God (the chief friend) and other friends that he wanted to make clear. It is not that a little help from one's friends is unimportant; it is just that our real help comes from God. And so Paul was prepared to express it in two sentences that seem to go together uncomfortably unless one understands the obligations of classic utilitarian friendship: "I can do all things through him who strengthens me. In any case, it was kind of you to share my distress" (Phil. 4:13–14).

The lesson is that a gift to Paul, or any other Christian, does not create an obligation on their part. Christian friendship is not *created by* the way a community shares its possessions; in fact, it is the reverse, in that the sharing should be seen as *the result of* friendship. In this way Paul *transposed the classic form of utilitarian friendship into a spiritual relationship*. Holy friendship is grounded in Christ and not any action of ours. So Christians should give freely and generously to others, but without expecting any return. And if someone does not have enough and others do not help him, this does not mean that the friendship is over. Instead, like Paul, learn to be content "in any and all circumstances" (Phil. 4:12). The equality of which Aristotle spoke is still a principle, but it is voluntary—a gift and not an obligation. It cannot be demanded. Inequality ought not to exist among Christians, but it cannot be legislated or compelled away. It is more important to note that "*God* will fully satisfy every need of yours" (4:19; emphasis added). However, those who do give to their friends will not find it a loss on their part; indeed, they will have "the profit that accumulates to your account" through generosity (4:17).

There is much to be considered, in light of this, in regard to financial relationships between Christians today. Significant inequalities exist in places, but there is also considerable sharing, and generous support is often provided freely to Christian ministries. The principles Paul put forward in his letter to the Philippians still have relevance today.

Holy friendship: rejoicing in the Lord

The second form of friendship, according to Aristotle, is friendship that shares in pleasure. This is what is most commonly understood as friendship—enjoying together the pleasure of diverse activities, such as sports and shopping, concerts, coffee, and conversation. Of course, good friends will then also share in their friend's times of difficulty and sadness, and this was intrinsic to the classic account of friendship as well. Paul, once again, utilized but transformed both of these dimensions—sharing both in pleasure and in suffering.

It was important for Paul that friendship included sharing in suffering (Phil. 1:7, 27, 29; 3:10; 4:3, 14). This was an important part of friendship with others ("it was kind of you to share my distress") and Christ (he wanted to know Christ, his resurrection, and "the sharing of his sufferings by becoming like him in his death," Phil. 4:14; 3:10). The emphasis placed on this sharing in Christ's suffering leads some to assume that suffering is *the* hallmark of being Christian. There are good reasons for this: it is a biblical attribute of believers that is quite distinctive; it connects us with Christ; and it resists the contemporary world's push toward self-satisfaction. So it is right to focus on suffering as an important theme, especially given that it is always in danger of being subsumed by the natural tendency to a preoccupation with power. But it is a mistake to focus on this alone and without reference to the joy that lies beyond the cross. Paul demonstrated the need to do this: in the very letter where he stressed suffering with Christ, he also spoke repeatedly of sharing in joy. It is, if anything, an even more prominent theme.

For Paul, joy and happiness are not to be denied, and just as one shares in suffering with both others and Christ, so, too, one rejoices in friendship with one another and in the Lord (Phil. 1:7; 2:2, 19; 4:4, 10). A holy friendship produces joy. It is this joy, and only this spiritual joy in the Lord, that makes Christian friendship a pleasure irrespective of the circumstances. In this way it fulfills, and even outshines, the second form of classic friendship as pleasure. In this higher form of friendship, it is not merely that friends can share in adversity *or* pleasure as determined by circumstances, but rather that one can rejoice *in* adversity because Christ is present in this friendship. This does not imply a mindless happiness that ignores the suffering of the world, or of one's friends, but it is also possible to know the joy of friendship with Christ. The ultimate goal of the Christian life is not suffering but the joy that comes from holy friendship with Christ.

Holy friendship: sharing in the fruit of the Spirit

In Philippians, Paul transformed not only the classic understanding of utilitarian friendship and friendship as pleasure but also the idea of friendship as the development of virtue. The highest form of classic friendship was a relationship focused on virtue and the common good, where one was encouraged in virtue by the teaching and the example of one's friend. This fit well with Paul's view of holy friendship in two ways.

First, it was important to learn from the example of Christ Jesus, with whom friends are encouraged to have the same mind, the same love, and the same humility. Adopting the humility and sacrifice that Christ demonstrated (Phil. 2:1–11) meant, quite radically, adopting virtues that were normally seen as appropriate for slaves, rather than for noble friends. In the classic Graeco-Roman context, friendship consisted of virtues such as courage, equality, and reciprocity. In a Christian context, the primary virtues are those nominated as "the fruit of the Spirit"—including, love, joy, peace, patience, kindness, goodness, faithfulness, gentleness, and self-control (Gal. 5:22–23)—and others—including grace, faith, hope, service, and so forth. It is possible to produce a much more extensive list of virtues that Scripture affirms, but Scripture itself nominates some as being of greater significance (Micah 6:8; 1 Cor. 13:13). These are theologically based values in the sense that God is the source and sustainer of them all. They are also specifically Christological virtues in that they are all demonstrated in the life of Christ. They include virtues that classic friendship saw as inappropriate but that are at the heart of Christian love.

Second, Paul encouraged the Philippians to learn from their other friends, with himself as an example. Paul established himself as a model for the Philippians to imitate. His determination to follow Christ and to press on toward the goal of the heavenly call should become theirs, and he nominated virtues that ought to be a part of their life that he said they had "learned and received and heard and seen in me"—that is, whatever is true, honorable, just, pure, pleasing, or commendable (Phil. 4:8–9). This is not arrogance or a misplaced sense of superiority. It is, as Paul showed, simply a cognition of maturity in faith, and part of the responsibility of Christian friendship (Phil. 1:27; 3:12, 15). It means learning not to focus on one's own goodness but on the way that God "is at work in you" (Phil. 2:13). It is a failure of friendship to not be willing to be taken as an example. Paul demonstrated his commitment to his friends. It was the kind of positive, enhancing friendship that Christians ought to adopt in order to build up friends, church, and society.

Holy friendship practiced

Holy friendship is not holy friendship if it does not actually build up holiness in oneself and one's friend. Holy friendship should bring about change. John Wesley saw very clearly the connection between holiness and friendship and was very concerned that his followers should understand this. By today's standards, his attitude toward friendship seems extreme. He established clear and detailed guidelines for friendships with both unbelievers and believers. He held that Scripture saw friendship with the ungodly as a sin in itself, but allowed that associations with them in business and for the sharing of the gospel were necessary. He provided guidelines for relations between the sexes and with lapsed Methodists. He even had concerns about friendship with believers (do not engage in friendship if they do not share one's spiritual passion; be sure the friendship is not going to detract from holiness in any way; do not love them too much), leading Jason Vickers to ask, "Are Wesley's extraordinary efforts to provide meticulous rules and guidelines to keep the Methodists from being overtaken by sin a form of wise counsel or of spiritual paranoia?"[10] While the specifics of the advice may not fit today, there is no doubting his fundamental motive—*a passion for holiness*. The reason for being wary of friendship with the ungodly was a concern that believers might unthinkingly adopt their way of life, and by that he did not simply mean obviously sinful behavior, but attitudes such as complacency with wealth, conformity, and a lessening in zeal for prayer. He was concerned about the subtlety of the influence, for "their spirit imperceptibly influences our spirit."[11] He was concerned about friendships with believers on the basis that even that which is good can detract from that which is best. Wesley understood that, at their deepest level, friendships should have no other aim than that of knowing and loving God and enhancing holiness. They should be entirely devoted to that task. Friendship with nonbelievers should focus on drawing them to Christ, and the purpose of engaging in friendship with believers was to love God more dearly. What Vickers describes as Wesley's main aim should be said of all Christian friends: "Wesley viewed service to God and the pursuit of holiness as the primary, if not sole purpose of friendship."[12]

Holy friendship and society

It is clear, then, that Christian friendship is specifically *holy* friendship, in that it is a mutual relationship that develops virtue and enhances holiness. For Wesley, holiness meant the indispensable necessity of having "the mind which was in Christ," and of "walking as Christ also walked."[13] Neither friendship nor holiness can be experienced by one person alone, and so, in that sense, they are both social qualities. But there is another sense of "social holiness" that focuses on the corporate life and values of a community in distinction from the virtues of the various individuals that make up the community. A society can, for instance, exercise justice in a way that is different from that of any of its individual members.

Civic virtue

This social dimension is found in the classic Graeco-Roman view of friendship. The qualities of goodness, trust, equality, respect, and justice referred to above were to operate both personally and publicly. They were the foundation for a flourishing common life as much as for an individual. Each city-state had its own particular virtues, but for Aristotle the ideal city combined justice and friendship as essential characteristics. Of course, this was an idealization, for the cities did not actually function as Aristotle would have liked them to. Important matters of life and occupation are neglected, and so "each man lives as he pleases," like the one-eyed Cyclops—seeing what is required for wife and children but neglecting broader matters of public concern.[14] Aristotle saw the various city-states as weak in commitment to virtue and the common good, and he believed that public, or civic, friendship was needed as the main part of the answer to this. In a similar manner, sometime later, Augustine of Hippo powerfully expounded on Christian virtues as the essential characteristics of the special city-state that was the city of God (*polei theou;* Heb. 12:22).

The present reality, however, is that this virtue-seeking, public dimension of friendship has been lost from the public sphere. Friendship has been privatized, and although it certainly exists everywhere, its place in public life is incidental. The friendships of public persons are not relevant to public life. Friendship is merely present as a personal adjunct to social life and not as an essential part of it. This is so much the case that there appears, to most people today, to be absolutely no connection between a personal relationship such as friendship and the very wide-ranging discipline of public theology where issues of justice, equality, freedom, and government prevail. Of course, anyone in the ancient world who was familiar with the writings of the philosophers would have immediately seen the connection between friendship and these themes. But that is generally not the case today.

However, the call for a shift toward a more explicit focus on friendship as a fundamental dimension of both the church and society does reflect the movement in social ethics that is often noted as beginning with Alasdair MacIntyre's *After Virtue: A Study in Moral Theory*. The connection between friendship and virtue comes to the fore here. MacIntyre argued that we live "after virtue," in that, modern, Enlightenment thought rejected the value of the classic moral tradition of virtue in favor of a search for a rational, objective foundation for morality. But this only led to what he famously described in terms of a catastrophe that destroyed most of the knowledge of the wisdom of the past and fragmented those pieces of understanding that remain. Now there is a proliferation of views that comes as a result of the expanding influence of individualism and the notion of the self as a rational, autonomous agent. In the light of this moral fragmentation, where a universal ethic is not possible and individualism leads to social chaos, "what matters at this stage is the construction of local forms of community within which civility and the intellectual and moral life can be sustained."[15]

The moral life of the community is grounded in virtue. While different cultures express the virtues—such as truth, courage, or friendship—in different ways, the simple fact is that no community can flourish without an affirmation of virtue. It is no doubt significant that MacIntyre turns to the virtues, including friendship, in the context of modern moral fragmentation in the same way that Aristotle turned to virtue and, even more explicitly, to friendship as civic virtues, in the light of the fragmentation of morality in Athens.

Friendship is *the* essential counter to the individualism and egoism of modern society. Individualism inevitably conceives of the good in individual terms and thus misunderstands the nature of a good life, which is not a thing to be possessed by an individual, but a life lived in joyful relationship. Without friendship, one may have a society but not a community. Rights and responsibilities are critical elements of every society because without them there would be complete social collapse, but they are not ends in themselves: the meaning and value of life is found in friendship, fellowship, and love.

Social holiness and prevenient grace

The term "social holiness" is frequently used with respect to John Wesley's well-known observation in the preface to the first volume of the Methodist hymnbook *Hymns and Sacred Poems*, that "the Gospel of Christ knows of no religion, but social; no holiness but social holiness. 'Faith working by love' is the length and breadth and height of Christian perfection."[16]

This is commonly connected with the historical reality that Methodism spoke out about the social injustices of the age, often interpreted as social justice and usually intended to be understood as one half of the phrase "personal and social holiness." However, while the intention is sound and it is true that Wesleyanism has a profound concern for social matters, it is likely that the phrase as used by Wesley in the hymnbook (and this is the only place he used it) should be interpreted as referring to the necessarily *social context* in which personal holiness is formed,[17] and thus to that which is discussed here in the previous section. Nonetheless, social holiness, in the sense of the corporate life of the community, is still a result of the work of the Spirit that ought to be expected as the result of the presence of divine grace and as an outworking of Christian virtue and the fruit of the Spirit. Although all traditions have a concern for the corporate life of the wider community, Wesleyanism's emphasis on prevenient grace provides a strong theological foundation for an expectation that society can be changed and transformed by divine grace, exercised through human discipleship.

M. Douglas Meeks remarked that "when sanctifying grace is applied to the economic and social structures of life, Methodism will experience another great revival."[18] Whether this optimism is justified or not, the prevenience of grace and the call to social holiness demands Christian involvement in evangelical, social witness, and action in regard to socio-political structures. The concept of the prevenience of grace provides a strong foundation for the relationship between the Christian community and the world. It means that God is at work in all parts of the world, and it means that God has enabled all people to receive the offer of salvation. God has not limited his love or excluded any from the possibility of receiving the grace of friendship. Through the friendship of believers, the love of God reaches out into society, bringing about personal and social transformation.

From virtue to value

This focus on friendship in the social domain directs attention toward the simple, though profound, everyday actions of friendship that influence the way society functions. Just as holy friendship builds individuals up, so, too, it can influence a community (both the church and wider society, albeit in different ways and to different extents). Communities, as well as individuals, can express virtues: an individual can be just, gracious, and caring (or unjust, greedy, and hateful), and so can a society. Consequently, a friendship model of engagement with the world looks at *developing attitudes* rather than *changing structures*. It is a very flexible approach that does not determine *a priori* the form of social or political structures because it can work with and within many of them.

When considering social mores, there is a tendency to refer to *values* rather than to *virtues*. While they are not exactly the same concept, they have a significant overlap, although, while the concept of virtues has diminished, the notion of values has increased. It is common today for all kinds of organizations to nominate their core values, but there is widespread reluctance to see anyone impose—or even propose—overall beliefs or values for others or society as a whole. But the attempt to avoid overall values really means replacing one set of values with another, such as the values of diversity, tolerance, and pluralism. This, in turn, accentuates the development of a multiplicity of values.

In a situation like this, what values can Christians offer? This is such an important question that there are any number of ways of avoiding it. Some models of engagement with society find it easier to leave this question aside and to focus intensively on single issues. But ultimately, every decision to act in a particular way needs to be grounded in some overall vision for society. Another way of avoiding the bigger issue is to simply agree with the notion that values are essentially personal, or are at least to be restricted to the life of a particular group. Some models of engagement assume that Christian values are for the church alone, and they have no expectation that society will adopt them or be interested in them.

But there are other models of engagement that seek to bridge the gap between church and world, and to bring to society what the church has to offer. They have a conviction that there are values that are not just personal and not just for the community of faith, but that are of value for society as a whole. These values are theologically and biblically derived, and they are capable of being explored at various levels of meaning or significance, including in ways appropriate for the wider community.

So, can the virtues that are understood to apply to individuals, such as love, joy, peace, patience, kindness, goodness, faithfulness, gentleness, self-control, grace, faith, hope, justice, and service, be expressed as public values? They are well understood in personal terms, but their public policy implications are not often addressed. It is generally assumed that any corporate value in these is simply what is achieved as the sum total of the behaviors of individuals, rather than as policies to be explicitly addressed. The exceptions that potentially demonstrate the falsity of this view are the virtues of peace, justice, and service. These are not only understood in terms of personal virtue, but also as public values that are strenuously sought. But it cannot be said that there is a widespread understanding of the public implications of virtues such as joy, patience, hope, gentleness, or kindness. And this is not because there are no such implications; it has more to do with the fact that they have not been recognized.

The value of values

What role is there here for developing the virtues of *generosity* in handling wealth, *equality* in public policy, and for refocusing the way to achieve *happiness*? Christian *joy*, to take a prominent example from Paul's letter to the Philippians, is not the same as happiness, but the concepts are connected. Being joyful is an important, though under-valued, Christian virtue. It is neglected as a social value. Joy is perhaps an old-fashioned word, but it expresses an important principle for indi-viduals, the community of faith, and wider society. God does not desire to have a joyless world or disspirited people. Joy is not just a by-product of other actions and values—it has significance in its own right. It is characteristic of the life of faith. It is a quality of being, rather than just an emotion; and so, although it is related to being happy, it is more fundamental than that and can be sustained when happiness is (hope-fully temporarily) diminished.

There is, of course, a theological foundation to Christian joy, just as there is to peace, justice, equality, and service. Joy comes from knowing God through Jesus Christ in the power of the Spirit. It also comes from participating in God's ministry in the world and seeing lives being positively changed and relationships enhanced. The theological founda-tions for the well-recognized public values of peace, justice, equality, and service do not prevent their acceptance by those of different or no faith. They are accepted on the basis that they can demonstrate in prac-tice their value to individuals and society as a whole. Those who lack conviction about the Christian foundation, or who have a completely different philosophical approach, may well present an alternative point of view about them, which can become a matter for public debate. But. But there can be an overlapping consensus as to what equity, justice, and peace involve. For instance, it has always been, in one sense, the aim of the modern, Western, liberal, democratic political system to enhance happiness and well-being, either directly through policy or legislation, or indirectly by creating the opportunity for people to seek it more freely. But well-being and happiness are not normally the explicit focus of policy or legislation, though they are the assumed end point of new policies, laws, or projects. However, sociological analysis and measurement of well-being and happiness are now to be utilized in directing government policy in a number of countries. The British prime minister, David Cameron, for instance, observed that while Western societies have seen fairly continuous growth in GDP, at the same time, levels of contentment have remained static or have even fallen. His government will start measuring progress "not just by how our economy is growing, but by how our lives are improving; not just by our standard of living, but by our quality of life."[19]

The aim is for the personal dimensions of happiness and well-being, which have always been of fundamental importance, to be more explicitly and directly located as guiding principles, rather than merely as implied outcomes. Clearly, there is scope here for aspects of Christian joy to infiltrate and influence secular concepts of well-being and happiness.

The same can surely be true of other Christian virtues, such as grace and hope, as they are practiced in the public sphere. There is great value for society in having a fundamental hope concerning life. *Hope* means that people are able to look beyond immediate problems and threatening scenarios and have confidence in God as the ultimate reality. Hope is not a guarantee that bad things will not happen, but it is a conviction that God has gone into the future before us and will always be with us. There are many aspects of our world that can cause people to despair. People worry about the threat of war, poverty, terrorism, environmental disaster, the spread of viruses, and the way technology such as genetic engineering may be used. Of course, in various parts of the world, many of these are not future projections but present realities. There are also many individual, personal problems that lead to despair over the future. Hope means having a realistic attitude toward the state of our world. It is not possible to deny either the present problems or the disastrous possibilities. But a friend, or a Christian community, that offers hope can encourage people to not overlook the many good and positive aspects of life. Hope sees many good things and people all around who are aware of God being at work in the world.

Again, there is a theological foundation. Christian hope is not just a subjective attitude, not simply positive thinking or looking on the bright side of life. It means having a trust in God, and believing that God is the Lord of all and is at work to bring about the future that he wants. Some will not want to adopt the theological foundation, and simple optimism is not the same thing. But if Christian hope can be demonstrated in public life as well as private faith, then those without faith may well be encouraged to consider it.

Grace can also be a social value. From a Christian point of view, it begins with the grace of God, but involves a calling for believers to express grace as a virtue in their own lives. The apostle Paul made the concept central to his theology and irrevocably tied it to the free gift of salvation that comes from God through Jesus Christ that works by creating faith (Eph. 2:5–8). In the life and death of Jesus of Nazareth, Christians see God at work. Jesus told stories about grace that have a powerful message. There was the father who welcomed the wayward son home again and the employer who made sure that even the late-coming workers got a full day's pay. In answer to the question about how often someone should be forgiven, the answer was "not seven times, but seventy times seven" (Matt. 18:22 NLT). In other words, don't bother counting. Grace is a social virtue that changes individuals, structures, and other assumed values. When grace is taken as a social virtue, it challenges other values, such as the most common contemporary understandings of tolerance and pluralism. This does not mean becoming less tolerant or more prejudiced, but recognizing that contemporary society has substituted the vague notion of "tolerance" for genuine grace. The idea of tolerating differences or certain groups of people or beliefs contains within it a begrudging acceptance of the right of a person or an idea to exist, while maintaining a stance of superiority. Grace is, at one and the same time, more accepting and forgiving of differences than mere tolerance, but it is also more transformative, seeking to change, enhance, and improve, rather than continuing to tolerate that which is personally or socially damaging. Christian virtues, when applied to society as a whole, are frequently culturally challenging as well as enhancing. These are only examples of the extensive possibilities for public life when Christian virtue is the primary content of Christian friendship and friendship is the principal vehicle by which virtue is formed.

PART V
The Future of Friendship

Destiny

The Meaning of Friendship for God

11

The grace of the Lord Jesus Christ, the love of God
and the friendship of the Holy Spirit be with you all,
evermore. Amen.

SEE 2 CORINTHIANS 13:13

Having come this far in our exploration of a theology of friendship, it seems that the imaginary gift book that was referred
to at the very beginning of chapter 1—the coffee-table book
filled with popular sayings about friendship and fine photographs of
smiling faces—was right in saying that "friends are the most important ingredient in this recipe of life." This providing, of course, that one
understands it as a spiritual friendship with God, who is, as Aquinas
said, our "chief friend." Friendship is, as C. S. Lewis reminded us, what
makes life worth living—but the meaning of this friendship has to be
informed by friendship with Jesus. It is *messianic* friendship that deepens
our relationships; it is a *transforming* friendship that is at the heart of our
understanding of the church; and as a *public* friendship, it is the foundation of mission and ministry to the world. Perhaps most important,

our friendship can become both a *holy* friendship that forms us into the image of God and an *eternal* friendship, for friendship with Jesus *is* salvation. That is, friendship with Jesus has implications that extend beyond this present life. Friendship with Jesus goes into eternity.

The most certain fact of life is that death comes to everyone. Those who have a friendship with Jesus will find in it great strength and encouragement in every situation and every stage of life, but especially in difficulty, pain, suffering, and death. Our friend Jesus is present when people have reached the end and know no other way out, no way of escape. As the hymn says, "What a friend we have in Jesus, all our sins and griefs to bear."[1] Our friendship with Jesus gives us courage for the present and hope for the future. It comforts us through death.

Death brings an end to every human friendship. The best friendship has a final conversation, a last time of sharing. One dies and one remains—a friendship separated by death. The disciples lost their friendship with Jesus when he was taken from them. Holy friendship, in its earthly form, is transient. Is this then the end of friendship altogether? Does death mean an end to love, affection, sharing, and special friendships? No, definitely not. Holy friendships extend beyond death. They may be, from the point of view of this world, interrupted, but they are able to be taken up again—although in a transformed way that is beyond our present comprehension. Perhaps it will be a world where friendship with all will be as enriching as the few particular and best friendships we have now.

But how can we know that our friendships will continue? After his death, the resurrected Lord Jesus returned to be with his friends for forty days (John 21; Acts 1:3). There were no public appearances during that time, but his friends knew him. He met with the two Marys, the disciples, and the five hundred in the garden, on the beach, in the country, at table, teaching, talking, eating together—their friendship continued and was not broken by death. No one need fear that friendship will cease forever.

Eternal life is nothing other than the life Jesus' friends share with him. This life is commonly thought of in terms of worship, rest, and the absence of pain and sorrow (Rev. 5:6–14; 6:9–17; 21:3–4; Heb. 4:9); but this "rest" is not mere inaction, and the absences are balanced by the positive presence of that which is holy, good, and reflective of the creative, life-giving character of God. This includes the continuation of holy friendships in the Lord. It is the Christian life intensified and perfected with good and creative activities and great joy and happiness. And holy friendship—living together in eternal friendship with God and his friends—is central to this precisely because it is important *to God*. This we can be sure of because the imagery of God as our Friend tells us, perhaps in a way that some other images of the divine-human relationship do not, that God values our friendship. The images of God as King and Master, Lord and Judge tell us much about both divine and human nature, but one could conceive of a King or a Judge as not having a personal interest in individual subjects or defendants. It is the very personal images of God, especially those of God as Father and Friend, that suggest that God cares about us and will not let us go.

The aim of this book has been to establish a biblical-theological foundation for spiritual friendship, and it has been shown that friendship means much to individuals and to the life of the church and society. So this one question remains: *what does friendship mean for God?*

Holy friendship and God

There is, one must concede, less that can be said about the inner life of God or the meaning of friendship for God than can be said about human friendship for God and others. Job reminds us of our limitations: "Can you find out the deep things of God? Can you find out the limit of the Almighty?" (Job 11:7). But a theology of friendship is not complete without some consideration of the meaning of friendship for God. I want to suggest that holy friendship is a significant relationship for God, without which God cannot be conceived as the Trinitarian God of Christian faith and thought.

Aelred pointed us in this direction, though he did not pursue it, in his declaration that "God is friendship." The importance of friendship between God and people is that this is a relationship that is not merely metaphorical, although, as noted earlier, all theological language is, in a general sense, metaphorical. But it is not the case that we have something "like" a friendship with God; we do indeed *actually have* a friendship with God. The term "friendship" is broad enough to encompass a divine-human relationship. And because of the kind of relationship that friendship is—an intimate, mutual, reciprocal relationship—it has definite meaning for God, or else it cannot be called a friendship. A completely one-sided relationship is not a friendship.

On the one hand, the inherent mutuality, the give-and-take between equals in all genuine friendships is, necessarily, a feature of friendship with God. But on the other hand, theological difficulties arise in a relationship with God that is characterized by equality and reciprocity. The equality that is an essential prerequisite for the depth of mutual sharing that good friendship involves seems to deny the transcendence of God, and the reciprocity of friendship implies that there must be something beneficial *for God* in the relationship, which seems to make God dependent upon the human other. It is the incongruity of these characteristics of friendship and the potential for it to detract from the essential differences in nature and status between God and humanity that has led some to question the appropriateness of using it as a primary model for relationship with God. In order not to diminish the understanding of God as transcendent Lord, some prefer that the relationship be expressed as master-servant, parent-child, king-subject, or in terms of some other unequal and nonreciprocal relationship.

Despite these theological issues, the early church gave room to the concept of friendship for two reasons. The first was the *biblical foundation* for friendship seen in the way in which Jesus, the incarnate Son of God, who presents to the world a window into the character and nature of God, related to his particular friends (such as the disciples, Mary, Martha, and Lazarus) and his general friends (the "sinners and tax-collectors" and all who followed him). The second was the way that *Trinitarian theology,* in the light of the incarnation, resisted philosophical notions of God as impassible and unchanging in every respect, and presented a view of a passionate, loving God. Friendship with God is impossible only if God is understood as one who has no need of others and who does not have the ability to feel joy or sadness or any other emotion as a result of the circumstances or feelings of their friends. Such a God, in fact, may be a Lord or a King but cannot be a Friend. But that would be a view based more on philosophical notions of what God can and cannot do or be, rather than on the radical and challenging biblical picture of a God who loves and cares for people, and who therefore is open to joy and delight in human life, as well as being open to disappointment, grief, and sadness.

Previous chapters explored the nature of the friendship between Jesus and his friends in terms of the implications for the friends, but now that the question is *What does friendship mean for God?*, it is helpful to briefly revisit it in order to view the other side of the relationship. The friendships that were experienced by Jesus were a real and authentic part of his incarnate life, but these are also an outworking of a principle of relationship that is related to the inner, or Trinitarian, friendship life of God as Father, Son, and Holy Spirit. And as we shall see, both the "outer" and "inner" expressions of divine friendship are related to the perfect future friendship that is the consummation of all friendship—human and divine. That is, these friendships have a future, a destiny, a *telos*, a purpose.

Jesus and his friends

What did friendship mean for Jesus? James Russell Miller was a Presbyterian pastor and author who wrote a number of popular devotional books. In 1897, he published *The Friendships of Jesus,* in which he explored the significance of friendship for both disciples and Jesus. He made some observations about the state of popular piety then that probably still apply today.

> We are apt to think of all the human life of Jesus as being in some way lifted up out of the rank of ordinary experiences. We do not conceive of him as having the same struggles that we have in meeting trial, in enduring injury and wrong, in learning obedience, patience, meekness, submission, trust, and cheerfulness. *We conceive of his friendships as somehow different from other men's.* We feel that in some mysterious way his human life was supported and sustained by the deity that dwelt in him, and that he was exempt from all ordinary limiting conditions of humanity.
>
> There is no doubt that with many people this feeling of reverence has been in the way of the truest understanding of Jesus, and ofttimes those who have clung most devoutly to a belief in his deity have missed much of the comfort which comes from a proper comprehension of his humanity.[2]

Was his experience of friendship different from that of others? Did Jesus really have a need or desire for human friendship? Did it fulfill some need for him, or was it purely a one-way relationship? Did it provide him with pleasure and enjoyment, or was it only a means by which to teach the disciples? Can we conceive, for example, of Jesus being tired of being away from home and wanting to get back to see John or Peter, Martha or Lazarus, and to be able to sit down and have a meal with them, and a laugh as well as a serious talk? Did he feel encouraged by them? Did he really care for personal relationships, and could he find, in this imperfect and sinful world, people who would truly be his friends?

If, in each of these cases, we consider the evidence in the Gospels, we will see that he did indeed appreciate and benefit from friendships in this way. He loved, was loved, and participated in a very human web of relationships. His friends contributed to his life, gave him companionship and pleasure, and supported his ministry. And, of course, it also means that he also suffered deeply as a result of the failures of friendship by those who were close to him and who should have done better at it. The conclusion is that we must not allow our awareness and appreciation of either his divinity or his universal love for all to overwhelm the thought that he had particular friendships that nourished his inner life.

The Christological principle of the incarnation—that God took human nature into the divine—tells us that God not only takes on the physical but also the emotional, the mental, and the relational dimensions of humanity. This surely includes all friendships, those experienced by the incarnate Christ and those experienced by the risen Christ through the mediation of the Holy Spirit. Is the life of God enriched by these friendships in some way that is analogous to the way friendships enrich our lives? The only possible answer is that this is, indeed, the case. The future of God, as we shall see, includes these friendships in consummated form. Friendship is part of the ultimate meaning of life. Friendship is important to God, who delights in friendships, rejoices with friends, and appreciates the activities that are shared together. All this is a part—perhaps the highest part—of God's experience of the created order.

The Trinity and holy friendship

These particular friendships are related to the inner, or Trinitarian, friendship life of God as Father, Son, and Holy Spirit. It is the doctrine of the Trinity that explains *how* it is possible that such friendly relationships between the incarnate Christ and his friends can exist. The fundamental theological statement that "God is love" is intimately connected with the understanding of God as Trinity. Love requires a relationship; it does not exist just on its own. It must be expressed by someone and received by another. Love simply could not exist if God were a solitary, undifferentiated being rather than the dynamic, loving community of Father, Son, and Spirit. Thus, love existed in divine friendship before the world was created. God did not need the world in order to be able to become love: the eternal, almighty God *is* love. This creative, outgoing love overflowed from the divine friendship and created the universe. This love then reached out to embrace and redeem humanity through the incarnation and friendship, and it continues to be inclusive, in that God now calls us to share in friendship and to be friends to others.

Friendship and love, therefore, do nothing less than define the very nature of the Trinity by specifying the inner relationships of God. In friendship with the world, God becomes committed and connected to people and voluntarily subjects himself to friendships that can be both enriching and frustrating. God participates fully in these relationships, and they are a part of divine experience. And this is no temporary state of affairs. After the incarnation, the Lord Jesus did not shrug off human nature and become again a God without human experience. The resurrected and ascended Lord Jesus has taken humanity into the divine life; and through the Holy Spirit, who unites us to Christ, it is possible to have a friendship with God. Friendship is not incidental for God; it is an essential part of God's creative and dynamic nature.

The future of holy friendship

A complete definition of holy friendship will not only answer the questions dealt with in earlier chapters ("What does a holy friend *do*?" and "What *is the nature* of a holy friendship?") and the question of the significance of friendship for God, but will also address the teleological question, "What is the future, the end, *the purpose* of holy friendship?"

It is often said that when Albert Einstein, one of the twentieth century's most quoted intellectuals, was asked "What is the most important question facing humanity today?" his reply was that it was finding an answer to the question, "Is the universe a friendly place?"

Unfortunately, this is a case of misplaced attribution because Einstein had nothing to do with this question or the alleged answer.[3] But even allowing for this mistaken attribution, the question is a useful tool with which to reflect, not only on the friendliness or otherwise of the universe, but also the reasons for our own fundamental attitude toward life and those around us. Will we live in fear? Do we live expecting threats? How far can our own friendship extend? And to what extent ought we to expect friendship from those around us?

This question of the friendliness of the universe is connected with the debate about what is called "the anthropic principle." The basic idea is that the universe is actually the result of the interaction of four very fundamental forces that are so finely tuned as to make it utterly astonishing that humanity ever came into being. The rate of expansion of the universe is so finely calibrated to allow for expansion: too fast and it would be unstable; too slow and basic elements like carbon simply would not emerge at all. Similarly, increasing the strong nuclear interaction by a very minute amount would make it impossible for any of the known chemical elements to form. But decreasing it by an even smaller amount would produce carbon atoms that would be unstable. This is not an argument that the universe looks as though it has been designed by God, but rather an argument that says simply that the universe is so amazingly constructed that it looks as though it was specifically oriented toward the emergence of human life. And it is possible to add to this argument from other fields as well. For example, it is argued that consciousness is intrinsic to the way things are. One of the world's leading biologists, Simon Conway Morris, maintains that "the emergence of human intelligence is a near-inevitability."[4] The question being debated in many circles today is whether an anthropic principle lies at the heart of what the universe is about.

With the eye of faith, I would suggest that when looked at this way, the issue is framed too narrowly. If the anthropic principle has validity, it is only as a part of what I would call the ecclesial principle. That is, the universe is not merely focused on producing sentient, rational beings; it is oriented much more fundamentally toward producing an ecclesia, a community of people, a church, an eschatological community of people who are united in friendship with Christ in one body. This is what the apostle Paul expounded in the first chapter of Ephesians. That God chose us, predestined us, redeemed us, and

> made known to us the mystery of his will according to his good pleasure, which he purposed in Christ, to be put into effect when the times will have reached their fulfillment—to bring all things in heaven and on earth together under one head [*anakephalaiosis*], even Christ. (vv. 9–10 NIV)

This is the ecclesial principle: a gathering of all things together in Christ, which is the aim, the goal, of creation. He described the mystery that is revealed as *anakephalaiosis*—a word that only occurs twice in the New Testament. It has the sense of "bringing things together" so that it can be translated "that he might gather together in one all things in Christ" or "to unite all things in him." The only other New Testament occurrence of this expression is in Romans, where Paul says that all the commandments of the law are *summed up* in this one rule: "Love your neighbor as yourself." If we draw a parallel here, we might say that just as Romans 13:9 shows that all that is true, meaningful, and significant for human discipleship in the myriad principles and commandments of the law is expressed in one single command, so Ephesians 1:10 shows how all of God's truth, goodness, and purpose that are found throughout the various elements and dimensions of the universe are summed up in union—let us say friendship—with Jesus Christ.

The answer, then, to the question that has been asked is that the universe is a fundamentally friendly place. Human destiny is bound up with being called into friendship with Jesus. This certainly tells us that friendship is important, not only to us, but also to God, for it is God's destiny and future as well as ours. We are to live together with God in eternal friendship. This is, as Paul exclaimed in the first chapter of Ephesians, "To the praise of his glorious grace[!]" (v. 6).

The "end" of friendship

It would be exciting to be able to say more about this future friendship, but what it is like is yet to be revealed. As Paul said, "For now we see in a mirror, dimly, but then we will see face to face" (1 Cor. 13:12). Happily, by expressing it in this way, Paul reminds us of the way that the final revelation of God will be like the revelation of Yahweh to Moses—"face to face, as one speaks to a friend" (Ex. 33:11). This "friendly" revelation, however, is an experience for the future. But we can be assured that it will be a continuation—albeit transformed and perfected—of our present friendship with Jesus. Yes, the best *is* yet to be!

In the meantime, my dear friends, there is little more to be said here. I thank you for sharing in this journey with me, and I pray that it has been, in some small way, a blessing to you. But now we have come to the "end"—and we have done so in more than one sense. Having reflected on the history of friendship, its biblical foundation, its theological meaning, and its spiritual significance, we have come to the end of this theology of friendship. But there can be no better place to end than this, for we have also come to the final end, or purpose, of life by being able to see holy friendship as the ultimate purpose of God, an eternal relationship of love that draws all things in heaven and on earth into union with Christ Jesus.

N O T E S

Chapter 1—Overture: The Changing Face of Friendship

1. Aristotle, *Nicomachean Ethics*, trans. Terence Irwin (Indianapolis: Hackett, 1985), bk. 9, chap. 8.

2. C. S. Lewis, *The Four Loves* (London: Collins, 1960), 67.

3. Michel de Montaigne, "Of Friendship," in *The Complete Essays of Montaigne*, ed. Donald M. Frame (Palo Alto: Stanford University Press, 1958).

4. L. M. Montgomery, *Anne of Green Gables*, 1st ed. (Toronto: Seal Books, 1983), chap. 8.

5. Ralph Waldo Emerson, "Friendship," in *Essays—First Series* (Charleston, SC: BiblioBazaar, 2008), 111–26; Elizabeth Telfer, "Friendship," *Proceedings of the Aristotelian Society* 71 (1970): 223–41; Lewis, *The Four Loves*, 55–84.

6. Groucho Marx, "To Gummo Marx," in *The Norton Book of Friendship*, eds. Eudora Welty and Ronald Sharp (New York: Norton, 1991), 58.

7. Montaigne, "Of Friendship."

8. John Ibson, *Picturing Men: A Century of Male Relationships in Everyday American Photography* (Washington, DC: Smithsonian Institution Press, 2002).

9. Miller McPherson, Lynn Smith-Lovin, and Matthew E. Brashears, "Social Isolation in America: Changes in Core Discussion Networks over Two Decades," *American Sociological Review* 71, no. 3 (June 1, 2006): 353–75.

10. One of the most influential books on this topic in recent times has been Robert D. Putnam, *Bowling Alone: The Collapse and Revival of American Community* (New York: Simon and Schuster, 2000). It produced a raft of responses that pointed to the complexity and diversity of the issue.

11. Liz Spencer and Ray Pahl, *Rethinking Friendship: Hidden Solidarities Today*, illustrated ed. (Princeton University Press, 2006).

12. Liz Carmichael, *Friendship: Interpreting Christian Love* (London: T. and T. Clark International, 2004), 32.

13. Aelred of Rievaulx, *Spiritual Friendship*, trans. Mary Eugenia Laker (Kalamazoo: Cistercian Publications, 1977).

14. Thomas Aquinas, *The Summa Theologica of St. Thomas Aquinas*, 2nd ed. (Trans. Fathers of the English Dominican Province, 1920), part II–II, on 27.8.

15. Alasdair MacIntyre, *After Virtue: A Study in Moral Theory* (Notre Dame: University of Notre Dame Press, 1981).

16. Søren Kierkegaard, "You Shall Love Your Neighbour," in *Other Selves: Philosophers on Friendship*, ed. Michael Pakaluk (Indianapolis: Hackett, 1991), 236; however, Lippitt argues that Kierkegaard has been misunderstood in this regard. John Lippitt, "Cracking the Mirror: On Kierkegaard's Concerns About Friendship," *International Journal for Philosophy of Religion* 61, no. 3 (June 2007): 131–50.

17. Ambrose of Milan, "Three Books on the Duties of the Clergy," in *Nicene and Post-Nicene Fathers*, 2nd series, vol. 2, bk. 3 (n.d.), chap. 21.

Chapter 2—Beginning: No Longer Servants

1. Richard Gillard, "The Servant Song," Scripture in Song/Maranatha Music, 1977.

2. Graham Kendrick, 'From Heaven You Came (The Servant-King)."

3. "Jesus, Friend of Little Children." Words: Walter Mathams, 1882. Music: William Griffith.

4. As in Mark 10:42–43: "You know that among the Gentiles those whom they recognize as their rulers lord it over them . . . But it is not so among you; whoever wishes to become great among you must be your servant."

5. See John 1:29, 36; 12:38. Also see Mark 10:43 compared with Isaiah 53:11–12; Luke 4:16–20 compared with Isaiah 61:1–2; and Matthew 12:15–21 compared with Isaiah 42:1–4. Steve Moyise and Maarten J. J. Menken, *Isaiah in the New Testament: The New Testament and the Scriptures of Israel* (London: Continuum, 2005).

6. Aristotle, *Nicomachean Ethics*, trans. Terence Irwin (Indianapolis: Hackett, 1985), bk. 8, chap. 11.

7. Robert K. Greenleaf, *Servant Leadership: A Journey into the Nature of Legitimate Power and Greatness*, 25th ed. (New York: Paulist Press, 1977).

8. Craig Blomberg, *1 Corinthians* (Grand Rapids: Zondervan, 1994), 257.

9. Janet O. Hagberg and Robert A. Guelich, *The Critical Journey, Stages in the Life of Faith*, 2nd ed. (Salem, WI: Sheffield, 2004), 113.

10. As, for example, seen in the four stages of the Christian life described in *The Cloud of Unknowing* (ca. 1370) which necessarily involves a monastic life. It describes the four stages as being Common ("living with your friends in the world"), Special (participation in religious orders), Solitary (the essence

of monasticism), and Perfect (true contemplation, humility, and love, a single-minded focus on God). Anonymous, *The Cloud of Unknowing and Other Works*, trans. Clifton Wolters (Harmondsworth, UK: Penguin, 1978), 58.

11. Aelred of Rievaulx, *Spiritual Friendship*, bk. 2, par. 14.

12. Ibid., par. 15.

Chapter 3—Growing: Friends of the King

1. There is some variation in the translation of the Hebrew word for "friend." While the NEB refers to Ahuzzah as "a friend of the king" (Gen. 26:26) the NRSV prefers to use "adviser" while the NIV uses "personal adviser." The NRSV ultimately agrees with the NEB when both translate the same Hebrew term in 1 Kings 4:1–6 as "king's friend" and in 1 Chronicles 27:32–34 the NRSV, NEB, and NIV have "King's Friend" and "king's friend." The context supports this translation.

2. Associated Press, "In Obama's Shadow, Friends Serve Key Role," *CBS News*, February 23, 2010.

3. James 2:21–23; emphasis added. In saying this James connects the Genesis account of Abraham's faithfulness (where Abraham is not actually described as a friend of God, Gen. 22:9–19) with a prophecy of Isaiah in which he describes the children of Israel as *"the offspring of Abraham, my friend"* (Isa. 41:8–10, emphasis added).

4. Flavius Josephus, *The Works of Flavius Josephus*, trans. William Whiston (Peabody, MA: Hendrikson, 1987), 15.6.7.

5. Eg., Sallie McFague, *Metaphorical Theology: Models of God in Religious Language* (Minneapolis: Fortress Press, 1982); John Hick, *The Metaphor of God Incarnate* (Louisville: Westminster John Knox Press, 1993).

6. McFague, *Models of God*, 34.

7. C. S. Lewis, *The Four Loves*, 73.

8. Ibid., 75.

9. Ibid., 81–82.

10. D. A. Carson, *The Gospel According to John* (Leicester, UK: Apollos, 1991), 522.

11. Ibid., 522.

12. Aristotle, *Nicomachean Ethics*, bk. 8, chap. 7.

13. It may be referred to as "Ben Sira" or "Sirach" or "Ecclesiasticus." It is a Hebrew writing that is not part of the Hebrew Scriptures and is deuterocanonical according to the Protestant tradition, but it is a part of the Catholic canon. See especially 6:5–17; 9:10–16; 13:15–23; 19:13–17; 22:19–26; 27:16–21; 37:1–6.

14. Gregory of Nyssa, *The Life of Moses* (Mahway, NJ: Paulist Press, 1978), 137.

15. Gary Lyons, *The Age* (Melbourne: Fairfax, September 18, 2010).

16. Dietrich Bonhoeffer, *The Cost of Discipleship*, rev. ed. (New York: Macmillan, 1959).

17. John Calvin, *Institutes of the Christian Religion* (London: Westminster Press, 1961), 494–502.

18. Jurgen Moltmann, *Open Church: Invitation to a Messianic Lifestyle*, 1st ed. (London: SCM Press, 1978), 54–57.

19. Aristotle, *Nicomachean Ethics*, bk. 9, chap. 8.

Chapter 4—Learning: God Is Friendship

1. Justin Martyr, "Dialogue with Trypho," in *The Apostolic Fathers with Justin Martyr and Irenaeus*, ed. Philip Schaff, Ante-Nicene Fathers (Grand Rapids: Eerdmans, 1980), chap. 8.

2. Ibid., chap. 28.

3. Clement of Alexandria, "Exhortation to the Heathen," in *Fathers of the Second Century*, vol. 2, eds. Alexander Roberts, James Donaldson, and A. Clevland Coxe, The Ante-Nicene Fathers (Grand Rapids: Eerdmans, n.d.), chap. 12.

4. From H. Chadwick, *The Sentences of Sextus* (Cambridge, UK: Cambridge University Press, 1959); cited by Steve Summers, *Friendship: Exploring Its Implications for the Church in Postmodernity* (London: T & T Clark, 2009).

5. Liz Carmichael, *Friendship: Interpreting Christian Love* (London: T. and T. Clark International, 2004), 70.

6. Marcus Tullius Cicero, *De Officiis*, Loeb Classical Library, trans. Walter Miller (Cambridge: Harvard University Press, n.d.), chap. 5.

7. Ibid., chaps. 6 and 7.

8. Which were ultimately derived from Plato's *Republic* Book IV and adopted by the Stoics.

9. Ambrose of Milan, "Three Books on the Duties of the Clergy," in *Nicene and Post-Nicene Fathers*, vol. 10, 2nd series, n.d., bk. I, chap. 28, par. 133.

10. Carmichael, *Friendship*, 48.

11. "Hence arises true love, which prefers others to self, and seeks not its own, wherein lies the pre-eminence of justice." Ambrose of Milan, "Three Books on the Duties of the Clergy," bk. I, chap. 27, par. 127.

12. Ibid., chap. 21; chap. 22, par. 127. With my comments in parentheses.

13. Ibid., chap. 22, par. 132.

14. Douglass Roby, "Aelred in the Tradition of Monastic Friendship," in *Spiritual Friendship*, trans. Mary Eugenia Laker (Kalamazoo: Cistercian Publications, 1977), 37. Also see A. Fiske, *Friends and Friendship in the Monastic Tradition* (Cidoc Cuaderno: CIDOC, 1970).

15. Anselm, "Cur Deus Homo," in *St. Anselm*, trans. S. N. Deane (Chicago: Open Court Publishers, 1926), bk. 2, chap. 6.

16. Aristotle, *Nicomachean Ethics*, bk. 9, chap. 4.

17. Anselm, "Epistle 16: To Henry," in *Cur Deus Homo: To Which Is Added a Selection from His Letters* (Charleston, SC: BiblioBazaar, 2009), 30.

18. John Henry Newman, *Lives of the English Saints*, vol. 14 (London: James Toovey, 1845).

19. Aelred of Rievaulx, *Spiritual Friendship*, bk. 1, par. 11.

20. Ibid., par. 1

21. Ibid., par 21. Compare with Cicero, *On Friendship*, 81, 92.

22. Ibid., bk. 2, par. 20.

23. Jonathan Edwards, *Christian Love and Its Fruit* (Lafayette, IN: Sovereign Grace Publishers, 2000), 10.

24. Aelred of Rievaulx, *Spiritual Friendship*, bk. 2, par. 19.

25. Ibid., bk. 1, par. 32.

26. Ibid., bk. 1, par. 59.

27. Ibid., bk. 3, par. 2.

28. Ibid., bk. 1, pars. 8, 10.

29. Ibid., bk. 1, par. 68.

30. Ibid., bk. 1, par. 70.

31. However, Johnson is not recorded as ultimately repudiating Mrs. Knowles's arguments to the contrary, which utilized the fact of Jesus' own friendships. James Boswell, *The Life of Samuel Johnson* (New York: George Dearborn, 1833), 168.

32. Anders Nygren, *Agape and Eros* (Philadelphia: Westminster Press, 1953).

33. As noted earlier he said, "Friendship is unnecessary, like philosophy, like art . . . It has no survival value; rather it is one of those things which give value to survival." C. S. Lewis, *The Four Loves* (London: Collins, 1960), 67.

34. My emphasis. "Love of Relations and Friends" in John Henry Newman, *Parochial and Plain Sermons*, vol. 2 (London: Longmans, Green, 1908), 54.

35. Newman, *Parochial and Plain Sermons*, 2:57.

36. The exclusivity and uniqueness of the marriage relationship give way to the believer's new, unique, spiritual marriage to Christ. This, however, does not mean a complete end to the relationship between those married in this world. It is theologically appropriate to believe that there will be ongoing, personal relationships in eternity—transformed, enriched, and perhaps even more extensive—but with the proviso that the one unique relationship a person has is with Christ.

37. Aelred of Rievaulx, *Spiritual Friendship*, bk. 3, par. 134.

38. Cicero, *De Officiis*, 1.51.

39. Ambrose of Milan, "Three Books on the Duties of the Clergy," bk. 1, chap. 15, 38–39.

40. John Cassian, "The Conferences of John Cassian," in *Nicene and Post-Nicene Fathers*, vol. 11 (Peabody: Hendrikson, 1999), Conference 11, chap. 7.

41. Ibid., Conference 1, chap. 4.

42. Ibid., Conference 1, chap. 8.

43. Ibid., Conference 1, chap. 7.

44. Ibid., Conference 11, chap. 8; and Conference 16, chap. 13.

45. Ibid., Conference 16, chap. 14.

46. Anna Silvas, *The Asketikon of St. Basil the Great* (Oxford University Press, 2005), 234.

47. Cassian, "The Conferences of John Cassian," Conference 16, chap. 11.

48. Ibid., Conference 1, chap. 6.

49. Aelred of Rievaulx, *Spiritual Friendship*, bk. 1, par. 38.

50. Ibid., par. 44.

51. Ibid., pars. 45 and 61.

52. Ibid., bk. 3, par. 85; bk. 2, par. 13.

53. Ibid., bk. 3, pars. 101–2.

54. Ibid., bk. 3, pars. 101, 104, and 106; bk. 2, pars. 38–40.

55. Ibid., bk. 2, par. 61.

56. Ibid., bk. 2, par. 14.

Chapter 5—History: The Privatization of Friendship

1. He makes no reference to *Spiritual Friendship* (or to Cicero's *On Friendship*). Nathan Lefler, *Saint Aelred of Rievaulx and Saint Thomas Aquinas on Friendship: A Comparison of Monastic and Scholastic Theology* (Washington, DC: Catholic University of America, 2008), 133.

2. Thomas Aquinas, *Summa Theologica*, 1920, part II–II, on 28.8.

3. See, for example, David Konstan, *Friendship in the Classical World* (Cambridge: Cambridge University Press, 1997); and John Fitzgerald, ed., *Friendship, Flattery, and Frankness of Speech: Studies on Friendship in the New Testament World* (Leiden, Neth.: E. J. Brill, 1996).

4. Aristotle, *Nicomachean Ethics*, bk. 8, chap. 3.

5. Ibid., bk. 9, chaps. 4 and 8.

6. Ibid., bk. 9, chap. 9.

7. Ibid., bk. 8, chap. 7.

8. Ibid.

9. Ibid., bk. 9, chap. 1.

10. Alasdair MacIntyre, *After Virtue: A Study in Moral Theory* (Notre Dame: University of Notre Dame Press, 1981).

11. Graham Little, *Friendship: Being Ourselves with Others* (Carlton North, Australia: Scribe Publications, 2000), 12.

12. Montaigne, "Of Friendship," 141.

13. Ibid., 128.

14. Francis Bacon, "Of Friendship," in *Other Selves: Philosophers on Friendship*, ed. Michael Pakaluk (Indianapolis: Hackett, 1991), essay 27.

15. Bacon, "Of Friendship," 207.

16. Michael Pakaluk, *Other Selves: Philosophers on Friendship* (Indianapolis: Hackett Pub. Co., 1991), 200.

17. Henri J. M. Nouwen, *Out of Solitude: Three Meditations on the Christian Life* (Notre Dame: Ave Maria Press, 1984), 38.

18. Immanuel Kant, "Lectures on Ethics," in *Other Selves: Philosophers on Friendship*, ed. Michael Pakaluk (Indianapolis: Hackett Publishing, 1991), 210–17.

19. Søren Kierkegaard, "You Shall Love Your Neighbour," in ibid., 233.

20. Kierkegaard, "You Shall Love Your Neighbour," 236.

21. Ibid., 238.

22. Jacques Derrida, *The Politics of Friendship* (London: Verso, 2005).

23. Ibid., 284.

24. Georg Simmel, *Sociology: Inquiries into the Construction of Social Forms*, vol. 1, trans. A. J. Blasi et al. (Leiden, Neth.: Brill, 2009), 307.

25. Georg Simmel, "Friendship, Love and Secrecy," in *The Substance of Sociology: Codes, Conduct and Consequences*, ed. Ephraim Mizruchi. (New York: Meredith, 1973), 167.

26. Ibid., 168.

27. Ibid., 167.

28. Putnam, *Bowling Alone.*

29. Liz Spencer and Ray Pahl, *Rethinking Friendship: Hidden Solidarities Today,* illustrated ed. (Princeton University Press, 2006).

30. Ibid., 203.

31. Carmichael, *Friendship*, 34.

32. Aquinas, *Summa Theologica*, part II–II, on qn. 27, art. 8, ob. 2.

33. Thomas Aquinas, *Commentary on the Sentences*, bk. III, d. 27, qn. 2, a. 1–4.

34. The Council of Trent, The Sixth Session, Decree on Justification, chaps. 7 and 10. Carmichael, *Friendship*, 126.

35. In 1932 Karl Barth (1886–1968) began his *Church Dogmatics* with a volume on "The Doctrine of the Word of God" which showed that "the doctrine of the Trinity itself belongs to the very basis of the Christian faith and constitutes the fundamental grammar of dogmatic theology." This is the editors' description of G. W. Bromily's English translation of Karl Barth, *Church Dogmatics,* eds. G. W. Bromily and T. F. Torrance (Edinburgh: T. and T. Clark, 1936), vol 1, part 1, ix.

Chapter 6—Church: Transforming Friendship

1. Peter Atkinson comments, "Evidently there was a profound and publicly acknowledged relationship between them. Their collegial, clerical and celibate status was clearly no barrier to this." Peter Atkinson, *Friendship and the Body of Christ* (London: SPCK Publishing, 2004), 35–36.

2. This prayer is found as part of a liturgy in the eighth-century MS Barberini 336, and the translation and Greek text can be found in John Boswell, *Same-Sex Unions in Premodern Europe* (New York: Vintage, 1995), 295.

3. Claudia Rapp, "Ritual Brotherhood in Byzantium," *Traditio* 52 (1997): 298.

4. See the acknowledgments in the unpublished thesis by Peter Drobac, "Christian Friendship and Adelphopoiesis" (New York: St Vladimir's Orthodox Theological Seminary, 2004).

5. Paul J. Wadell, *Friendship and the Moral Life* (Notre Dame: University of Notre Dame Press, 1989), xiii.

6. Jeremy Corley, *Ben Sira's Teaching on Friendship* (Providence: Brown Judaic Studies, 2002).

7. Nathan Solomon, "David and Jonathan in Iraq," in *Probing the Frontiers of Biblical Studies* (Eugene: Pickwick, 2009), 21–32.

8. Ibid., 30.

9. Ibid., 32.

10. Plato, *Republic* 424a; Aristotle, *Nicomachean Ethics* 1159b, 116b; and also in Plutarch, Cicero, Seneca, Philo, and others.

11. A. C. Mitchell, "The Social Function of Friendship in Acts 2:44–47 and 4:32–47," *Journal of Biblical Literature* 111 (1992): 255–72.

12. Christine D. Pohl, *Making Room: Recovering Hospitality as a Christian Tradition* (Grand Rapids: Eerdmans, 1999), 62.

13. John Fitzgerald, ed., *Friendship, Flattery, and Frankness of Speech: Studies on Friendship in the New Testament World* (Leiden, Neth.: E. J. Brill, 1996).

14. Douglas Hume, *Friends of God: Portrayals of the Early Christian Community in Acts 2:41–47 and 4:32–35* (Princeton: Princeton Theological Seminary, 2009), 185.

15. Hume, *Friends of God*, 188. The original makes reference to Acts 2:39; 2:38; 3:19; 3:20; 3:21; 3:16; and 4:12.

16. Pohl, *Making Room*, 73.

17. James M. Houston, *The Transforming Friendship: A Guide to Prayer* (Vancouver: Regent College Publishing, 2010).

18. Clement of Alexandria, "Exhortation to the Heathen," chap. 12.

19. Richard Heitzenrater, "The Imitatio Christi and the Great Commandment: Virtue and Obligation in Wesley's Ministry with the Poor," in *The Portion of the*

Poor: Good News to the Poor in the Wesleyan Tradition, ed. M. Douglas Meeks (Nashville: Kingswood, 1995), 54.

20. Benjamin Jowett, *Sermons on Faith and Doctrine* (London: John Murray, 1901), "Sermon on Friendship," 351.

21. Ben Witherington III, *Grace in Galatia* (Edinburgh: T. and T. Clark, 1998), 280.

22. Richard N. Longenecker, *Word Biblical Commentary*, vol. 41, *Galatians* (Nashville: Thomas Nelson, 1990), 157.

23. Richard Wilkinson and Kate Pickett, *The Spirit Level: Why More Equal Societies Almost Always Do Better* (London: Allen Lane, 2009), 76.

24. Ibid., 84; and also see chapter 6.

25. Jürgen Moltmann, *The Church in the Power of the Spirit: A Contribution to Messianic Ecclesiology* (New York: Harper and Row, 1977), 316.

26. Ibid., 116.

27. The three calls were discerned in, respectively, John 1:35–39 ("They said to him, where are you staying?" He said to them, "Come and see"); Luke 5:10 ESV ("From now on you will be catching men") and Matthew 4:18. Thomas Aquinas, *Commentary on the Gospel of St John*, trans. J. A. Weisheipl (Albany: Magi Books, n.d.), lecture 15 on chapter 1.

28. John Wesley, "Letter to Mr. John Smith" in *The Works of John Wesley*, ed. Thomas Jackson (Grand Rapids: Baker, 1979) 12:57, cited in Jason E. Vickers, "On Friendship: John Wesley's Advice to the People Called Methodists," *Wesleyan Theological Journal*, 42, no. 1 (Spring 2007): 43.

29. Vickers, "On Friendship," 43.

30. Wesley, *The Works of John Wesley*, vol. 12: 295–6.

31. John Wesley, Sermon 33: "Sermon on the Mount VIII" in *The Works of John Wesley*, vol. 3 (Nashville: Abingdon, 1984), 697.

32. John Wesley, Sermon 81, "In What Sense Are We to Leave the World," in *The Bicentennial Edition of the Works of John Wesley* (Nashville: Abingdon, 1984) as noted by Vickers, "On Friendship: John Wesley's Advice to the People Called Methodists," 34, who provides a most helpful overview of Wesley on friendship.

Chapter 7—Ministry: What a Friend We Have in Jesus

1. John Fitzgerald, "Christian Friendship: John, Paul, and the Philippians," *Interpretation: A Journal of Bible & Theology* 61 (July 2007): 290. Fitzgerald notes that Hesychius of Alexandria gives *philia* ("friendship") as one meaning for *katallage* ("reconciliation"), which is used in 2 Corinthians 5:18–20; and "to make a friend" (*philon poiesai*) as the meaning of "to reconcile" (*apokatallaxai*), which is used in Ephesians 2:16; Colossians 1:20, 22. He quotes Spicq, who says, "For

pagans and Christians alike, reconciliation is the action of reestablishing friend-ship between two persons who are on bad terms, to replace hostility with peaceful relations."

2. William Barclay, *The New Testament: A New Translation*, vol. 2 (London: Collins, 1969), 72. Cited by Fitzgerald, "Christian Friendship," 290. Emphasis added.

3. Desmond Tutu, *Report of the Truth and Reconciliation Commission*, vol. 1 (Cape Town: The Truth and Reconciliation Commission, 1998), 108.

4. Maxie D. Dunnam, *Galatians, Ephesians, Philippians, Colossians, Philemon*, vol. 8, The Communicator's Commentary (Waco: Word Books, 1982), 401.

5. Philip Hallie, *Lest Innocent Blood Be Shed: The Story of the Village of Le Chambon and How Goodness Happened There*, repr. (New York: Harper Perennial, 1994). The reaction of Mme. Barraud is recoded by Grace Scales Yoder in "The Town that Defied the Holocaust," n.d.

6. Cited in J. R. Miller, *Personal Friendships of Jesus* (New York: Thomas Y. Crowell, 1897).

7. Eric Metaxas, *Bonhoeffer: Pastor, Martyr, Prophet, Spy*, 1st ed. (Nashville: Thomas Nelson, 2010), 375.

8. Frank Woggan, "'For the Hatching of Our Hearts': Friendship, Pastoral Care, and the Formation for Ministry," *Journal of Pastoral care and Counseling* 57, no. 3 (Fall 2003): 237.

9. Donald M. Scott, *From Office to Profession* (Philadelphia: University of Pennsylvania, 1978), 154–55.

10. Stanley Hauerwas and William Willimon, "Ministry as More Than a Helping Profession," *The Christian Century*, March 15, 1989.

11. See David F. Wells, "The D-Min-ization of the Ministry" in *No God but God*, eds. Os Guiness and John Seel (Chicago: Moody, 1992). The same mate-rial also appears in David Wells, *No Place for Truth: Or Whatever Happened to Evangelical Theology?* (Grand Rapids: Eerdmans, 1993).

12. Wayne E. Oates, *The Christian Pastor* (Philadelphia: Westminster John Knox Press, 1982), 196.

13. Alan Booth, distinguished professor of sociology, human development, and demography at Penn State University, cited in Florence Isaacs, *Toxic Friends True Friends: How Your Friendships Can Make or Break Your Health, Happiness, Family, and Career* (New York: William Morrow, 1999), 1.

14. Matthew Messner, "Leadership That Cares: How Intentional Friendship Revolutionizes Leadership" (D.Min. thesis, Massachusetts: Gordon-Conwell Theological Seminary, 2005), 94.

15. Ibid., 142.

16. Jeremy Taylor, *The Whole Works of the Right Reverend Jeremy Taylor*, vol. 1 (London: Longman, Brown, Green and Longmans, 1854), 73. Emphasis added.

17. John Swinton, *Resurrecting the Person: Friendship and the Care of People with Mental Health Problems* (Nashville: Abingdon, 2000), 37.

18. David Shields, "Friendship: Context and Content of Christian Religious Education," *Religious Education* 91, no. 1 (Winter 1996): 111–12.

19. Ibid., 118.

20. Dale Carnegie, *How to Make Friends and Influence People* (New York: Simon & Schuster, 1981).

Chapter 8—Theology: Public Friendship

1. Nicholas A. Christakis and James H. Fowler, *Connected: The Surprising Power of Our Social Networks and How They Shape Our Lives* (New York: Little, Brown and Company, 2009).

2. Russel Ward, *The Australian Legend* (Melbourne: Oxford University Press, 1958); James S. Page, "Is Mateship Virtue?," *Australian Journal of Social Issues* 37, no. 2 (May 2002): 193–200. A larrikin is a good-natured, boisterous, and often misbehaving youth.

3. Interview, *Lingua Franca*, ABC Radio National (April 24, 1999).

4. H. R. Niebuhr, *Christ and Culture* (New York: Harper and Bros., 1951).

5. Stanley Hauerwas, *The Hauerwas Reader*, eds. John Berkman and Michael G. Cartwright (Durham: Duke University Press, 2001), 113.

6. Abraham Kuyper, "Sphere Sovereignty," in *Abraham Kuyper: A Centennial Reader*, ed. James D. Bratt. (Grand Rapids: Eerdmans, 1998), 488. Emphasis added.

7. Karl Barth, "The Christian Community and the Civil Community," in *Community, State and Church* (New York: Anchor Books, 1960).

8. Marcus Tullius Cicero, *On Friendship*, trans. Alexander Inglis (New York: Newton and Cartwright, 1908), 7, section 23.

9. Graham Smith, "Friendship and the State" (presented at the 9th Congrès de l'Association Francaise de Science Politique, Toulouse, Fr., 2007), 104–5.

10. Aristotle, *Nicomachean Ethics*, bk. 8, chap. 1.

11. Ibid., bk. 8, chap. 9.

12. Ibid., bk. 8, chap. 1.

13. Ibid., bk. 8, chap. 11.

14. Michael Gordon, "Encounter with Debbie Mortimer: Rebel with a Cause," *The Age* (Melbourne: Fairfax, November 27, 2010), Insight, 10.

15. Michael Schluter and John Ashcroft, *Jubilee Manifesto: A Framework, Agenda & Strategy for Christian Social Reform* (Leicester, UK: Inter-Varsity, 2005).

16. Peter Slade, *Open Friendship in a Closed Society: Mission Mississippi and a Theology of Friendship* (Oxford: Oxford University Press, 2009), 134.

17. Gilbert Meilaender, *Friendship, a Study in Theological Ethics* (Notre Dame: University of Notre Dame Press, 1981), 74–75. The italics have been added.

18. Ibid., 77.

19. E. M. Forster, *Two Cheers for Democracy* (New York: Harcourt Brace, 1951).

20. Newman, cited in William Oddie, ed., *After the Deluge: Essays Towards the Desacralization of the Church* (London: SPCK, 1987), 13-14.

21. Jacques Ellul, *The New Demons* (New York: Seabury, 1975), 199.

22. Emily Langer, "Boyhood Pals Reshaped Major Faiths," *The Age* (Melbourne: Fairfax, January 10, 2012).

Chapter 9—Mission: Friendship and the Scattered Church

1. Ruth Rouse and Stephen Neill, *A History of the Ecumenical Movement* (London: SPCK, 1954), 359. Emphasis added.

2. J. R. Miller, *Personal Friendships of Jesus* (New York: Thomas Y. Crowell, 1897), loc. 582–87.

3. Deborah Bruce, "Are All Your friends in Church? Leaving No One to Invite?," *Beyond the Ordinary: Insights into US Congregational Life* (Louisville: US Congregational Life Survey, December 6, 2011).

Chapter 10—Virtue: Holy Friendship

1. Jason E. Vickers, "On Friendship: John Wesley's Advice to the People Called Methodists," *Wesleyan Theological Journal*, 42, no. 1 (Spring 2007): 41.

2. Janet L. Ramsey, "Holy Friendship: Reimaging Ministry with Homebound Older Adults," *Word and World* 26, no. 3 (Summer 2006): 259.

3. Ibid., 259–60.

4. John White, for instance, analyzed 117 ancient letters and categorized them as letters of introduction and recommendation; letters of petition; and family letters, out of which grew "cultivated letters of friendship." For a thorough review see John Fitzgerald, ed., *Friendship, Flattery, and Frankness of Speech*. For the contrary view, that sees Philippians as a family rather than friendship letter, see Ben Witherington, *Paul's Letter to the Philippians: A Socio-Rhetorical Commentary*, (Grand Rapids: Eerdmans, 2011), 17–21.

5. Aristotle, *Eudemian Ethics*, 7.6.9.

6. Aristotle, *Nicomachean Ethics*, bk. 9, chap. 8.; Diogenes Laertius 5.20.

7. Luke Timothy Johnson, "Making Connections," *Interpretation,* April 2004, 164.

8. Aristotle, *Nicomachean Ethics,* bk. 8, chap. 4.

9. Ibid., bk. 8, chaps. 3, 4, 9.

10. Vickers, "On Friendship," 49.

11. John Wesley, "The Wisdom of God's Counsels," *The Works of the Rev. John Wesley* (London: Wesleyan Methodist Book Room, 1872).

12. Vickers, "On Friendship," 41.

13. John Wesley, "A Plain Account of Christian Perfection," in *The Works of John Wesley,* vol. 11, ed. Thomas Jackson., n.d., 366–446.

14. Aristotle, *Nicomachean Ethics,* bk. 10, chap. 9.

15. Alasdair MacIntyre, *After Virtue: A Study in Moral Theory* (Notre Dame: University of Notre Dame Press, 1981), 263.

16. John and Charles Wesley, *Hymns and Sacred Poems,* in John Wesley, *The Works of the Reverend John Wesley, A.M.,* vol. 7 (New York: J. Emory and B. Waugh, 1831), preface, par. 5, p. 593.

17. Andrew C. Thompson, "From Societies to Society: The Shift from Holiness to Justice in the Wesleyan Tradition," *Methodist Review* 3 (2011): 141–72.

18. M. Douglas Meeks, *The Future of the Methodist Theological Tradition* (Nashville: Abingdon, 1985), 131.

19. David Cameron, "Speech on Wellbeing," Number10.gov.uk, November 25, 2010.

Chapter 11—Destiny: The Meaning of Friendship for God

1. "What a Friend We Have in Jesus," words by Joseph Scriven, 1855; music by Charles Converse, 1868.

2. J. R. Miller, *Personal Friendships of Jesus* (New York: Thomas Y. Crowell, 1897); emphasis added.

3. Ralph E. Luker eliminates Einstein but traces the widespread use of this question in sermons by Martin Luther King, Vernon Johns, Harry Emerson Fosdick, and Leslie D. Weatherhead, and further back to apparently independent sources in English, poet and literary critic Frederic William Myers (1843–1901) and German zoologist Ernst H. P. Haeckel (1834–1919). George Mason University, History News Network, *Cliopatria: a Group Blog* (August 22, 2004).

4. Simon Conway Morris, *Life's Solution: Inevitable Humans in a Lonely Universe* (Cambridge: Cambridge University Press, 2003).

SELECTED BIBLIOGRAPHY

Aelred of Rievaulx. *Spiritual Friendship*. Translated by Mary Eugenia Laker. Kalamazoo, MI: Cistercian Publications, 1977.

Ambrose of Milan. "Three Books on the Duties of the Clergy." In *Nicene and Post-Nicene Fathers*, 2nd series. Edited by P. Schaff. Vol. 10. Grand Rapids: Eerdmans, 1956.

Anselm. "Cur Deus Homo." In *St. Anselm*. Translated by S. N. Deane. Chicago: Open Court Publishers, 1926.

Aquinas, Thomas. *The Summa Theologica of St. Thomas Aquinas*. 2nd ed. Translated by Fathers of the English Dominican Province. New York: Benziger, 1920.

Aristotle. *Nicomachean Ethics*. Translated by Terence Irwin. Indianapolis: Hackett, 1985.

Atkinson, Peter. *Friendship and the Body of Christ*. London: SPCK, 2004.

Augustine of Hippo. *Confessions*. Translated by R. S. Pine-Coffin. Harmondsworth, UK: Penguin Books, 1961.

Bacon, Francis. "Of Friendship." In *Other Selves: Philosophers on Friendship*. Edited by Michael Pakaluk. Indianapolis: Hackett, 1991.

Barth, Karl. "The Christian Community and the Civil Community." In *Community, State and Church*. New York: Anchor Books, 1960.

Batten, Alicia. *Friendship and Benefaction in James*. Blandford Forum, UK: Deo, 2010.

Bellah, Robert Neelly. *Habits of the Heart: individualism and commitment in American life*. Berkeley, CA: University of California Press, 1985.

Bloom, Allan. *Love and Friendship*. New York: Simon and Schuster, 1994.

Bonhoeffer, Dietrich. *Life Together*. New York: Harper and Row, 1954.

Bruce, Deborah. "Are All Your Friends in Church? Leaving No One to Invite?", in *Beyond the Ordinary: Insights into US Congregational Life*. Louisville: US Congregational Life Survey, 2011.

Carmichael, Liz. *Friendship: Interpreting Christian Love*. London: T. and T. Clark International, 2004.

Carnegie, Dale. *How to Make Friends and Influence People*. New York: Simon & Schuster, 1981.

Cassian, John. "The Conferences of John Cassian." In *Nicene and Post-Nicene Fathers*. Edited by P. Schaff. Vol. 11. Peabody, MA: Hendrikson, 1999.

Christakis, Nicholas A., and James H. Fowler. *Connected: The Surprising Power of Our Social Networks and How They Shape Our Lives*. New York: Little, Brown, 2009.

Cicero, Marcus Tullius. *De Officiis*. Loeb Classical Library. Translated by Walter Miller. Cambridge, MA: Harvard University Press, n.d.

———. *On Friendship*. Translated by Alexander Inglis. New York: Newton and Cartwright, 1908.

Clement of Alexandria. "Exhortation to the Heathen." In *The Ante-Nicene Fathers*. Vol. 2. Edited by Alexander Roberts; James Donaldson; A. Clevland Coxe. Grand Rapids: Eerdmans, 1952.

Conway Morris, Simon. *Life's Solution: Inevitable Humans in a Lonely Universe*. Cambridge: Cambridge University Press, 2003.

Corley, Jeremy. *Ben Sira's Teaching on Friendship*. Providence, RI: Brown Judaic Studies, 2002.

Derrida, Jacques. *The Politics of Friendship*. London: Verso, 2005.

Desai, Amit, and Evan Killick. *The Ways of Friendship: Anthropological Perspectives*. New York: Berghahn Books, 2010.

Dunnam, Maxie D. *Galatians, Ephesians, Philippians, Colossians, Philemon.* Vol. 8. The Communicator's Commentary. Waco: Word Books, 1982.

Echeverria, Eduardo J. "The Friendship of Charity." *Calvin Theological Journal* 33, no. 2 (1998): 350–74.

Edwards, Jonathan. *Christian Love and Its Fruit.* Lafayette, IN: Sovereign Grace, 2000.

Ellul, Jaques. *The New Demons.* New York: Seabury, 1975.

Emerson, Ralph Waldo. "Friendship." In *Essays—First Series.* Charleston, SC: BiblioBazaar, 2008.

Enright, D. *The Oxford Book of Friendship.* Oxford: Oxford University Press, 1991.

Fitzgerald, John, ed. *Friendship, Flattery, and Frankness of Speech: Studies on Friendship in the New Testament World.* Leiden, Neth.: E. J. Brill, 1996.

——— "Christian Friendship: John, Paul, and the Philippians." *Interpretation: A Journal of Bible and Theology* 61 (July 2007): 284–96.

Gordon, Michael. "Encounter with Debbie Mortimer: Rebel with a Cause." *The Age.* Melbourne: Fairfax, November 27, 2010.

Greely, Andrew. *The Friendship Game.* New York: Image Books, 1971.

Hallie, Philip. *Lest Innocent Blood Be Shed: The Story of the Village of Le Chambon and How Goodness Happened There.* New York: Harper Perennial, 1994.

Hauerwas, Stanley. "Happiness, the Life of Virtue and Friendship: Theological Reflections on Aristotelian Themes," *Asbury Theological Journal* 45, no. 1 (Spring 1990): 5–48.

Herman, Gabriel. *Ritualised Friendship and the Greek City.* Cambridge: Cambridge University Press, 1987.

Heuertz, Christopher, and Christine Pohl. *Friendship at the Margins: Discovering Mutuality in Service and Mission.* Downers Grove, IL: IVP Books, 2010.

Hilkert, Mary Catherine. "I call you friends." *Spiritus* 2, no. 2 (Fall 2002): 244–47.

Houston, James M. *The Transforming Friendship: A Guide to Prayer.* Vancouver: Regent College Publishing, 2010.

Johnson, Luke Timothy. *Brother of Jesus, Friend of God: Studies in the Letter of James.* Grand Rapids: Eerdmans, 2004.

Johnson, Mark. "Friends of God: Virtues and Gifts in Aquinas." *Thomist* 59, no. 3 (1995): 508–12.

Jowett, Benjamin. "Sermon on Friendship." In *Sermons on Faith and Doctrine.* London: John Murray, 1901.

Kant, Immanuel. "Lectures on Ethics." In *Other Selves: Philosophers on Friendship.* Edited by Michael Pakaluk. Indianapolis: Hackett Publishing, 1991.

Kerr, Fergus. "Charity as Friendship." In *Language, Meaning and God: Essays in Honour of Herbert McCabe.* Edited by Brian Davies. London: Chapman, 1987.

Kierkegaard, Søren. "You Shall Love Your Neighbour." In *Other Selves: Philosophers on Friendship.* Edited by Michael Pakaluk. Indianapolis/ Cambridge: Hackett Publishing, 1991.

King, Preston. *The Challenge to Friendship in Modernity.* London: F. Cass, 2000.

Konstan, David. *Friendship in the Classical World.* Cambridge: Cambridge University Press, 1997.

Kuyper, Abraham. "Sphere Sovereignty," in *Abraham Kuyper, A Centennial Reader.* Edited by James D. Bratt. Grand Rapids: Eerdmans, 1998.

Langer, Emily. "Boyhood Pals Reshaped Major Faiths." *The Age.* Melbourne: Fairfax, January 10, 2012.

Leaman, Oliver. *Friendship East and West: Philosophical Perspectives.* Richmond, Surrey (UK)/London: Curzon, 1995.

Leech, Kenneth. *Soul Friend: Spiritual Direction in the Modern World.* London: Darton, Longman and Todd, 1994.

Lefler, Nathan. *Saint Aelred of Rievaulx and Saint Thomas Aquinas on Friendship: A Comparison of Monastic and Scholastic Theology.* UMI Microfilm. Washington, DC: Catholic University of America, 2008.

Longenecker, Richard N. *Galatians.* Nashville: Thomas Nelson, 1990.

Lepp, Ignace. *The Ways of Friendship.* New York: Macmillan, 1966.

Lewis, C. S. *The Four Loves.* London: Collins, 1960.

Lippitt, John. "Cracking the Mirror: On Kierkegaard's Concerns About Friendship." *International Journal for Philosophy of Religion* 61, no. 3 (June 2007): 131–50.

Little, Graham. *Friendship: Being Ourselves with Others.* Carlton North, VIC, Australia: Scribe Publications, 2000.

Long, Thomas G. "Making Friends." *Journal for Preachers* 30, no. 4 (2007): 52–57.

MacIntyre, Alasdair. *After Virtue: A Study in Moral Theory.* Notre Dame, IN: University of Notre Dame Press, 1981.

Marty, Martin. *Friendship.* 1st ed. Allen, TX: Argus Communications, 1980.

McFague, Sallie. *Metaphorical Theology: Models of God in Religious Language.* Minneapolis: Fortress, 1982.

McNamara, Marie. *Friends and Friendship for Saint Augustine.* New York: Alba House, 1964.

McPhee, Arthur. *Friendship Evangelism.* Eastbourne, UK: Kingsway, 1980.

Meilaender, Gilbert. *Friendship, a Study in Theological Ethics.* Notre Dame, IN: University of Notre Dame Press, 1981.

Metaxas, Eric. *Bonhoeffer: Pastor, Martyr, Prophet, Spy.* 1st ed. Nashville: Thomas Nelson, 2010.

Miller, J. R. *Personal Friendships of Jesus.* New York: Thomas Y. Crowell, 1897.

Mitchell, A. C. "The Social Function of Friendship in Acts 2:44–47 and 4:32–47." *Journal of Biblical Literature* 111 (1992): 255–72.

Moltmann, Jurgen. *Open Church: Invitation to a Messianic Lifestyle.* 1st ed. London: SCM, 1978.

————*The Church in the Power of the Spirit: A Contribution to Messianic Ecclesiology.* New York: Harper and Row, 1977.

Montaigne, Michel de. "Of Friendship." Chapter 28 in *The Complete Essays of Montaigne.* Edited by Donald M. Frame. Palo Alto, CA: Stanford University Press, 1958.

Newman, John Henry. "Love of Relations and Friends." In *Parochial and Plain Sermons.* Vol. 2. London: Longmans, Green and Co., 1908.

Niebuhr, H. R. *Christ and Culture.* New York: Harper and Bros., 1951.

Nygren, Anders. *Agape and Eros.* Philadelphia: Westminster, 1953.

O'Day, Gail. "Jesus as Friend in the Gospel of John." *Interpretation* 58, no. 2 (2004): 144–57.

————. "Preaching as an Act of Friendship: Plain Speaking as a Sign of the Kingdom." *Journal for Preachers* (Pentecost 2005): 15–20.

Oddie, Wiliam. ed. *After the Deluge: Essays Towards the Desacralization of the Church.* London: SPCK, 1987.

Page, James S. "Is Mateship Virtue?," *Australian Journal of Social Issues* 37, no. 2. (2002): 193–200.

Pakaluk, Michael. *Other Selves: Philosophers on Friendship.* Indianapolis: Hackett, 1991.

Pohl, Christine D. *Making Room: Recovering Hospitality as a Christian Tradition.* Grand Rapids: Eerdmans, 1999.

Prager, Marcia, and Rebecca Kratz Mays. "Friendship Counts Most." *Journal of Ecumenical Studies* 43, no. 2 (March 1, 2008): 121–31.

Ramsey, Janet L. "Holy Friendship: Reimaging Ministry with Homebound Older Adults." *Word and World* 26, no. 3 (Summer 2006): 259–68.

Roby, Douglass. "Aelred in the Tradition of Monastic Friendship." In *Spiritual Friendship.* Translated by Mary Eugenia Laker. Kalamazoo, MI: Cistercian Publications, 1977.

Rouner, Leroy. *The Changing Face of Friendship*. Notre Dame, IN: University of Notre Dame Press, 1994.

Schluter, Michael, and John Ashcroft. *Jubilee Manifesto: A Framework, Agenda and Strategy for Christian Social Reform*. Leicester, UK: Inter-Varsity, 2005.

Schwartz, Daniel. *Aquinas on Friendship*. Oxford: Oxford University Press, 2007.

Scorza, Jason. "Liberal Citizenship and Civic Friendship." *Political Theory* 32, no. 1 (2004): 85–108.

Shields, David. "Friendship: Context and Content of Christian Religious Education." *Religious Education* 91, no. 1 (Winter 1996): 104–21.

Simmel, Georg. "Friendship, Love and Secrecy." In *The Substance of Sociology: Codes, Conduct and Consequences*. Edited by Ephraim Mizruchi. New York: Meredith Corporation, 1973.

——. *Sociology: Inquiries into the Construction of Social Forms*. Vol. 1. Translated by A. J. Blasi, Anton Jacobs, and Mathew Kanjirathinkal. Leiden, Neth.: Brill, 2009.

Slade, Peter. *Open Friendship in a Closed Society: Mission Mississippi and a Theology of Friendship*. Oxford; New York: Oxford University Press, 2009.

Smith, Graham. "Friendship and the State" (presented at the 9th Congrès de l'Association Francaise de Science Politique, Toulouse, 2007.

Solomon, Nathan. "David and Jonathan in Iraq." In *Probing the Frontiers of Biblical Studies*. Edited by J. Harold Ellens and John T. Greene. Eugene, OR: Pickwick, 2009.

Spencer, Liz, and Ray Pahl. *Rethinking Friendship: Hidden Solidarities Today*. Illustrated ed. Princeton, NJ: Princeton University Press, 2006.

Stern-Gillet, Suzanne. "Epicurus and Friendship." *Dialogue* 28, no. 2 (April 2010): 275.

Stortz, Martha E. "Geographies of Friendship: Arendt and Aristotle." *Dialog: A Journal of Theology* 41, no. 3 (Fall 2002): 225.

Stortz, Martha Ellen. "Beyond Justice: Friendship in the City." *Word and World* 14, no. 4 (Fall 1994): 409–18.

Summers, Steve. *Friendship: Exploring Its Implications for the Church in Postmodernity.* London: T. and T. Clark, 2009.

Swinton, John. *Resurrecting the Person: Friendship and the Care of People with Mental Health Problems.* Nashville: Abingdon, 2000.

Taylor, Charles. *Sources of the Self: The Making of the Modern Identity.* Cambridge, MA: Harvard University Press, 1989.

Taylor, Jeremy. "Discourse of the Nature, Offices and Measures of Friendship." In *The Whole Works of the Right Reverend Jeremy Taylor.* 10 vols. London: Longman, Brown, Green and Longmans, 1854.

Telfer, Elizabeth. "Friendship." *Proceedings of the Aristotelian Society* 71 (1970): 223–41.

Vernon, Mark. "The Ambiguity of Friendship." *Theology* 109, no. 852 (2006): 403–11.

Vickers, Jason E. "On Friendship: John Wesley's Advice to the People Called Methodists." *Wesleyan Theological Journal* 42, no. 1 (Spring 2007): 32–49.

Wadell, Paul J. *Friendship and the Moral Life.* Notre Dame, IN: University of Notre Dame Press, 1989.

Ward, Russel. *The Australian Legend.* Melbourne: Oxford University Press, 1958.

Weatherhead, Leslie. *The Transforming Friendship.* London: Wyvern Books, 1956.

Wesley, John. "A Plain Account of Christian Perfection." In volume 11 of *The Works of the Rev. John Wesley.* Edited by Thomas Jackson, London: Wesleyan Methodist Book Room, 1881.

———. "The Wisdom of God's Counsels." In volume 6 of *The Works of the Rev. John Wesley.* Edited by Thomas Jackson, London: Wesleyan Methodist Book Room, 1872.

Wilkinson, Richard, and Kate Pickett. *The Spirit Level: Why More Equal Societies Almost Always Do Better.* London: Allen Lane, 2009.

Witherington, Ben. *Grace in Galatia.* Edinburgh: T. and T. Clark, 1998.

————. *Paul's Letter to the Philippians: a Socio-Rhetorical Commentary.* Grand Rapids: Eerdmans, 2011.

Woggan, Frank. "'For the Hatching of Our Hearts': Friendship, Pastoral Care, and the Formation for Ministry." *Journal of Pastoral Care and Counseling* 7, no. 3 (Fall 2003): 257–67.

INDEX